REVISION WORKBOOK

Equity and Trusts

Third Edition

MICHAEL DOHERTY
BA Law, MA Criminology,
Senior Lecturer in Law, University of Glamorgan

OLD BAILEY PRESS

OLD BAILEY PRESS
at Holborn College, Woolwich Road,
Charlton, London, SE7 8LN

First published 1997
Third edition 2002

ISBN 1 85836 462 0

British Library Cataloguing-in-Publication.

A CIP Catalogue record for this book is available from the British Library.

Printed and bound in Great Britain.

Contents

Contents

Acknowledgement

Some questions used are taken or adapted from past University of London LLB (External) Degree examination papers and our thanks are extended to the University of London for their kind permission to use and publish the questions.

Caveat

The answers given are not approved or sanctioned by the University of London and are entirely our responsibility.

They are not intended as 'Model Answers', but rather as Suggested Solutions.

The answers have two fundamental purposes, namely:

a) to provide a detailed example of a suggested solution to an examination question; and

b) to assist students with their research into the subject and to further their understanding and appreciation of the subject.

Introduction

This Revision WorkBook has been designed specifically for those studying equity and trusts to undergraduate level. Its coverage is not confined to any one syllabus, but embraces all the major equity and trust topics to be found in university examinations.

Each chapter contains a brief introduction explaining the scope and overall content of the topic covered in that chapter. There follows, in each case, a list of key points which will assist the student in studying and memorising essential material with which the student should be familiar in order to fully understand the topic.

Additionally in each chapter there is a key cases and statutes section which lists the most relevant cases and statutory provisions applicable to the topic in question. These are intended as an aid to revision, providing the student with a concise list of materials from which to begin revision.

Each chapter usually ends with several typical examination questions, together with general comments, skeleton solutions and suggested solutions. Wherever possible, the questions are drawn from the University of London external Law of Trust papers, with recent questions being included where possible. However, it is inevitable that, in compiling a list of questions by topic order rather than chronologically, not only do the same questions crop up over and over again in different guises, but there are gaps where questions have never been set at all.

Undoubtedly, the main feature of this Revision WorkBook is the inclusion of as many past examination questions as possible. While the use of past questions as a revision aid is certainly not new, it is hoped that the combination of actual past questions from the University of London LLB external course and specially written questions, where there are gaps in examination coverage, will be of assistance to students in achieving a thorough and systematic revision of the subject.

Careful use of the Revision WorkBook should enhance the student's understanding of equity and trusts and, hopefully, enable you to deal with as wide a range of subject matter as anyone might find in an equity and trusts examination, while at the same time allowing you to practise examination techniques while working through the book.

Studying Equity and Trusts

Students often embark on the study of equity and trusts with a sense of dread or, at best, resignation. It is seen as both difficult and boring. Admittedly, some of the principles are quite complicated and difficult to grasp initially, but this is true of most areas of the law. It is a myth, however, that the law of trusts is boring. The subject raises many interesting moral, political and general issues – in particular, the political aspect of charitable trusts (Chapter 11) and the division of jointly owned property under resulting and constructive trusts (Chapter 7). Indeed equity and trusts have something for everyone. For those students who are dissatisfied with the fact that the law never produces concrete answers, trusts comes closer to doing so than any other area of the law – it is a very analytical subject. For those students who prefer more abstract discussions about whether the law is 'fair', the subject raises this question in many areas such as that of charitable trusts.

In equity and trusts, in particular, there exists no substitute for hard work. A student who hopes to do well must not limit his study to textbooks. Knowledge of source material is vital – statutes and cases (judgments; not just headnotes!).

The subject divides itself quite neatly into two parts, as does this book. The first half – the principles of trusts – is based mainly on the development of case law. The role of the trustee in the second half, on the other hand, derives itself primarily from statute although cases do offer important interpretation. Students tend to find the principles of trusts more complicated but more interesting than the law regarding the trustee's role. It is important to remember, however, that most syllabuses will require knowledge and understanding of both aspects of the subject.

Revision and Examination Technique

Revision Technique

Planning a revision timetable

In planning your revision timetable make sure you do not finish the syllabus too early. You should avoid leaving revision so late that you have to 'cram' – but constant revision of the same topic leads to stagnation.

Plan ahead, however, and try to make your plans increasingly detailed as you approach the examination date.

Allocate enough time for each topic to be studied. But note that it is better to devise a realistic timetable, to which you have a reasonable chance of keeping, rather than a wildly optimistic schedule which you will probably abandon at the first opportunity!

The syllabus and its topics

One of your first tasks when you began your course was to ensure that you thoroughly understood your syllabus. Check now to see if you can write down the topics it comprises from memory. You will see that the chapters of this WorkBook are each devoted to a syllabus topic. This will help you decide which are the key chapters relative to your revision programme, though you should allow some time for glancing through the other chapters.

The topic and its key points

Again working from memory, analyse what you consider to be the key points of any topic that you have selected for particular revision. Seeing what you can recall, unaided, will help you to understand and firmly memorise the concepts involved.

Using the WorkBook

Relevant questions are provided for each topic in this book. Naturally, as typical examples of examination questions, they do not normally relate to one topic only. But the questions in each chapter will relate to the subject matter of the chapter to a degree. You can choose your method of consulting the questions and solutions, but here are some suggestions (strategies 1–3). Each of them pre-supposes that you have read through the author's notes on key points and key cases and statutes, and any other preliminary matter, at the beginning of the chapter. Once again, you now need to practise working from memory, for that is the challenge you are preparing yourself for. As a rule of procedure constantly test yourself once revision starts, both orally and in writing.

Strategy 1

Strategy 1 is planned for the purpose of quick revision. First read your chosen question carefully and then jot down in abbreviated notes what you consider to be the main points at issue. Similarly, note the cases and statutes that occur to you as being relevant for citation purposes. Allow yourself sufficient time to cover what you feel to be relevant. Then study the author's skeleton solution and skim-read the suggested solution to see how they compare with your notes. When comparing consider carefully what the author has included (and concluded) and see whether that agrees with what you have written. Consider the points of variation also. Have you recognised the key issues? How relevant have you been? It is possible, of course, that you have referred to a recent case that is relevant, but which had not been reported when the WorkBook was prepared.

Strategy 2

Strategy 2 requires a nucleus of three hours in which to practise writing a set of examination answers in a limited time-span.

Select a number of questions (as many as are normally set in your subject in the examination you are studying for), each from a different chapter in the WorkBook, without consulting the solutions. Find a place to write where you will not be disturbed and try to arrange not to be interrupted for three hours. Write your solutions in the time allowed, noting any time needed to make up if you are interrupted.

After a rest, compare your answers with the suggested solutions in the WorkBook. There will be considerable variation in style, of course, but the bare facts should not be too dissimilar. Evaluate your answer critically. Be 'searching', but develop a positive approach to deciding how you would tackle each question on another occasion.

Strategy 3

You are unlikely to be able to do more than one three hour examination, but occasionally set yourself a single question. Vary the 'time allowed' by imagining it to be one of the questions that you must answer in three hours and allow yourself a limited preparation and writing time. Try one question that you feel to be difficult and an easier question on another occasion, for example.

Misuse of suggested solutions

Don't try to learn by rote. In particular, don't try to reproduce the suggested solutions by heart. Learn to express the basic concepts in your own words.

Keeping up-to-date

Keep up-to-date. While examiners do not require familiarity with changes in the law during the three months prior to the examination, it obviously creates a good impression if you can show you are acquainted with any recent changes. Make a habit of looking through one of the leading journals – *Modern Law Review*, *Law Quarterly Review* or the *New Law Journal*, for example – and cumulative indices to law reports, such as the *All England Law Reports* or *Weekly Law Reports*, or indeed the daily law reports in *The Times*. The *Law Society's Gazette* and the *Legal Executive Journal* are helpful sources, plus any specialist journal(s) for the subject you are studying.

Examination Skills

Examiners are human too!

The process of answering an examination question involves a communication between you and the person who set it. If you were speaking face to face with the person, you would choose your verbal points and arguments carefully in your reply. When writing, it is all too easy to forget the human being who is awaiting the reply and simply write out what one knows in the area of the subject! Bear in mind it is a person whose question you are responding to, throughout your essay. This will help you to avoid being irrelevant or long-winded.

The essay question

Candidates are sometimes tempted to choose to answer essay questions because they 'seem' easier. But the examiner is looking for thoughtful work and will not give good marks for superficial answers.

The essay-type of question may be either purely factual, in asking you to explain the meaning of a certain doctrine or principle, or it may ask you to discuss a certain proposition, usually derived from a quotation. In either case, the approach to the answer is the same. A clear programme must be devised to give the examiner the meaning or significance of the doctrine, principle or proposition and its origin in common law, equity or statute, and cases which illustrate its application to the branch of law concerned. Essay questions offer a good way to obtain marks if you have thought carefully about a topic, since it is up to you to impose the structure (unlike the problem questions where the problem imposes its own structure). You are then free to speculate and show imagination.

The problem question

The problem-type question requires a different approach. You may well be asked to advise a client or merely discuss the problems raised in the question. In either case, the most important factor is to take great care in reading the question. By its nature, the question will be longer than the essay-type question and you will have a number of facts to digest. Time spent in analysing the question may well save time later, when you are endeavouring to impress on the examiner the considerable extent of your basic legal knowledge. The quantity of knowledge is itself a trap and you must always keep within the boundaries of the question in hand. It is very tempting to show the examiner the extent of your knowledge of your subject, but if this is outside the question, it is time lost and no marks earned. It is inevitable that some areas which you have studied and revised will not be the subject of questions, but under no circumstances attempt to adapt a question to a stronger area of knowledge at the expense of relevance.

When you are satisfied that you have grasped the full significance of the problem-type question, set out the fundamental principles involved.

You will then go on to identify the fundamental problem (or problems) posed by the question. This should be followed by a consideration of the law which is relevant to the problem. The source of the law, together with the cases which will be of assistance in solving the problem, must then be considered in detail.

Very good problem questions are quite likely to have alternative answers, and in advising a party you should be aware that alternative arguments may be available. Each stage of your answer, in this case, will be based on the argument or arguments considered in the previous stage, forming a conditional sequence.

If, however, you only identify one fundamental problem, do not waste time worrying that you cannot think of an alternative – there may very well be only that one answer.

The examiner will then wish to see how you use your legal knowledge to formulate a case and how you apply that formula to the problem which is the subject of the question. It is this positive approach which can make answering a problem question a high mark earner for the student who has fully understood the question and clearly argued their case on the established law.

Examination checklist

a) Read the instructions at the head of the examination carefully. While last-minute changes are unlikely – such as the introduction of a compulsory question or an increase in the number of questions asked – it has been known to happen.

b) Read the questions carefully. Analyse problem questions – work out what the examiner wants.

c) Plan your answer before you start to write.

d) Check that you understand the rubric before you start to write. Do not 'discuss', for example, if you are specifically asked to 'compare and contrast'.

e) Answer the correct number of questions. If you fail to answer one out of four questions set you lose 25 per cent of your marks!

Style and structure

Try to be clear and concise. Fundamentally this amounts to using paragraphs to denote the sections of your essay, and writing simple, straightforward sentences as much as possible. The sentence you have just read has 22 words – when a sentence reaches 50 words it becomes difficult for a reader to follow.

Do not be inhibited by the word 'structure' (traditionally defined as giving an essay a beginning, a middle and an end). A good structure will be the natural consequence of setting out your arguments and the supporting evidence in a logical order. Set the scene briefly in your opening paragraph. Provide a clear conclusion in your final paragraph.

Table of Cases

Table of Statutes

Part One
The Principles of Trusts

Chapter 1

Classification of Trusts

1.1　Introduction

1.2　Key points

1.3　Key cases and statute

1.4　Questions and suggested solutions

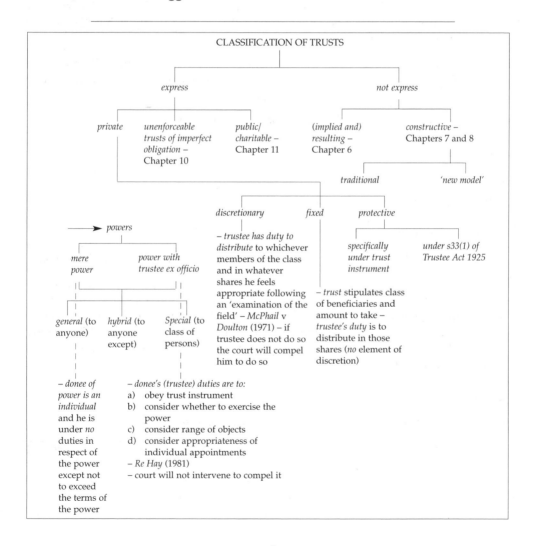

CLASSIFICATION OF TRUSTS

express / not express

express:
- private
- unenforceable trusts of imperfect obligation – Chapter 10
- public/ charitable – Chapter 11

not express:
- (implied and) resulting – Chapter 6
- constructive – Chapters 7 and 8
  - traditional
  - 'new model'

traditional:
- discretionary
- fixed
- protective

discretionary – trustee has duty to distribute to whichever members of the class and in whatever shares he feels appropriate following an 'examination of the field' – *McPhail* v *Doulton* (1971) – if trustee does not do so the court will compel him to do so

fixed – *trust* stipulates class of beneficiaries and amount to take – *trustee's duty* is to distribute in those shares (*no* element of discretion)

protective:
- specifically under trust instrument
- under s33(1) of Trustee Act 1925

powers:
- mere power
- power with trustee ex officio

- general (to anyone)
- hybrid (to anyone except)
- Special (to class of persons)

– donee of power is an individual and he is under *no* duties in respect of the power except not to exceed the terms of the power

– donee's (trustee) duties are to:
a) obey trust instrument
b) consider whether to exercise the power
c) consider range of objects
d) consider appropriateness of individual appointments
– Re Hay (1981)
– court will not intervene to compel it

1.1 Introduction

This chapter aims simply to provide an overview of the trust concept by showing the different types of trust which can exist. The relationship between trusts and powers is also considered, as is the nature of a trustee's duties under a trust and a donee's duties under a power, as these topics do not fit neatly anywhere else in the book. An understanding of these things is a vital prerequisite to the study of the rest of the law of trusts. In the key points section below, references are made to later chapters when material is particularly relevant to a specific area.

1.2 Key points

Trusts can arise either by express creation or by operation of the law. A trust of the latter description will either be an (implied or) resulting trust – Chapter 6 – or a constructive trust – Chapters 7 and 8.

An express trust – one created by the settlor, either inter vivos or by will – may be a public or charitable trust – Chapter 11 – an unenforceable trust of imperfect obligation – Chapter 10 – or a private trust for specific person(s).

An express private trust will fall into one of three categories.

A *fixed trust*

Eg to X on trust for my nephews in equal shares.

The trustee has no element of discretion.

A *discretionary trust*

Eg to X on trust for such of my nephews and in such shares as he shall in his absolute discretion determine.

The trustee has discretion as to the division of the trust. He may select the beneficiaries from within a specified class and then decide the amount of each person's share. Whilst normally distribution has to take place it is possible, as in *Re Beatty* [1990] 1 WLR 1503, that it may have to: for example, if the property were to go to residue instead, if it was not distributed within two years.

A *protective trust*

Eg on protective trusts to X for life remainder to Y absolutely.

The terms of the trust will be those contained in the trust instrument or, if none, as provided by s33(1) Trustee Act 1925. Section 33(1) provides that whenever a protective trust exists, to X for life (or shorter), then the income for that period will be held on trust for X provided that X does nothing in conflict with the existence of the protective trust.

If he in fact does so, the protective trust will end and will be replaced by a discretionary trust in favour of:

a) X and his spouse and issue if any; or if none

b) X and the remainderman Y.

The importance of the distinction between discretionary and fixed trusts is of primary importance in the sphere of certainty of objects – Chapter 2. Although this distinction is straightforward to draw, the distinction between discretionary trusts and powers is more confusing and also important (although less so since *McPhail* v *Doulton* [1971] AC 424). The courts use the term discretionary trust and trust power interchangeably to mean the same thing. However, clearly a difference does exist between trusts and other forms of powers, and it must be recognised in order to determine the nature of the trustee's obligations regarding a trust or a donee's obligations regarding a power.

Fixed trust

Clearly the nature of the trust means that the trustee is under an obligation to distribute the trust property in accordance with the terms of the trust. There is no element of discretion.

Discretionary trust

The trustee has a discretion as to the manner of distribution but a duty to actually distribute – *McPhail* v *Doulton* [1971] AC 424. There is a related duty to survey the range of objects before making the distribution. In an exhaustive discretionary trust, the trustees must actually distribute, but if the trust is non-exhaustive, they have a power to accumulate part or all of the trust property instead of distributing it.

Powers

Mere power – donee is not a trustee

There are no duties in relation to the power except not to act beyond the authority conferred by it.

Power where the donee is a trustee

Although in general terms a power imposes no obligation on the donee, it was pointed out in *Re Hay* [1981] 3 All ER 786, that by virtue of his fiduciary position as a trustee, albeit ex officio, means that certain obligations will be imposed upon him. Apart from the fact that, as with a mere power, the trustee must not exceed his authority, he must also survey the range of beneficiaries from time to time and consider whether to exercise the power bearing in mind the range and the appropriateness of individual appointments.

Unlike trusts, if no appointment is made, the court will not step in and enforce the power.

Power in the nature of a trust

This is sometimes referred to as a trust power, or a power with a trust in default of appointment.

Eg to X for life with power to appoint the remainder among X's children in such shares as X shall think fit.

If X fails to make an appointment, the property will either revert on resulting trust to the settlor or pass to X's children in equal shares. The crucial factor is the intention of the original settlor. If he intended that X's children would benefit in any event, and that X merely had a discretion to fix the shares, the property will pass to X's children in equal shares, if no appointment is made, as in *Burrough* v *Philcox* (1840) 5 My & Cr 72. If the settlor intended that X's children would benefit if, and only if, X exercised the power in their favour, the property reverts to the original settlor if X fails to make appointment, as in *Re Weekes' Settlement* [1897] 1 Ch 298. This latter situation is sometimes referred to as a mere power, in contrast to the power in the nature of a trust, or trust power, in the *Burrough* v *Philcox* case. If the instrument contains a gift in default of appointment, the power must be a mere power. The case of *Mettoy Pension Trustees Ltd* v *Evans* [1990] 1 WLR 1587 is a more recent example of the difficulties involved in distinguishing trusts and powers.

1.3 Key cases and statute

- *Burrough* v *Philcox* (1840) 5 My & Cr 72
  Trust power – power with a trust in default of appointment

- *McPhail* v *Doulton* [1971] AC 424
  Discretionary trust – duty to distribute

- Trustee Act 1925, s33(1) – protective trust; income held for the beneficiary

1.4 Questions and suggested solutions

QUESTION ONE

By his will, a testator who died last year left certain valuable land to his trustees upon trust to sell the same and invest the proceeds in investments authorised by law and to pay the income thereof to Daphne for life and subject thereto to hold the capital and income upon trust for such one or more of Daphne's children and if more than one in such shares as Daphne should by deed appoint. The testator left his residuary estate to his son, Eric.

Advise the trustees in the event of Daphne dying tomorrow leaving three children but without having made any appointment, for whom they should hold the capital and income of the trust fund.

University of London LLB Examination
(for External Students) Law of Trusts June 1990 Q4(b)(ii)

General Comment

A standard type of problem on this area. Students are not expected to come to a definite conclusion whether a trust power or mere power is created, but to set out the two possibilities and state the appropriate test to be applied.

Skeleton Solution

Who is entitled to the property? – if trust power; children take in equal shares – if mere power; reverts to testator's estate on resulting trust – rest depends on intention of settlor.

Suggested Solution

This problem turns on the true nature of the 'power' granted to Daphne by the testator's will. If, indeed, it is, on its true construction, merely a power of appointment that power would be extinguished on Daphne's death so that the property concerned, not being appointed, would go on resulting trust to the testator's estate.

It may possibly be, however, that, on the true construction of the testator's instructions, Daphne has been granted not a simple power but 'a power in the nature of a trust', ie a 'trust-power' which is in reality a trust. If this is the correct conclusion such trust must be enforced, but since Daphne obviously cannot make a selection between the potential beneficiaries the court will enforce the trust on the footing of the maxim 'equity is equality' and will thus divide the property equally between the three children. See in this context *Burrough* v *Philcox* (1840) 5 My & Cr 72. As Lord Cottenham pointed out in this case, where there appears to be a general intention to benefit a class, subject to a power of selection, and for some reason no selection is made, the court will carry out the testator's intention and divide the property equally between the possible beneficiaries.

The difficulty with a case like this is in deciding whether a power simpliciter or a trust-power is involved and this, as indicated above, is a matter of construction. Since a trust is imperative the settlor, if he did intend a trust, would not have contemplated that the trust might not be carried out so would not have provided for a gift-over in default of appointment. If he has made such a provision it follows that he must have been contemplating a power of appointment only. On the other hand, if there is no gift over in default of appointment, as in *Burrough* v *Philcox*, the disposition in question may or may not amount to a trust power; it still remains a matter of construction. In *Burrough* v *Philcox* the disposition was held to be a trust-power but in *Re Weekes' Settlement* [1897] 1 Ch 298, where likewise there was no gift over, on the wording used the court was unable to spell out a trust-power, merely a power. So, on failure to exercise that power by the donee, the potential objects were entitled to nothing: see also *Re Combe* [1925] Ch 210.

But although, as stated above, the presence of a gift over will preclude a trust-power, this is not so if the gift over is a gift of residue. This was made clear in *Re Brierley* (1894) 43 WR 36, where it was pointed out that a gift over which precludes the finding of a trust-power must be in regard to specific property and not to residue. In the present problem, the power given to Daphne could be a trust power rather than simply a power of appointment. The test is whether the testator intended Daphne's children to benefit in any event or whether he intended them to benefit only if Daphne exercised the power in their favour. The distinction is notoriously difficult to draw, and it will be necessary to consider the exact words used in the will.

QUESTION TWO

Is there any longer a difference between discretionary trusts and powers of appointment?

University of London LLB Examination
(for External Students) Law of Trusts June 2000 Q2

General Comment

This question requires consideration of both the basic distinctions between trusts and powers outlined in this chapter, and of the three certainties, as since *McPhail* v *Doulton* [1971] AC 424 the tests for discretionary trusts and powers have become the same and this suggests that the gaps between the two concepts has narrowed.

Skeleton Solution

The traditional approach – the classifications of trusts and powers – the effect of the decision in *McPhail* v *Doulton* on the distinction – comments on and criticisms of the courts' and commentators' classifications – the distinction between the duties imposed by trusts and by powers.

Suggested Solution

The traditional approach to the distinction between trusts and powers is that a trust is imperative, a power discretionary. Whether or not this remains true, this approach is too simplistic to be of any real use. There is not a single trust concept or a single type of power; many variations of each exist. There are two main classifications of an express private trust: a fixed trust and a discretionary trust. Powers divide themselves in two ways. Firstly, a power may be general (the donee can appoint in anyone's favour, including his own), hybrid (the donee can appoint in anyone's favour except for named persons) and special (possible appointments are limited to a specific class of persons).

Secondly, the donee of the power maybe a trustee ex officio or a mere individual (a mere power). Whilst, strictly speaking, it is true that all types of powers are voluntary – no appointment need be made – whereas both types of trust are imperative – a distribution must be made or the court will interfere – it is doubtful whether any other practical distinction remains between the two middle concepts – the discretionary trust and the special power with a trustee ex officio. Indeed, in view of the practical elimination of the distinction by the courts, it is debatable whether this arbitrary distinction should in fact remain.

The similarity between the two concepts stems from the decision in *McPhail* v *Doulton* [1971] AC 424. Prior to this case the test for the certainty of objects was the same for both fixed and discretionary trusts, and was that laid down in *IRC* v *Broadway Cottages Trust* [1955] Ch 20 – that due to the imperative nature of a trust, it must be possible to ascertain all the potential beneficiaries. A different test existed for powers – the *Re Gestetner Settlement* [1953] Ch 672 test affirmed in *Re Gulbenkian* [1970] AC 508 that it is only necessary to be able to say with certainty whether any given individual is or is not a member of the class. The test was wider because powers were not considered to be imperative. In *McPhail* v *Doulton* [1971] AC 424, however, the court decided that discretionary trusts were, in fact, very similar in nature to powers and thus, that the same test for certainty of objects should apply to both: that being the existing test for powers in *Re Gulbenkian* [1970] AC 508. Thus, in the sphere of the three certainties, no important distinction exists between discretionary trusts and powers.

The problem of distinguishing between trusts and powers and of the place of discretionary trusts in the context is not helped by further classifications put forward by the courts and by commentators. Two terms, in particular, which are used are 'trust powers' and 'powers with trusts in default of appointment'. The former term is used by the courts to mean the same thing as a discretionary trust, and it is submitted that the two terms refer to the same concept – the trustee has a discretion as to how distribution is to be made but a duty to distribute in that if he does not do so, the court will step in and enforce the trust. Pettit distinguishes between a 'trust power' and a 'power with a trust in default of appointment' and similarly concludes that a 'trust power' is simply different terminology for a discretionary trust. He also concludes, however, that a 'power with a trust in default of appointment' is a different species of power which has elements of a trust. With a discretionary trust there is a duty to distribute, and if the trustee does not do so the court will do so. A power with a trust in default of appointment has, in fact, the same result. The donee has a discretion regarding appointment. However, if he does not appoint the court will step in and do so.

The only area, therefore, in which a distinction between trusts and powers can exist is that of the trustee's duties under a discretionary trust and those of a donee under a power, and the related question of what will happen if no appointment or distribution is made. The position was considered in *McPhail* v *Doulton* [1971] AC 424 and *Re Hay* [1982] 1 WLR 202. It is clear from *McPhail* v *Doulton* that a trustee under a discretionary trust is under an obligation to distribute the trust property and to act responsibly in doing so – he must survey the range of objects and consider carefully how to exercise his discretion before doing so. If he does not distribute, the court will enforce the trust and compel him to do so. *Re Hay* [1982] 1 WLR 202 considers the position of the donee of a power. If the donee is a mere individual, he is under no duties whatsoever except that he must not act beyond the authority conferred by the power. If, however, he is a trustee ex officio then he must act as a fiduciary in that he must survey the range of beneficiaries periodically and consider whether to exercise the power. If he does not exercise it, the court will not interfere. Thus, in effect, the only distinction between a discretionary trust and a special power with a trustee ex officio is that only in the former case will the court step in if the trustee fails to distribute. In the case of *Mettoy Pension Trustees Ltd* v *Evans* [1991] 2 All ER 513, a company was viewed as holding a mere power as a fiduciary, circumstances in which all the remedies available in the case of a discretionary trust were thought to be applicable. This case was concerned with pension funds and had some other distinctive features. These factors may limit the importance of the decision, but it provides some further indication that the distinction between discretionary trusts and powers is narrowing. The discretion between discretionary trusts and powers is further blurred by the fact that the trustee of a discretionary trust may well have a power not to make a distribution at all. If he fails to distribute in exercise of this power the court will not interfere unless he exercises the power improperly.

Chapter 2
The Three Certainties

2.1   Introduction

2.2   Key points

2.3   Key cases

2.4   Questions and suggested solutions

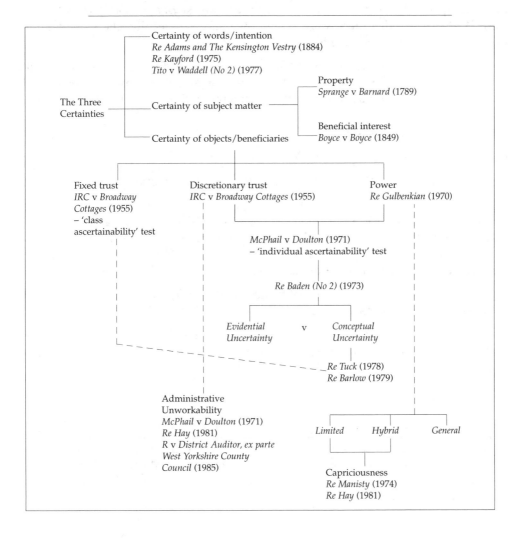

2.1 Introduction

The three certainties is one of the most conceptually difficult areas of the law of trusts. Much of the difficulty stems from the problems involved in distinguishing between trusts and powers (see Chapter 1). At first sight, the topic seems to be a jumble of different rules; once understood it will be seen that the topic is strictly structured with the various rules fitting neatly into place.

2.2 Key points

Certainty of words/intention

Language must be sufficiently mandatory to infer intention to impose a trust; precatory words will generally not be sufficient: *Re Adams and The Kensington Vestry* (1884) 27 Ch D 394. The test is whether there was an intention to impose a legally binding obligation as opposed to a morally binding one.

The words 'in trust for' are indicative but not conclusive of the existence of a trust: *Tito v Waddell (No 2)* [1977] Ch 106. All circumstances are relevant: eg opening of separate bank account is a helpful indication of intention: *Re Kayford* [1975] 1 All ER 604.

Certainty of subject matter

Property

The property subject to the trust must be certain: *Sprange v Barnard* (1789) 2 Bro CC 585.

In this case, the testatrix left £300 to her husband for his sole use and at his death the remaining part of what was left which he did not use to be divided between her brother and sister. It was held that this was an absolute gift to her husband and not a trust as no certainty as to what would be left on his death.

In *Re Golay* [1965] 1 WLR 1969 'reasonable income' was sufficiently certain as the court could determine what is reasonable.

Where a settlor declares himself to be trustee of '5 per cent of the shares' in a company, and there is only one class of shares, it was held by the Court of Appeal that the subject matter was certain: *Hunter v Moss* [1994] 3 All ER 215.

Beneficial interest

The size of the beneficial interests must be certain: *Boyce v Boyce* (1849) 16 Sim 476.

In this case, the testator left several houses on trust for his wife for life and on her death to convey one to his daughter A as she might choose and the remaining houses to his daughter B. A died before making a choice. As a result the trust was void for uncertainty of B's beneficial interest.

(There will be no such uncertainty if it is possible to apply the maxim 'equity is equality'.)

Re Harvard Securities [1997] 2 BCLC 369 followed the decision in *Hunter v Moss* [1994] 3 All ER 215. It was decided that it was possible to create a trust of a particular number of shares even where they formed an unidentified part of a bulk of shares.

Certainty of objects/beneficiaries

Fixed trusts

The test is the 'class ascertainability' test in *IRC v Broadway Cottages Trust* [1955] Ch 20 – the whole range of objects must be ascertained or ascertainable in the light of the circumstances at the date the instrument came into force. It must be possible to draw up a complete and exhaustive list of all beneficiaries.

Powers

The test is the 'individual ascertainability' test in *Re Gulbenkian* [1970] AC 508 (affirming *Re Gestetner Settlement* [1953] Ch 672) – must be able to say with certainty whether any given individual is or is not a member of the class.

The class of beneficiaries can be as wide as the testator wishes except that it must not be 'capricious': *Re Manisty* [1974] 1 Ch 17; *Re Hay* [1981] 3 All ER 786.

Discretionary trusts

Until 1971, the test was the 'class ascertainability' test as for fixed trusts. However, in *McPhail v Doulton* [1971] AC 424, it was held that the test was the same as that for powers – the 'individual ascertainability' test.

In *Re Baden's Deed Trusts (No 2)* [1973] Ch 9 a distinction was drawn between 'evidential' and 'conceptual' uncertainty. See also *Re Tuck's Settlement Trusts* [1978] Ch 49; *Re Barlow's Will Trusts* [1979] 1 All ER 296.

Even if a discretionary trust passes the 'individual ascertainability' test, it will nevertheless be void if it is 'administratively unworkable': *McPhail v Doulton*; *R v District Auditor, ex parte West Yorkshire Metropolitan County Council* (1985) 26 RVR 24.

Care must be taken with trusts which appear to be for the benefit of an association, or a purpose, which will make them invalid. See *Re Lipinski's Will Trusts* [1976] Ch 235 (Oliver J) where the purpose is actually for the benefit of a definable body of persons, the trust can be analysed as a 'people trust' and therefore found to be valid.

2.3 Key cases

- *Boyce* v *Boyce* (1849) 16 Sim 476
  Certainty of subject matter – beneficial interest uncertain – selection process never materialised

- *IRC* v *Broadway Cottages Trust* [1955] Ch 20
  Certainty of objects – fixed trusts – complete list

- *McPhail* v *Doulton* [1971] AC 424
  Certainty of objects – discretionary trust – individual ascertainability

- *Re Adams and The Kensington Vestry* (1884) 27 Ch D 394
  Certainty of words – precatory words – intention

- *Re Gestetner Settlement* [1953] Ch 672
  Certainty of objects – powers – individual ascertainability

- *Re Kayford* [1975] 1 All ER 604
  Certainty of words – separate bank account

- *Sprange* v *Barnard* (1789) 2 Bro CC 585
  Certainty of subject matter – property uncertain – absolute gift

2.4 Questions and suggested solutions

QUESTION ONE

Advise the intended beneficiaries in each of the following cases whether a valid and enforceable trust has been created in their favour:

a) A sent a cheque for £20,000 to his brother, B, together with a note saying: 'I wish you to use this sum towards educating your three children';

b) C, on the occasion of his girlfriend, D, moving into his house, said: 'Darling, from this day forward this house and all its contents are yours';

c) E sent a cheque for £5,000 to his undergraduate granddaughter, F, together with a note saying: 'Please divide this money amongst such of your University Student Societies as you consider most deserving';

d) G receives an inheritance of £10,000 with which he opens a bank account in the name of his girlfriend H, telling her that he has done this in case his latest business venture fails. The business succeeds but G and H have now fallen out and H has refused to transfer the money to G.

University of London LLB Examination
(for External Students) Law of Trusts June 1992 Q1

General Comment

A standard type of question which should give few problems to a well-prepared student. Those who have studied past examination papers will have an advantage as very similar questions have been asked in the past.

Skeleton Solution

a) Certainty or intention: is there an absolute gift to B or a trust in favour of his children? – if a trust: what are its terms and what should happen to any surplus remaining when children's education has been completed?

b) Does C's statement have any legal effect? – is it intended as a gift or declaration of trust? – what formalities are required?

c) Certainty of intention – absolute gift or discretionary trust? – if discretionary trust; certainty of objects? – are purposes wholly and exclusively charitable?

d) Is there a gift to H or resulting trust in favour of G? – presumptions of resulting trust and advancement – what evidence is admissible to rebut presumptions?

Suggested Solution

a) The first issue to be resolved is whether A has made an absolute gift in favour of B with a non legally binding request that he use the money in a particular way, or whether he has created a trust of which B is the trustee and his three children beneficiaries. This question depends on A's intention in making the gift and whether he intended to impose a legally binding obligation on B. In *Re Adams and The Kensington Vestry* (1884) 27 Ch D 394 a testator gave property 'unto and to the absolute use of my dear wife, Harriet … in full confidence that she will do what is right as to the disposal thereof between my children, either in her lifetime, or by will after her decease'. It was held that the wife took absolutely. It is not simply a matter of the particular words used but the intention of the donor.

The words used in this case sound uncertain since A has said 'I wish you to use' rather than 'you must use' and it could also be argued that as B is A's brother, A might not have felt any necessity to impose a binding legal obligation on him, as A could have relied on B using the money in the desired way. On the other hand the purpose for which the gift is made seems reasonably clear – the education of B's children – in contrast to *Re Adams and The Kensington Vestry*, where, had the court held a trust to exist, it would have been very unclear what its precise terms were. On balance it is suggested that no trust has been created here and that B takes absolutely, free from any legal obligation to use the money for the education of his children, although subject to a very strong moral obligation to do so.

If, however, a trust has been created, it might become necessary to consider what should happen to any surplus remaining after B's children have all completed their education. There are two possibilities. The first is that the surplus should return to

A by way of resulting trust, and the second that the surplus should belong to B's children absolutely. Again this is a question of A's intention. Did he intend to make an out and out gift on trust for B's children, his motive being to provide for their education, or did he intend that the money should be used only for their education? In *Re Abbott Fund (Trusts of the)* [1900] 2 Ch 326 money was collected to be used for the maintenance of two deaf and dumb ladies. It was held that the surplus remaining on the death of both ladies should return to the subscribers on resulting trust. By contrast, in *Re Andrews Trust* [1905] 2 Ch 48 a fund was subscribed for the infant children of a deceased clergyman and a letter showed that the contributions were made 'for or towards their education' but it was held that the surplus remaining when all children had completed their education should go to the children in equal shares and not return to the donors. Again, in *Re Osoba* [1979] 1 WLR 247, where there was a gift to the widow on trust 'for her maintenance and for the training of my daughter up to University grade and for the maintenance of my aged mother …' it was held that the intention had been to make absolute gifts and the surplus remaining after the death of the widow and mother and the completion of the daughter's education, belonged to the surviving beneficiary, the daughter, absolutely. It is always difficult to distinguish between gifts made for the particular purpose only and gifts made out and out but from a particular motive, but on balance it is suggested that if a trust has been created, any surplus remaining after the education of B's children has been completed, should go to the children outright and not return to the donor, A. It seems more likely that A intended to make an outright transfer of the money.

b) Again the first issue is what was C's intention when he made this statement? Did he intend to make a gift to D or did he intend to declare himself a trustee in favour of D? It seems far more likely from the contract that he intended to make a gift in favour of D. There seems no evidence that he intended to impose on himself the onerous duties of trusteeship. It is not sufficient that he had an intention to benefit C. In *Jones* v *Lock* (1865) 1 Ch App 25 and *Richards* v *Delbridge* (1874) LR 18 Eq 11, although there was a clear intention to benefit the child in each case, the court refused to construe what had happened as a declaration of trust, since the words used were consistent only with the intention to make a gift. In any event there can be no effective declaration of trust concerning the house as there is no evidence of any written evidence signed by the settlor to satisfy s53(1)(b) Law of Property Act 1925. Declarations of trust concerning pure personalty do not require any particular formality.

If C's intention was to make an outright gift, has he made an effective gift? Transfers of land should be by deed or transfer and C's oral statement will not affect the legal title to the house. Chattels are transferable by delivery and in special cases, as in *Jaffa* v *Taylor Gallery* (1990) The Times 21 March without any physical transfer at all. In *Re Cole* [1964] Ch 175 a husband showed his wife the house and said 'It's all yours', but the court refused to accept that there had been a sufficient act of delivery to make an effective gift of the contents of the house. It seems likely here that there has not been a sufficient act of delivery and that D has acquired nothing, unless C has done something to show clearly that a delivery was being made.

c) It seems unlikely here that there was an intention to make an outright gift to F as F's intention seems clear that the money should be divided amongst the student societies. Therefore it seems that a discretionary trust has been created with F as the trustee and the issue is then whether the objects of the discretionary trust are sufficiently certain and in particular whether the objects are wholly and exclusively charitable. In *London Hospital Medical College* v *IRC* [1976] 1 WLR 613 a students union was held to be charitable as its predominant object was to further the purposes of the college, even though other objects were to confer private and personal benefits on members. Individual student societies, however, are more likely to have as a main objective promoting individual interests and the social welfare of students, although it could still be argued that any student society exists to further the interests of students and that the opportunity to belong to such groups is part of the wider educational process and therefore charitable.

In any event there is no reason why a discretionary trust should not include charitable and non-charitable objects provided those objects are certain. Some student societies may be incorporated bodies and others are likely to be unincorporated associations. Whilst gifts to non-charitable unincorporated associations fail, if construed as gifts for the purposes of the association, the modern tendency is to construe the gift as being in favour of the members of the association as in *Re Recher's Will Trusts* [1972] Ch 526.

Thus it is suggested that a discretionary trust has been created, either in favour of wholly charitable objects, or more likely, in favour of charitable and non-charitable objects. It is not a trust for non-charitable purposes as such and will not fail.

d) In this case G has clearly transferred legal title to the £10,000 to H since the account is in her name alone and the question is whether he is entitled in equity under a resulting trust. The presumption is that a voluntary transfer to a third party raises an inference of a resulting trust in favour of the transferor. In *Re Vinogradoff* [1935] WN 68 a grandmother transferred certain stock into the joint names of herself and her four-year-old granddaughter. On the grandmother's death it was held that her estate was entitled under a resulting trust. There was nothing to rebut the presumption. Hanbury suggests that in the case of a transfer to a sole transferee, the slightest possible evidence will be sufficient to rebut the presumption. In this case G's intention was to safeguard the money from his creditors and no doubt, had his business venture failed, he would have asserted to his creditors that the money belonged to H.

In certain cases there is a counter presumption of advancement, that a gift was intended, but this applies from husband to wife and father to child but not in favour of a girlfriend. In *Tinker* v *Tinker* [1970] P 136 property was transferred by voluntary transfer to a wife, in an attempt to safeguard the property from the husband's creditors. The court refused to allow evidence of a fraudulent intention to rebut the presumption of advancement and the wife kept the property. G's position is different in that he does not wish to rebut the presumption of resulting trust but to rely upon it in his favour. However, despite the presumption, the natural interpretation of what has happened is surely that G intended to make a gift to H and it seems unlikely that once all the evidence is heard, the court will allow him to reclaim the money. G's purpose in making the transfer could only have been achieved had he made an outright gift to H, as otherwise the property would still be his and any creditors would be entitled to it. Therefore it is suggested that H is entitled to retain the £10,000 and there is no trust in favour of G.

QUESTION TWO

Consider the effect of the following testamentary gifts:

a) £100,000 to my sister Maria on trust first, to spend as she pleases so that she can live out her days in comfort, and secondly, to leave what is left to her children, Paul and Frederick, on her death;

b) the trustees shall give in such amounts as they shall in their absolute discretion see fit any of the books or pictures in my law library to such of my children, nieces, or nephews, who have made a good start at the Bar within ten years of the coming into effect of this will, the remaining books or pictures, if any, to go to Lincoln's Inn;

c) £20,000 to my trustees to advance the same on interest-free loan, such loan to be repaid not later than 21 years after the operation of this will, to my brother-in-law Hugo solely for the purpose of acquiring new premises for his haberdashery business;

d) the residue of my estate to my trustees on trust to distribute such residue during a period not exceeding 21 years from my death to such persons and in such proportions as they in their absolute discretion see fit with preference to be given, first, to any barrister under 35 years of age, and secondly, to any other member of the legal profession, save that no distribution whatsoever shall be made to my wife or children or any other relation of mine.

University of London LLB Examination
(for External Students) Law of Trusts June 1998 Q7

General Comment

This is a fairly straightforward question on certainties, but with the possibility for an able candidate to argue alternatives. Part (a) is concerned with precatory words and uncertainty of subject matter, part (b) with certainty of objects in a discretionary trust, part (c) with the status of loans from a trust, and part (d) with administrative workability. This question gives plenty for the student to work on in some depth.

Skeleton Solution

a) Imperative/precatory words: *Wright* v *Atkyns*; *Re Adams*; *Lamb* v *Eames*; *Palmer* v *Simmonds* – possibility of a 'floating trust' – *Ottaway* v *Norman*; *Birmingham* v *Renfrew*; *Re Goodchild*.

b) Discretionary trust/mere power: *McPhail* v *Doulton* – conceptual certainty: *Re Barlow*.

c) Loan, not a purpose: *Re Denley* – status of loan if refused or unused in whole or in part: *Quistclose*; *Re ETVR*.

d) Discretionary trust – administrative workability: *McPhail* v *Doulton*; *R* v *District Auditor* – *Denley* trust?

Suggested Solution

a) In order to create a valid trust, the words must be imperative (*Wright* v *Atkyns* (1823) 1 Tur & Rus 143): the testator must require the trustee to hold it for the benefit of others. The words used here are precatory words. It cannot be said that on a true construction of the testator's words, Maria must hold the property on trust for Paul and Frederick. Instead, she is given the money to spend as she pleases and to leave what is left to her children. In *Re Adams and The Kensington Vestry* (1884) 27 Ch D 394 property left to a wife 'in full confidence' that she would do what was right by the testator's children was held to be the absolute property of the wife. The wording in this bequest does not even use words of confidence. It is similar to the words used in *Lamb* v *Eames* (1871) 6 Ch App 597; a direction to a widow to dispose of property 'in any way she may think fit' was considered by the court to be insufficiently certain.

There is no certainty of subject matter. 'What is left', coupled with an injunction to 'spend as she pleases' gives no indication of on what property the trust is to fall. The trust fund must be identifiable. In *Palmer* v *Simmonds* (1854) 2 Drew 221 it was held that there was no certainty of subject matter when the testator tried to declare a trust of 'the bulk of my estate'. The wording here is akin to that used in *Sprange* v *Barnard* (1789) 2 Bro CC 585 where the husband was directed to hold 'the remaining part of what is left' at his death on trust.

The objection here is that the property would only be ascertainable at the date of Maria's death. However, if this were a mutual will, the court might be prepared to impose a floating trust, since it would be inequitable for Maria to take the benefit of the legacy during her lifetime without assuming the obligation to leave the remaining money as directed. This was the solution suggested in *Ottaway* v *Norman* [1972] 3 All ER 1325 – that such a trust was suspended during the donee's lifetime. This was a suggestion which was first made in the Australian case of *Birmingham* v *Renfrew* (1937) 57 CLR 666. However, the subject matter of the trust in *Ottaway* v *Norman* was a house, and there was thus certainty of subject matter. In *Re Goodchild*

[1996] 1 All ER 670 the Court of Appeal refused to impose a floating trust on a mere expectation of inheritance, but said that if a contractual arrangement could be established between testator and donee, then the floating trust solution could be accepted.

b) This is a discretionary trust rather than a mere power: the trustees are directed to exercise the discretion ('the trustees shall'). Following *McPhail v Doulton* [1971] AC 424 the trustees do not have to draw up a complete list of potential beneficiaries, but as a class the beneficiaries must be conceptually certain.

Although children, nieces and nephews are conceptually certain, the condition precedent 'who have made a good start at the bar' is equivocal and requires definition. The court may be prepared to supply a definition, but if they are not prepared to do so, the gift may fail for uncertainty of objects. However, it was suggested in *Re Barlow's Will Trusts* [1979] 1 WLR 278 that it would be enough to validate the trust if it could be shown that a number of persons fell within the category of beneficiary specified. Thus, the requirement of conceptual certainty in relation to conditions may be less strict than that applicable to the beneficiaries themselves.

There is a time limit of ten years, which means the gifts must vest well within the perpetuity period. The gift over to Lincoln's Inn means that there is a body which can step in to enforce the trust (one of the underlying tenets of the beneficiary principle). This is therefore likely to be construed as a valid trust.

c) The loan is to be advanced for the sole purpose of enabling Hugo to acquire premises. Although the gift is stated to be for a purpose, there is an ascertainable beneficiary in Hugo so that, under the rule in *Re Denley's Trust Deed* [1969] 1 Ch 373 in fact the trust has an ascertainable beneficiary.

If Hugo refuses the loan, or if it does not take effect for some other reason, the money will be held on resulting trust for the estate as a *Quistclose* trust: see *Barclays Bank Ltd v Quistclose Investments Ltd* [1970] AC 567. There has been academic argument as to the nature of such trusts, but in *Re ETVR* [1987] BCLR 646 the court stated that such trusts were resulting trusts, rather than a primary and secondary trust. This means that if the loan is not made, or if there is a surplus after the purchase of the premises, the money must be returned to the estate.

If Hugo accepts the loan, this will take effect as an unsecured debt to the estate, repayable within 21 years.

d) This is another discretionary trust, but the class of beneficiaries is drawn very wide. The class is only defined by the stipulation that preference shall be given to barristers and members of the legal profession, and by the prohibition on distribution to members of the testator's family. Is this too wide to be administratively unworkable?

It was established in *McPhail v Doulton* [1971] AC 424 that, if it can be said with certainty of any given postulant that they were, or were not, a member of the class, that would be sufficient. The problem here is that it would be difficult to say whether an ordinary member of the public, who was not a lawyer and not a member of the testator's family, was not a member of the class. If this is the case, the class will be too wide to be administratively workable (see dicta in *McPhail v Doulton* [1971] AC 424 which were followed in *R v District Auditor, ex parte West Yorkshire Metropolitan County Council* (1985) 26 RVR 24) and would thus fail for uncertainty of objects.

Could this be construed on the *Re Denley's Trust Deed* [1969] 1 Ch 373 principle? Barristers under 35 years of age could be ascertained from the records of the Bar Council, as could other members of the legal profession from similar sources. They would have locus standi to enforce the trust. The gift is specifically limited to within the perpetuity period. A gift of the residue is sufficiently certain subject matter, and the bequest is expressed using words of trust, so that the testator's intention to create a trust is sufficiently certain. The court might be prepared to construe the trust as a trust power to benefit the barristers and lawyers with a mere power to benefit others. This might depend on the court's willingness to imply severance between the gifts from residue from the use of the words 'preference to be given' and 'firstly' and 'secondly' to divide the potential beneficiaries into three groups. This was the approach taken in *Denley*, where it was stipulated that the provision of sports facilities was to be 'primarily' for the benefit of employees and 'secondarily' for the benefit of unspecified others. In any event, the trustees should take out a construction summons so that they would not be personally liable for breach of trust.

The trustees should also note that the excluded relatives might have a claim under the Inheritance (Provision for Family and Dependants) Act 1975.

QUESTION THREE

Advise whether a valid and enforceable trust has been created by Grimstone in each of the following circumstances.

a) He conveyed his seaside villa, Sandcastles, to his brother, Sam, absolutely. Immediately prior to doing so, he orally informed Sam that he wished Sam to hold Sandcastles upon trust for his (Grimstone's) secretary, Fiona, absolutely.

b) He transferred shares in a public company worth £50,000 to his sister, Sarah, and at the same time orally informed Sarah that he was confident that she would use the income from the shares for the education and benefit of Sarah's daughter, Sally.

c) He sent a cheque for £20,000 to his son and daughter-in-law, Stephen and Stella, payable to them. Prior to doing so, he had orally informed Stephen, but not Stella, that he intended to give them £20,000 to be distributed by them amongst such charities as they should think fit. Stephen informed Stella of this two weeks after the cheque had been paid into their joint account.

d) He handed £10,000 to his nephew, Stanley, for the express purpose of enabling Stanley to pay his children's school fees at Greyfriars School. Before the fees were paid, Stanley was adjudicated a bankrupt with debts of £100,000. The £10,000 given to him by Grimstone is Stanley's only asset.

University of London LLB Examination
(for External Students) Law of Trusts June 1990 Q2

General Comment

This question has been included here since it is very largely concerned with certainty of intention, although it does contain a minor issue on formalities and an analogy can be drawn with secret trusts.

Skeleton Solution

a) Formality – land; s53(1)(b) LPA 1925 – equally will not allow a statute to be used as an instrument of fraud – certainty of intention – trust or moral obligation?

b) Certainty of intention – disposition of capital if trust in favour of Sally?

c) Certainty of intention – gift or resulting trust – compare secret trust for rules on communication.

d) Certainty of intention – gift for a particular purpose only.

Suggested Solution

a) The first point to note regarding this transaction is that for an express trust inter vivos concerning any interest in land, s53(1)(b) Law of Property Act 1925 requires that a declaration of trust concerning land (including leaseholds) must be manifested and proved by some writing signed by a person who is able to declare such trust.

Section 53(1)(b) does not require the declaration of trust actually to be in writing, merely to be evidenced in writing. Thus, for example, the necessary written evidence might be found in correspondence, see *Forster* v *Hale* (1798) 3 Ves Jun 696, or in a telegram, see *McBlain* v *Cross* (1871) 25 LT 804. On the facts made available here, however, it does not appear that anything more than an oral declaration of trust has been made – which would not satisfy s53(1)(b).

However, there is an extremely important maxim of equity that equity will not allow a statute to be an engine of fraud. Thus, if it could be shown that Grimstone conveyed Sandcastles to Sam on the clear understanding that Sam should hold the property for the benefit of Fiona and Sam received it on that footing, the court would probably be prepared to impose a trust (ie a constructive trust) to this effect. Cases in which the court has been prepared to enforce a trust in respect of land despite the lack of written evidence include *Davies* v *Otty (No 2)* (1865) 35 Beav 208;

Rochefoucauld v *Bousted* [1897] 1 Ch 196 and *Bannister* v *Bannister* [1948] 2 All ER 133. See also, in this context, *Binions* v *Evans* [1972] Ch 359 and *Re Sharpe* [1980] 1 WLR 219.

The above cited cases show clearly that the court will, despite non-compliancy with s53(1)(b), impose a trust when justice demands this. Relating this to the present problem, the court would have to be satisfied that Sam had led Grimstone to believe (possibly even by his silence) that he, Sam, would hold the property on trust as requested.

But even if the obstacle presented by s53(1)(b) can be overcome, it does appear that the words Grimstone has used are 'precatory words' (ie 'wish') and, if this is the correct construction, would be insufficiently certain for the imposition of a trust. This point is discussed in more detail in part (b), below, but it is appropriate to state at this point that in *Re Hamilton* [1895] 2 Ch 370 the word 'wish' was held not to be sufficiently imperative for the imposition of a trust. On this footing, Sam would take beneficially. However each case must be judged in its own context. Although the word wish may sound vague, Grimstone did apparently say that Sam was to hold the property 'upon trust' for Fiona and the use of the word trust does sound more definite. Given that Sam would owe no moral obligation to Fiona, it seems more likely that Grimstone intended to impose a legally binding obligation on Sam.

b) In this case the property involved is not land or any interest therein so the question of compliance with s53(1)(b) does not arise in declaring an inter vivos trust, although, obviously, evidence of the oral delcaration of trust would be required. The main problem here, however, is that 'precatory words' appear to have been used in attempting to create a trust.

It is axiomatic that express trusts must comply with the 'three certainties' set out by Lord Langdale MR in *Knight* v *Knight* (1840) 3 Beav 148, viz certainly of words, certainty of subject matter, certainty of objects. Whereas the latter two certainties appear to be present in regard to this gift, it is quite likely that Grimstone's statement that he was 'confident' that Sarah would use the income for Sally's education would not be regarded as sufficiently imperative to create a trust in favour of Sally.

However, what is important is the donor's intention to create a trust and the court must be convinced of this intention from the words used and the context of their use. Usually, words such as 'in full confidence', 'feeling confident', 'desire', 'wish', 'request' will be judged to be too imprecise to create a trust: see eg *Re Adams and The Kensington Vestry* (1884) 27 Ch D 394; *Mussoorie Bank* v *Raynor* (1882) 7 App Cas 321; *Re Diggles* (1888) 39 Ch D 253; *Re Hamilton* [1895] 2 Ch 370; *Re Johnson* [1939] 2 All ER 458.

On the other hand, taking the instrument as a whole (or where, as here, there is no instrument, considering all the relevant surrounding circumstances), sometimes an intention to create a trust can be discerned by the court from what, prima facie, are precatory words. See in particular the conclusion of the House of Lords in *Comiskey* v *Bowring-Hanbury* [1905] AC 84.

In the present question the words used would probably be regarded as too uncertain to create a trust, in which case Sarah, though under a moral obligation to use the income for Sally's education and benefit, would be under no legal obligation. It could be argued that Grimstone would have felt it unnecessary to impose a legal obligation on Sarah and would have been content to rely on a moral obligation. If there is a trust, it seems that Sally is entitled only to the income and that there would be a resulting trust of the capital in favour of Grimstone.

c) It is submitted that this problem can be solved by following, by analogy, the principle in *Re Stead* [1900] 1 Ch 237, although this case was concerned with secret trusts arising out of wills and not inter vivos trusts.

In *Re Stead*, Farwell J showed that a promise made by one of several prospective joint tenants before a will is made that the relevant property would, when received, be held for the benefit of another party, would be binding on the other joint tenants (the position differs with regard to tenants-in-common). In this case, Stephen and Stella, being joint payees of the sum of £20,000 and having paid the cheque into their joint account, appear to be joint tenants in regard to the £20,000 received. It appears that Stephen has, at least by implication, agreed to hold the money received on discretionary trusts for charity. Since this is personal property no problem under s53(1)(b) arises. Certainly, therefore, Stephen's share will be bound, and, if the principle in *Re Stead* is extended, so will Stella's. Even if this principle is not extended to this situation it would appear that Stella (assuming she is unwilling to use the fund as Grimstone requires) will hold her share on a resulting trust for Grimstone if, as seems at least possible, an intention on the part of Grimstone could be deduced that if the fund were not used for the purpose he had specified it should be returned to him.

d) Since the sum of £10,000 was given by Grimstone to Stanley expressly to pay Stanley's children's school fees, and since it appears that Stanley acquiesced in receiving the money for this purpose, he would receive it as trustee on the terms indicated. No question of compliance with s53(1)(b) would arise and, of course, there would be no need for the word 'trust' to appear in connection with the transaction.

This fund would, therefore, on receipt, be the subject of a trust in favour of Stanley's children. Compare the positions in *Re Kayford* [1975] 1 WLR 279, in which money paid to a company in advance by customers and held by the company in a separate bank account, was held on trust for individual customers, and so free from the claims of the company's general creditors. Although in this problem there is no indication that Stanley has placed the fund in a separate account, the express instructions received by Stanley from the donor, presumably agreed to by Stanley, would in any event be likely to create a trust. Assuming then a trust has arisen, where a trustee is adjudicated bankrupt it is clear that any funds or other property which he holds on trust cannot be claimed by his trustee in bankruptcy: see s283(3)(a) of the Insolvency Act 1986, formerly s38(1) Bankruptcy Act 1914.

QUESTION FOUR

Consider the effect of each of the following events.

a) As he is very much in love, Romeo whispers in Juliet's ear that his house and all its contents are 'as much yours as mine'.

b) Norman dies and in his will states that one of his collection of ten classic cars should be given to each of his 'good friends'. The will further states that in cases of doubt the decision of Norman's wife (the residuary legatee) 'is to be final'.

c) Basil orally declares that he holds one quarter of his stock of wine on trust for Rodney.

d) Margot orally declares herself a trustee for Sarah of her (Margot's) beneficial interest under a trust of shares.

e) Zach dies and in his will leaves his wife, Flo, £50,000 in 'full confidence that she will use it as she thinks fit to assist our two children' and the rest of his estate (comprising a further £50,000) to Flo 'absolutely'.

University of London LLB Examination
(for External Students) Law of Trusts June 1996 Q7

General Comment

This question concerns the three certainties and s53 Law of Property Act 1925.

Skeleton Solution

a) Section 53(1)(b) invalidates the purported trust of the house but not of the chattels.

b) The subject matter of this gift is uncertain – 'good friends' may or may not be sufficiently certain, but there is no mechanism to resolve this.

c) This is prima facie a valid gift, but there may be a problem whether the subject matter is sufficiently certain.

d) This declaration is invalidated under s53(1)(c).

e) Flo takes absolutely, because there is insufficient certainty of words to create a trust.

Suggested Solution

a) The question is whether this constitutes a valid trust.

Clearly if it is otherwise valid, this is a declaration of trust and thus the trust is completely constituted. Equally clearly the object of the trust is certain – Juliet. The subject matter is probably sufficiently certain as the words probably establish a 50:50 division of the equity of the house and of its contents. It is submitted that the words are sufficiently imperative to constitute a trust: *Re Adams and The Kensington Vestry* (1884) 27 Ch D 394.

The problem is that a declaration of trust in respect of land has to be in writing: s53(1)(b) Law of Property Act 1925. Therefore, the purported declaration of trust of the house is invalid. This, however, does not apply to the chattels in the house. Thus, it seems that the rather bizarre situation has arisen, where the trust of the house itself is invalid, while the trust of the contents is valid.

b) Norman's will exhibits two problems. First the subject matter appears to be uncertain, since it is not clear who is to have which car: *Boyce* v *Boyce* (1849) 16 Sim 476 (where the testator devised all his houses, but without making it clear which house or how many houses each beneficiary was to have. The court held that the trust failed and there was a resulting trust to the settlor). Second, there is a question as to whether 'good friends' are a sufficiently certain object. The dicta in *Whishaw* v *Stephens* [1970] AC 508 (*Re Gulbenkian* [1970] AC 508) clearly suggest that it is not. However, a different conclusion was reached in *Re Barlow's Will Trusts* [1979] 1 WLR 278 (where Browne-Wilkinson J held that 'friends' and 'family' were not so uncertain as to make a disposition void). It seems, though, that even if either or both of these are a problem, Norman has set up a mechanism to resolve this by appointing his wife as arbitrator. The likelihood is that the court will uphold this: *Re Tuck's Settlement Trusts* [1978] Ch 49. Therefore, it seems likely that this gift will be upheld.

c) Since the wine is not land, Basil's oral declaration of trust is prima facie valid. The problem is whether the subject matter of the trust is sufficiently certain. If the wine is all of one type, there seems unlikely to be any problem. However, if the wine is of various different types, there may be some difficulty in determining which wine is to be allocated to Rodney's quarter.

d) This declaration is invalid since it is a purported oral declaration of trust of a beneficial interest, albeit of a beneficial interest in personalty. As such it would need to be in writing under s53(1)(c) Law of Property Act 1925.

e) The words 'in full confidence that' are precatory words and do not create a trust: *Re Adams and The Kensington Vestry* (1884) 27 Ch D 394 (where the words used were the same). Therefore, Flo takes the entire estate absolutely and the children are entitled to nothing. However, there is nothing to stop Flo (if she wishes) from making a gift to the children. She should, though, do so within two years of the death and under a deed of family arrangement, in order to obtain the tax advantages which may accrue from so doing.

QUESTION FIVE

Roland, who spent much of his working life as an executive of British Coal plc, has just died. Consider the validity of the following dispositions to trustees contained in his will:

a) £100,000 to be distributed as the trustees in their absolute discretion think fit to any residents of, or institutions or bodies based in, any community in Great Britain which depends financially or did so depend on the coal industry;

b) £200,000 to be distributed as the trustees in their absolute discretion think fit to persons or dependants of persons who have had coal miners in their family for at least three generations;

c) the trustees shall pay £500 from the residue of my estate to any person they consider to have assisted me in my career;

d) the trustees shall in their absolute discretion distribute one each of my three residences Blackacre, Whiteacre and Greenacre to my daughters, Fran and Zelda, subject to the choice of my wife, Madge, of one of the three residences to occupy for the remainder of her life.

University of London LLB Examination
(for External Students) Law of Trusts June 1997 Q6

General Comment

This is a problem question concerning the validity (or otherwise) of various dispositions under a will.

Skeleton Solution

a) It is really a question of fact whether this gift can meet the test for certainty of objects.

b) This gift probably does satisfy the test for certainty of objects.

c) This gift is probably valid if only because the testator has set up a mechanism to resolve any ambiguity.

d) The first limb of the gift is probably valid as a discretionary trust – the second limb is probably valid provided Madge exercises her right of choice.

Suggested Solution

a) The question here is whether or not the objects of the gift are sufficiently certain. The gift is a discretionary trust, so that the test is the newer and more relaxed test, namely whether it can be said with certainty of any prospective object that they are or are not a member of the class: *McPhail v Doulton* [1971] AC 424; and *Re Baden's Deed Trusts (No 2)* [1973] Ch 9.

Clearly it would be impracticable to draw up a compete list of such persons (the old test), but it might be possible to apply the newer test successfully. This is very much a question of fact rather than a question of law, but areas of possible difficulty include whether any such communities are sufficiently clearly defined that one can say with certainty where the boundaries are, and whether it can be said with sufficient certainty that any given community does or did (or does or did not) depend on the coal industry. Examples of these problem areas would be a large conurbation, part of which might be said to depend on the coal industry, or a community which depended on one or more other industries as well as coal.

b) This gift will be subject to the same test. The term 'dependants' is no longer a term which is void for uncertainty: *Re Baden's Deed Trusts (No 2)* [1973] Ch 9; and contrast *Re Ball, Hand v Ball* [1947] Ch 228 (where it was held to be void). There should be no difficulty in saying whether or not someone is (or was) a coal miner. Three generations is a clearly definable concept. Plainly it covers the instant generation plus parents and grandparents. There might be a slight difficulty as to whether it requires that the present generation, plus parents and grandparents must all have included coal miners, or whether if, for example, the present generation had no coal miners while the generations of their parents, grandparents and great-grandparents all included coal miners they would qualify. This, however, is a problem which a court of construction should be able to resolve.

c) This gift is more difficult. Though it is not entirely clear, presumably it is a discretionary trust and thus subject to the above test. Though it looks like a fixed trust at first blush, the words 'any person they consider' could be construed so as to import an element of discretion and it would be perfectly possible to give £500 to all those who can satisfy the newer test, while withholding it from any who could not satisfy that test. Assuming this to be correct, the difficulty is whether or not it can be said with certainty that someone has or has not assisted the testator's career. More evidence is needed of the factual matrix surrounding this problem. It may, for example, be obvious on the facts known to the testator who the possible candidates are. If so, this may well be admissible as extrinsic evidence under s21 Administration of Justice Act 1982. If so, there might be sufficient evidence to satisfy the older and more stringent test that one must draw up a complete list, in case the court construes this as a fixed gift. If not, there is a greater difficulty and it may be that the gift is void. However, in *Re Barlow's Will Trusts* [1979] 1 WLR 278 (where Browne-Wilkinson J held that 'friends' and 'family' were not so uncertain as to make a disposition void). If 'friends' and 'family' are sufficiently certain, why not those who have helped someone with their career?

Either way it is submitted that the gift can be validated by arguing that the testator has set up a mechanism by which any ambiguity can be resolved, by appointing the trustees as adjudicators to determine who is qualified to take – the words 'any person they consider'. If so, this mechanism will validate the gift: eg *Re Tuck's Settlement Trusts* [1978] Ch 49.

d)   The difficulties with this gift are that it is not clear which daughter is to have which residence and the life interest to Madge is an unspecified residence.

The problem here is certainty of subject matter. Under the second limb of this rule the law is that the beneficial interests which each beneficiary is to take must be certain: *Boyce* v *Boyce* (1849) 16 Sim 476. In this case, the testator devised all his houses, but without making it clear which house or how many houses each beneficiary was to have. The court held that the trust failed and there was a resulting trust to the settlor. In the instant case it is clear that each daughter is to have one house, but it is not clear which house each is to have. It is submitted, however, that this ambiguity can be resolved by the trustees in exercising the discretion which the testator has given them and therefore that this is a valid discretionary trust: *Re Tuck's Settlement Trusts* [1978] Ch 49.

There is a similar problem with Madge's life interest in that it is not clear which house she is to have, but here there is a mechanism to resolve the ambiguity, in that Madge is given the right to choose her house: *Re Tuck's Settlement Trusts*. It is submitted, therefore, that provided she exercises her right of choice this part of the gift is valid.

Chapter 3

Formal Requirements for Creating a Trust

3.1 **Introduction**

3.2 **Key points**

3.3 **Key cases and statute**

3.4 **Questions and suggested solutions**

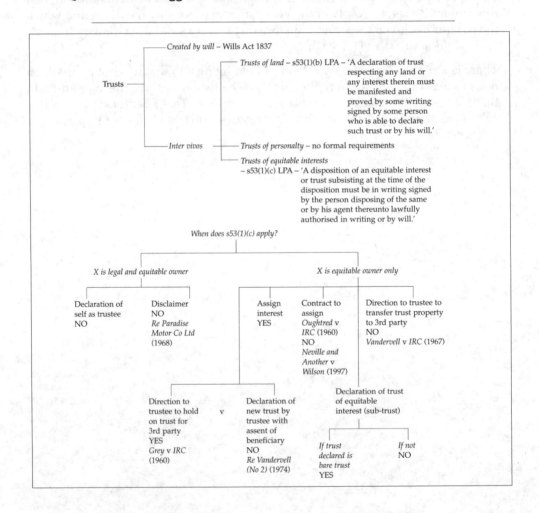

3.1 Introduction

The words 'formal requirements' and in particular the phrase 's53(1)(c)' commonly provide subject matter for students' nightmares. In fact, it is this fear which often creates the obstacle in understanding this topic. Rather like learning to ride a bicycle, s53(1)(c) Law of Property Act 1925 requires a lot of time and (mental) energy to master, but once done it will appear to be simplicity itself and will never be forgotten.

3.2 Key points

The Law of Property Act (LPA) 1925, s53(1)(b) and s53(1)(c) apply only to express trusts (ie not constructive, implied or resulting trusts – s53(2)) created inter vivos. The formal requirements for trusts created by will are governed by the Wills Act 1837.

Trusts of land

Section 53(1)(b) applies:

a) there must be written evidence of the trust (the trust itself need not be in writing) at the time of or subsequent to the trust being declared; and

b) the writing must be signed by the settlor.

Trusts of personalty

No formal requirements are necessary provided there is clear intention to create a trust.

Trusts of equitable interests

Section 53(1)(c) provides that a 'disposition' of an equitable interest must be in writing and signed by the person disposing or by his authorised agent. Thus, if a transaction concerning an equitable interest constitutes a 'disposition' the requirements under s53(1)(c) must be satisfied.

If X is both the legal and the equitable owner the following applies.

a) If he declares himself trustee of or assigns the equitable interest, there is no 'disposition' but instead the creation of an equitable interest.

b) If he disclaims the property, there is no disposition within s53(1)(c): *Re Paradise Motor Co Ltd* [1968] 2 All ER 625.

If X is the equitable owner only the following applies.

a) If he assigns the interest to a third party, clearly there is a 'disposition' and so s53(1)(c) applies.

b) If he directs the trustee (legal owner) to hold the equitable interest on trust for a third party, there is a 'disposition' within s53(1)(c): *Grey v IRC* [1960] AC 1.

Note, however, following *Re Vandervell's Trusts (No 2)* [1974] Ch 269, if the trustee declares a new trust with the assent of the beneficiary, there is no such 'disposition'. However, see *Re Brooks Will Trusts* [1939] 1 Ch 993 where this has been considered theoretically impossible.

c) If he contracts to assign his equitable interest to a third party, s53(1)(c) will not operate because s53(2) provides an exception for implied, constructive and resulting trusts. This point, which was previously uncertain, was decided in *Neville and Another* v *Wilson* [1997] Ch 144.

See also *Oughtred* v *IRC* [1960] AC 206 and *Re Holt's Settlement* [1969] 1 Ch 100.

d) If he declares a trust of the equitable interest (a sub-trust):

   i) if the trust declared is a bare trust and the trustee (X) has no active duties to perform, the result is that the equitable interest is, in effect, transferred by X to the third party and so s53(1)(c) applies;

   ii) if X has some active duties to perform, there is no 'disposition' of the equitable interest but rather the creation of a 'sub-equitable interest' and so s53(1)(c) does not apply;

   iii) if he directs the trustee (legal owner) to transfer the trust property to a third party (ie to transfer the legal estate), s53(1)(c) does not apply: *Vandervell* v *IRC* [1967] 2 AC 291.

   iv) The discussion in Underhill & Hayton (*Law of Trusts and Trustees*) explains that *Grey* v *IRC* [1960] AC 1 found that there is a disposition of an equitable interest where that interest alone is transferred to another beneficiary. However, after *Vandervell* v *IRC* [1967] 2 AC 291 it is possible that there is no disposition of the equitable interest. Rather, the beneficiary might create a sub-trust of that interest (remaining as trustee of the sub-trust). There would not be a disposition (or transfer) of the interest here.

   See also *Re Vandervell's Trusts (No 2)* [1974] Ch 269 where it was held by Lord Denning that, in some circumstances, the trustees can declare the terms of the trust. There would not be a disposition of an equitable interest where the trustees' actions are simply declaring the terms of the trust.

3.3 Key cases and statute

- *Grey v IRC* [1960] AC 1
  Direction to trustee to hold for third party – disposition

- *Re Vandervell's Trusts (No 2)* [1974] Ch 269
  New trust-assent of beneficiary – declaration of the terms by the trustee

- *Vandervell* v *IRC* [1967] 2 AC 291
  Instruction to transfer to third party – no disposition

- Law of Property Act 1925

  - s53(1)(b) – inter vivos gift; trust of land (need for writing)

  - s53(1)(c) – inter vivos gift; equitable interest (need for writing)

3.4 Questions and suggested solutions

QUESTION ONE

A holds a parcel of land, Blackacre, on trust for B. B declares that he holds his beneficial interest in Blackacre on trust for C. He later writes to C to confirm what he has done. Upon receipt of B's letter, C immediately telephones him to say that he wants nothing from B and that he refuses to accept the gift of Blackacre. B then decides to make D the owner of Blackacre, orally directs A to transfer the legal title of Blackacre to D, and telephones D to tell him what he has done. Both B and C in the meantime have had a change of heart and now claim that D holds Blackacre on trust for one or other of them.

Advise D.

University of London LLB Examination
(for External Students) Law of Trusts June 1999 Q1

General Comment

This question deals comprehensively with the formalities necessary for the transfer of an existing beneficial interest under s53(1)(c) Law of Property Act 1925, and with the creation of trusts of land. It would be advisable to have copies of these provisions available if your institution permits candidates to take statute books into the examination room. If you are permitted to use statutes in the examination, do not quote the provisions in your answer.

Skeleton Solution

Irrevocability of valid declaration of trust – rules of formality; beneficial interest; s53(1)(c) – *Grey* v *IRC*; *Vandervell* – separation of legal and beneficial interest – disclaimer – rules of formality; land: s53(1)(a) – advice to D.

Suggested Solution

In the absence of an express contrary intention, a properly constituted trust is irrevocable. If there has been a valid declaration of trust in favour of C, and B has then complied with the formalities required for an effective transfer of the property into the trust, B cannot later change his mind and declare a trust in favour of D.

B's initial declaration that he holds the beneficial interest on trust for C is subject to the requirements of formality contained in s53(1)(c) Law of Property Act (LPA) 1925, which provides that a disposition of an existing equitable interest must be in writing, signed by the person disposing of the interest. It was established by the House of Lords in *Grey v IRC* [1960] AC 1 that the term 'disposition' was to be given its ordinary dictionary meaning. Although we are told later that B could direct A to transfer the legal title, by this stage (as in *Grey*) B had already transferred the legal title to A but had retained the beneficial interest. This disposition is therefore caught by the requirements of s53(1)(c). If the declaration is in writing and signed by B, there is a valid disposition of the equitable interest in land. If the declaration itself is oral, it will not be valid: the later written communication of the disposition to C will not satisfy the requirements of s53(1)(c).

However, C disclaims the gift of Blackacre. It was held in *Re Paradise Motor Co Ltd* [1968] 2 All ER 625 that a disclaimer of an equitable interest is not a disposition within s53(1)(c): it is an avoidance of the disposition and the property is never received. *Re Paradise Motor Co Ltd* concerned a gift of shares, but on the basis that the disposition never took effect, the court might well feel itself bound to follow the decision where the trust property was a beneficial interest in land. However, there might be difficulty in adducing evidence of an oral disclaimer.

After a valid disclaimer, B would be free once more to dispose of his interests in Blackacre. This time he directs the transfer of both the legal title and the equitable interest. If B has retained control of the legal title, and disposes of both legal and equitable titles together, the transaction is not caught by s53(1)(c), since the equitable interest is not 'subsisting' separately from the legal title at the time of the disposition, but is treated as one title. This was established by the House of Lords in *Vandervell* v *IRC* [1967] 2 AC 291. However, the property in *Vandervell* was shares in a private company. B is purporting to transfer land, so that s53(1)(a) LPA 1925 applies to the transfer of Blackacre to D. Since we are told that B directed A orally to transfer the legal title, and telephones D to inform him, the requirements under s53(1)(a) that interests in land must be created or disposed of in writing and signed by the person creating or disposing of the interest have not been complied with, and the transfer will be invalid.

This appears to be a purported outright gift rather than a declaration of trust, and my advice to D is that, since equity will not perfect an imperfect gift, he acquires no interest in Blackacre for want of formality. A holds the legal title to B's direction, and B can either direct A to hold the property for C under a disposition of the beneficial interest under the existing trust, or direct the transfer of the legal title to C. In either case, the direction to A must be in writing signed by B (although under s53(1)(a), an agent can sign on B's behalf).

It was argued in *Grey* v *IRC* [1960] AC 1 that s53(1)(c) should not apply in a case where no fraud was intended, on the basis that the 1925 provision was based on s9 Statute of Frauds 1677. This argument was rejected, because the trustee and the court need to be able to ascertain the beneficiaries.

QUESTION TWO

a) 'The effect of s53(1)(c) of the Law of Property Act 1925 on dealings with equitable interests is in many ways thoroughly obscure.'

Discuss.

b) Albert held shares on trust for Billy. Consider the effect of the following alternative events:

 i) on the oral instructions of Billy, Albert declared himself trustee of the shares for Owen;

 ii) on the oral instructions of Billy, Albert transferred legal title to the shares into the name of Owen. Owen had previously undertaken to Billy that he would hold the shares, when transferred, on trust for Peter to whom Billy had previously contracted to assign his interest.

University of London LLB Examination
(for External Students) Law of Trusts June 1994 Q5

General Comment

This question enables the student to display both general knowledge of s53(1)(c) Law of Property Act (LPA) 1925 and to apply that knowledge to particular circumstances. The problem question is always easier to amass marks on. In the essay section, the candidate must be careful to structure an answer tightly.

Skeleton Solution

a) Discussion of s53(1)(c).

b) i) Transfer of the beneficial interest.

 ii) Structured transfer.

Suggested Solution

a) There are a number of possible readings of s53(1)(c) Law of Property Act (LPA) 1925 which have been brought to light by the case law which seem to go against the seemingly unequivocal wording of the section. On its face the subsection would seem to provide that a disposition of a beneficial interest in land cannot be assigned other than by signed writing (all the hypothetical examples posited below relate to land).

In a case where there is clear intention on the part of the beneficiary that the equitable interest is to be passed to another beneficiary under the same trusts, this will require signed writing to dispose of the equitable interest: *Grey* v *IRC* [1960] AC 1. This appears to be in line with the plain words of the section.

Where the whole interest (both equitable and legal) has passed to new trustees in favour of new beneficiaries, this will not constitute a disposition of a beneficial interest alone: *Vandervell* v *IRC* [1967] 2 AC 291.

This is not the result of the *Vandervell* case. In this case, it was found that there was no transfer of the interest and that the beneficial interest resulted to the original trusts. However, the thinking in this example works by analogy with *Saunders* v *Vautier* (1841) 4 Beav 115. The decision in that case was that a beneficiary who is absolutely entitled to property, is entitled to call for the property to be delivered to him or her by the trustees. Therefore, in this example, the beneficiary could be said to be calling for the trust property from the trustees of the original trust and to be settling those legal and beneficial interests on new trusts.

While the beneficial interest is still being disposed of, it is not being disposed of simply as a beneficial interest. Rather it is subsumed in the legal interest and settled. If the beneficiary under the original trust was both legal and equitable owner, there would be no suggestion that s53(1)(c) applied. Therefore, it is argued that it cannot apply in this example where the beneficiary actually calls for property. The argument made by analogy with *Vandervell* v *IRC* is that the beneficiary would be impliedly acting as though the legal and beneficial owner of the land.

The alternative analysis is that a sub-trust of the original trust is being created. This would mean that the original beneficiary was taking his own beneficial interest and settling it on sub-trust for another on the same terms and held by the same trustee as the original trust. In this instance there could be no argument that the *Saunders* v *Vautier* argument applied because there is no settling on new trusts.

It could be argued that the alternative analysis only works where the beneficiary retains some office as trustee of the sub-trust. However, in *Re Lashmar* [1891] 1 Ch 258, this second analysis would apply even where the original beneficiary dropped out of the trust altogether. Therefore it will be a matter of strict interpretation on the facts whether the *Saunders* v *Vautier* or the *Re Lashmar* analysis applies. The beneficiary would have to show an intention to call for the property and resettle it, rather than simply creating a trust over the same interest held.

The case of *Oughtred* v *IRC* [1960] AC 206 posits the situation where the disposition occurs by operation of a contract for sale of the interest rather than by a straightforward disposition of the interest. Once a contract is created, the vendor of the interest holds that interest on constructive trust for the purchaser. This was found to be a disposition of the equitable interest which is outside the requirements of s53(1)(c).

The case of *Re Vandervell's Trusts (No 2)* [1974] Ch 269, decided in the Court of Appeal by Lord Denning, is a difficult case because Lord Denning suggests that, contrary to *Re Brooks Will Trusts* [1939] 1 Ch 993 and other authority, the trustees have the ability to declare the terms on which the trust property is held. This is to argue that the trustees can go outside the limits set upon them by the settlor. Lord

Denning was eager in that case to end a series of cases when the settlor had died in untimely circumstances and it would be impossible to resettle the property. This has thrown further doubt on the applicability of s53(1)(c) because it appears that where the trustees alter the status of the beneficial interest, there is no s53(1)(c) disposition.

b) i) Where Albert declares the trusts of the shares, this would generally be in breach of the powers of the trustee, unless the trust deed can be read to permit it. On an analogy with *Re Vandervell's Trusts (No 2)* [1974] Ch 269 however, it would mean that the beneficiary is not disposing of the equitable interest and therefore it does not fall within the prescription of s53(1)(c).

If Billy called for the property to be delivered to him and then declared that the property is to be transferred to a trust under the terms of which Albert is to hold the shares for Owen, there would be no need for writing under s53(1)(c).

ii) Where Albert transfers legal title on Billy's instructions, he must be acting impliedly on the basis of Billy's powers under *Saunders v Vautier* (1841) 4 Beav 115, otherwise there would be a breach of trust. As such, there is not a disposition of the beneficial interest on analogy with *Vandervell v IRC* [1967] 2 AC 291 and *Saunders v Vautier* (as discussed at (a) above).

The difficulty is that with Billy having reached a prior agreement with Owen as to the treatment of the shares after the transfer it could be argued that Billy disposes of his beneficial interest at this time. However, it would be impossible for Billy to direct Owen as to the legal title when he does not have a right to the legal title at the time. Therefore this analysis will not interfere with the *Saunders v Vautier* argument set out above.

Where Billy has contracted with Peter for the disposition of the beneficial interest before invoking *Saunders v Vautier* rights, the case falls by analogy with *Oughtred v IRC* [1960] AC 206. The vendor of the interest holds that interest on constructive trust for the purchaser. This is a disposition of the equitable interest which is outside the requirements of s53(1)(c).

QUESTION THREE

Is there, and if so, should there be a difference between the formality requirements of the following:

a) a declaration of a bare sub-trust and other sub-trusts;

b) a disclaimer at the outset of a beneficial interest under a trust and a surrender of an existing beneficial interest under a trust;

c) a direction to trustees to transfer the legal title in trust property to X, and a direction to trustees to transfer the legal title in trust property to Y on trust for X;

d) a declaration of a trust of land and a declaration of a trust of personality?

University of London LLB Examination
(for External Students) Law of Trusts June 1997 Q7

General Comment

This is a problem question concerning the need (or otherwise) for writing on certain dispositions.

Skeleton Solution

a) Declarations of bare sub-trusts need to be and should be in writing – where the sub-trust is not a bare trust of personalty, however, writing is arguably not needed.

b) A subsequent surrender of a beneficial interest certainly needs to be in writing – an initial disclaimer does not need to be in writing.

c) The actual transfer of the legal title has to be by the appropriate formality – how the direction is done only matters if it could be used to transfer the equitable interest, in which case it needs to be in writing.

d) A declaration of trust of land does need to be in writing – a declaration of trust of personalty does not.

Suggested Solution

a) In practice most trusts are created by a deed. Among other advantages, this means that any requirement for writing is automatically satisfied.

The requirement for writing is laid down by s53 Law of Property Act 1925. Subsection (1)(a) requires writing for the creation or disposal of any interest in land. Subsection (1)(b) requires any declaration of trust relating to land to be evidenced in writing. Subsection (1)(c) requires the transfer of any subsisting equitable interest or trust to be in writing.

The rationale behind these rules is to prevent fraud. That being so, the courts have been careful not to allow the absence of writing to be used as an engine for fraud: eg *Bannister* v *Bannister* [1948] 2 All ER 133.

A declaration of a bare sub-trust must in almost every case (if not every case) constitute the disposition of an equitable interest, so that it will have to be in writing under s53(1)(c). If, for example, T holds on trust for A who declares that he holds on bare trust for B, then arguably writing is needed because A drops out of the picture leaving T holding on bare trust for B, so that A is disposing of his equitable interest to B within s53(1)(c): *Grainge* v *Wilberforce* (1889) 5 TLR 436; *Re Lashmar* [1891] 1 Ch 258. If, however, the sub-trust is a true sub-trust and leaves A with duties as a sub-trustee (eg for B for life with remainder to C), then there is arguably no disposition of an equitable interest and thus no need for writing if the trust concerns personalty: *Onslow* v *Wallis* (1849) 1 Mac & G 506. If land is involved the creation of the sub-trust will, however, need to be evidenced in writing under s53(1)(b).

There can thus be a difference between a declaration of a bare sub-trust and any other type of sub-trust. It is submitted, however, that there is no logical reason why there should be any difference.

b) It is submitted that an initial disclaimer by a beneficiary does not need to be in writing, because it is not a disposition of an equitable interest within s53(1)(c) – rather it is simply declining to accept a beneficial interest. It 'operates by way of avoidance and not by way of disposition': *Re Paradise Motor Co Ltd* [1968] 1 WLR 1125.

A subsequent surrender of a beneficial interest must clearly be in writing, since it is unquestionably a disposition of an equitable interest. It has been argued that a surrender takes effect by way of extinguishment of the pre-existing equitable interest and therefore is not a disposition. It is submitted, though, that the surrender in fact disposes of the interest to the person to whom it is surrendered.

Thus there probably is a difference between an initial disclaimer and a subsequent surrender. It is submitted that again there is no logical reason why there should be any such difference.

c) A direction by the beneficial owner of property to the trustees to hold that trust property on trust for someone else does have to be in writing: *Grey* v *IRC* [1960] AC 1. However, a transfer of the legal ownership (which carries the beneficial interest with it) as distinct from a transfer of the beneficial interest by itself, which is made by the trustee at the instigation of the beneficiary, does not have to be in writing: *Vandervell* v *IRC* [1967] 2 AC 291.

Here in both cases we are concerned with the transfer of the legal title in property. The transfer of the legal title itself would have to be done by the method appropriate to the nature of the property (eg transfer of shares and transfer or conveyance of land). Unless and until this is done the direction will have no effect on the legal title. Nor will it (of itself) give rise to any right on the part of the recipient to enforce the transfer of the legal title, because there is no specifically enforceable contract for transfer. Nor will the direction alone affect the equitable interest because of s53(1)(c). Once the transfer of the legal title had been put into effect, it is submitted that the direction would probably be otiose. Presumably what is envisaged here is a *Saunders* v *Vautier* (1841) 4 Beav 115 situation. If so, the transfer of the legal title to X would carry the beneficial ownership with it under *Vandervell* v *IRC*. The transfer to Y on trust for X is more complicated. Arguably the transfer of the legal title carries with it the beneficial ownership within *Vandervell* v *IRC*, and *Grey* v *IRC* is distinguishable. Thus the trust of personalty could be created without writing, though if the trust were of realty writing would be needed under s53(1)(b). However, depending on the status quo before the direction, it might be arguable that there is a transfer of the equitable interest which requires writing within s53(1)(c). If the trust for X commenced after the transfer the legal title to Y, then the transfer of the equitable interest would certainly need to be in writing to satisfy s53(1)(c): *Grey* v *IRC* [1960] AC 1.

Thus there is some doubt as to whether or not there is any difference between the formality requirements. It is submitted that if there is, this is anomalous and could profitably be removed.

d) A declaration of trust of land does have to be in writing: s53(1)(b). A declaration of trust of personalty, on the other hand, does not: *Benbow* v *Townsend* (1833) 1 My & K 596.

Here, therefore, there is a clear difference in the formalities required. It is certainly possible to argue that this distinction is outdated under modern conditions, but it is submitted that on balance the distinction is justified since, even under modern conditions, land is a more complex commodity and dealings in land need to be approached in a more serious fashion than those of mere personalty.

Chapter 4

Completely and Incompletely Constituted Trusts

4.1   Introduction

4.2   Key points

4.3   Key cases and statute

4.4   Questions and suggested solutions

4.1 Introduction

Commonly considered to be another 'nightmare', this topic seems, at first sight, to be a maze of cases with no logical route to follow when trying to solve a problem. This is further confounded by the fact that many aspects of the law in this area are by no means settled and have been the subject of much discussion and dispute. The key to mastering the topic is to gain an overall view, to impose on this a structure (such as that contained in the flowchart: see p43) and finally to insert the case law into the relevant parts. Without some sort of structured view of the subject, students will find it impossible to produce a good answer in an examination.

4.2 Key points

A settlor can create a trust in two main ways. In the case of *Choithram (T) International SA and Others* v *Pagarani and Others* [2001] 1 WLR 1, the House of Lords found a third method of settlement. What appeared to be an outright gift was viewed as being a gift on trust. The circumstances in which such an approach would operate are likely to be very rare indeed.

Declaration of self as trustee

To do so, there must be more than a dramatic gesture; there must be a clear manifestation of the settlor's intention to create a trust: *Jones* v *Lock* (1865) 1 Ch App 25.

Intention may be shown by a combination of words and conduct and the court will look at all the circumstances: *Paul* v *Constance* [1977] 1 WLR 527.

The trust is created by the declaration and no transfer of property is necessary.

By giving property to trustees upon a declaration of trust

To create a trust in this way, the settlor must intend to do so and must 'do everything which, according to the nature of the property comprised in the settlement, was necessary to be done in order to transfer the property and render the settlement binding upon him': *Milroy* v *Lord* (1862) 4 De GF & J 264 per Turner LJ.

What is necessary depends on the nature of the property.

a) Land – by deed.

b) Leaseholds – by deed if for at least three years.

c) Chattels – delivery.

d) Shares – execution of share transfer form and registration of shares in name of trustee. However, as the registration is outside the power of the settlor, the cases *Re Rose* [1952] Ch 499 and *Re Rose* [1949] Ch 78 qualify the rule in *Milroy* v *Lord* (1862) 4 De GF & J 264 so that the settlor need only do what it is in his power to do.

e) Choses in action (including debts, beneficial interests and contractual rights) – can be assigned at law under s136 Law of Property Act (LPA) 1925 or in equity.

   i) Section 136 requires that the whole interest in the chose is assigned; that the assignment is in writing; and that written notice is given from whom the assignor would have been entitled to claim the chose in action.

   ii) In equity, the whole interest need not be assigned and written notice is not necessary. If the chose is equitable, the assignment must be in writing to satisfy s53(1)(c) LPA 1925. If it is legal, writing is not necessary but some form of consideration, is due to the maxim that 'equity will not assist a volunteer': *Olsson* v *Dyson* (1969) 120 CLR 265.

Note: if a trust is intended to be created by one mode, the court will not give effect to it by applying the other mode: *Richards* v *Delbridge* (1874) LR 18 Eq 11.

If the settlor has done all that is necessary, then a completely constituted trust exists which can be enforced by the beneficiary in equity.

If the settlor has not, then there are two possible interpretations of what exists.

a) Trust of the benefit of a promise (completely constituted), enforceable in equity by the beneficiary: *Fletcher* v *Fletcher* (1844) 4 Hare 67.

b) Incompletely constituted trust (generally, a covenant to settle).

Whether a beneficiary in this situation has a remedy against a settlor who refuses to settle the property on the trustees (and thereby completely constitute the trust) depends on various factors.

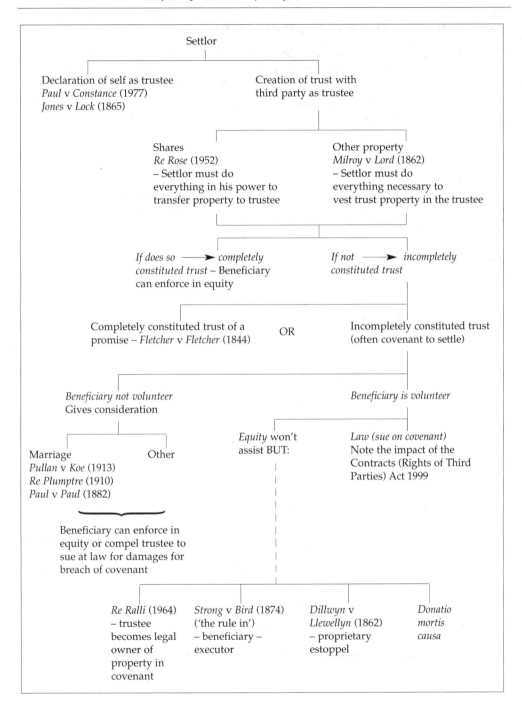

In equity (the remedy of specific performance)

If the beneficiary has given consideration (including marriage consideration: *Pullan* v *Koe* [1913] 1 Ch 9; *Re Plumptre's Marriage Settlement* [1910] 1 Ch 609; *Paul* v *Paul* (1882) 20 Ch D 742) he will have a remedy in equity. If he has not, then he will generally have no such remedy due to the maxim that 'equity will not assist a volunteer'. This is subject to a number of exceptions.

The rule in Strong v Bird

The donor must intend to make an immediate lifetime gift to the donee which fails for lack of compliance with the appropriate formalities. If the donor continues to intend to make this gift until his death and the donee becomes the executor or administrator of the estate, the gift is perfected.

The rule in Re Ralli's Will Trusts

The rule in *Strong* v *Bird* was extended to trustees. If the trust appears incompletely constituted but the trustee acquires title to the trust property, even if in a different capacity, the trust is constituted.

Proprietary estoppel – Dillwyn v Llewellyn

There are many cases on this topic now and since each case turns on its own facts, it is difficult to generalise. If A makes a representation to B about B's existing of future legal rights and B acts to his detriment in reliance on that representation, an equity arises in favour of B. The court will not allow A to enforce his strict legal rights and devise an appropriate remedy for B.

Donatio mortis causa

The donor, in contemplation of death, intends to make a gift which is conditional on his death and not fully effective until his death. He must transfer 'dominion' over the asset to the donee. He need not comply with the normal formalities for gifts. Thus if the necessary intent is present, a donatio of land may be made by handing over the deeds to the donee. In *Woodard* v *Woodard* [1995] 3 All ER 980 there was a gift of a car to his son by a man who died shortly afterwards. The father said 'you can keep the keys I will not be driving it any more'. The gift of the car without its logbook was upheld as a valid donatio mortis causa. As a result of the case of *Sen* v *Headley* [1991] Ch 425 it is now possible for land to form the subject matter of a donatio mortis causa.

At law (the remedy of damages for breach of covenant)

If the beneficiary is party to the covenant, he can sue on the covenant for damages: *Cannon* v *Hartley* [1949] Ch 213.

Another possibility is for the trustee to sue the settlor on the covenant on the beneficiary's behalf. It is unsettled as to whether this is possible. As is noted below, the matter is now much less significant.

It is clear that the trustees will not be able to do so if the subject matter of the covenant is future property as this is not recognised at law. If, however, the subject matter is existing property one line of cases suggest that the trustees should not, at least, sue on the covenant: *Re Pryce* [1917] 1 Ch 234; *Re Kay's Settlement* [1939] Ch 329; *Re Cook's Settlement Trusts* [1965] Ch 902. The case of *Re Cavendish-Browne's Settlement Trusts* [1916] WN 341, on the other hand, suggests that trustees can obtain a remedy for the beneficiary in this way. Furthermore, this case shows that if the trustees do so, they can obtain substantial damages (ie the amount of the beneficiary's loss) and not simply nominal damages (the amount of their own loss). However, this case is poorly reported and its authority is now regarded as doubtful.

It is important to note the impact of the Contracts (Rights of Third Parties) Act 1999. This Act grants rights to third parties to contracts, in that it allows those who are to have the benefit of a contract to sue. Covenants to settle property on trust will be similarly directly enforceable by the intended beneficiaries: *Re Pryce* [1917] 1 Ch 234 and *Re Kay's Settlement* [1939] Ch 329 will no longer need to be relied upon.

4.3 Key cases and statute

- *Dillwyn* v *Llewellyn* (1862) 4 De GF & J 517
  Proprietary estoppel – representation – detriment

- *Fletcher* v *Fletcher* (1844) 4 Hare 67
  Action by beneficiary – in equity – trust of the promise

- *Milroy* v *Lord* (1862) 4 De GF & J 264
  Transfer – all that has to be done

- *Paul* v *Constance* [1977] 1 WLR 527
  Declaration of self as trustee – no need for transfer

- *Re Rose* [1949] Ch 78
  Shares – everything in his power

- *Strong* v *Bird* (1874) LR 18 Eq 315
  Intention of gift in lifetime – formalities problem – donee the executor – gift perfected

- Contracts (Rights of Third Parties) Act 1999 – covenant to settle; directly enforceable by intended beneficiary

4.4 Questions and suggested solutions

QUESTION ONE

Is there an interpretation of the maxim 'Equity will not assist a volunteer' that both explains the decisions in the cases, and provides a principled justification for them? If not, what reforms are indicated?

University of London LLB Examination
(for External Students) Law of Trusts June 1998 Q1

General Comment

Although in their report the examiners described this question as 'fairly open-ended and standard', the requirements for a good answer are quite complex, requiring a detailed knowledge of the case law and the ability to analyse the application of the principles. The question requires the student's own interpretation of the maxim 'equity will not assist a volunteer' and proposals for reform. There is a danger that the well-prepared student will not have enough time to do justice to this question.

Skeleton Solution

Circumstances in which 'equity will not assist a volunteer' is invoked – review and explain the decisions: 'will not perfect an imperfect gift' where no consideration from beneficiary – your interpretation of the maxim – principled justification – exceptions: *Strong* v *Bird*; donatio mortis causa; proprietary estoppel – conclusion: your proposals for reform – Contracts (Rights of Third Parties) Act 1999.

Suggested Solution

The equitable maxim 'equity will not assist a volunteer' is usually invoked when a trust has been incompletely constituted. This may arise when the formalities for the passing of legal title to the property have not been fully complied with, or if the intention of the donor is uncertain, or if the promisor has failed to act upon a covenant.

Where the formalities necessary to pass title to the property have not been complied with, or the donor's intention to create a trust rather than make a gift is uncertain, this is often expressed as 'equity will not assist a volunteer to perfect an imperfect gift'. This arose in the 'baby' case *Jones* v *Lock* (1865) 1 Ch App 25 where a father's gesture in offering his baby son a cheque was held to be an invalid gift, because he had failed to carry out the formality of endorsing the cheque in his son's favour before his death some time later. His declaration 'Look you here, I give this to baby' was held to be an expression of an intention to make a gift, not create a trust, and equity could not therefore be invoked to supply a trust of the cheque when the formalities for transfer of ownership had not been complied with, causing the gift to fail. By contrast, in *Paul* v *Constance* [1977] 1 WLR 527, the Court of Appeal held that a declaration that 'the money is as much yours as it is mine' in relation to a bank account in the sole name of one party was a sufficiently certain declaration of trust, and the argument that this was an imperfect gift failed.

In *Milroy* v *Lord* (1862) 4 De GF & J 264 the formalities for the transfer of bank shares, which were intended to be made over to Lord as trustee, had not been complied with at the time of the settlor's death. The settlor had not executed a formal share transfer and the transfer had not been registered with the bank. However, the settlor had given Lord power of attorney to enable him to carry out these formal requirements, which he failed to do. The judge held that, for the transfer to be valid, the settlor must have done everything which, according to the nature of the property, must be done to transfer title. The court did not accept that giving the trustee the means to comply with the necessary formalities discharged this requirement, despite the fact that the settlor had done all he could to enable the transfer of the shares to be effected.

This case was followed in *Re Fry* [1946] Ch 312, but by contrast in *Re Rose* [1949] Ch 78 it was held to be sufficient that the settlor had done everything in his power to transfer the shares. The settlor in that case had executed a share transfer form and handed it to the beneficiary, but the beneficiary had failed to register the transfer. The court took the view that there was nothing else the settlor could have done, and that this was the correct test of validity. The judge concluded that the settlor's intention to transfer the shares was plain from the course of action which he took. One of the arguments in favour of this proposition is that the settlor, in effect, has declared himself a trustee of the shares pending the completion of registration in the name of the new owner. If it was not the settlor's intention to declare a trust of the shares, is this not, in effect, perfecting an imperfect gift in favour of a volunteer? Nevertheless, this precedent was applied in *Mascell* v *Mascell* (1984) 81 LS Gaz 2218 in relation to an incomplete transfer of registered land.

'Equity will not assist a volunteer' is also an expression of the principle that a court of equity will not enforce a promise for which nothing has been given in return. It is an example of the application of another maxim, 'equity follows the common law'. At common law a covenant, contract or promise will only be binding if there is good consideration, or if the recipient is a party to a deed by which the promise is given (since a deed is considered to be a solemn form of covenant, where the deed itself is proof enough that the promise is intended to be binding). If the promise is given by deed, the parties can enforce it at common law. However, if no consideration has been given for the promise, the recipient cannot seek specific performance in equity, because the promise is voluntary, and in equity the promisor is then free to withdraw the promise even if it has been given by deed.

Good consideration in this context is construed as money or money's worth or marriage consideration. The marriage consideration arises where a promise is given to settle money or property in return for an agreement to marry. The requirements necessary for marriage to be deemed good consideration were laid down in *Re Densham* [1975] 1 WLR 1519, and are as follows:

a) the promise must be made before and in consideration of the marriage or pursuant to an ante-nuptial agreement;

b) it must be conditional upon the marriage taking place;

c) it must be made in order to encourage or facilitate the marriage.

The marriage settlement is then enforceable by the parties to the marriage and by their issue (ie children and grandchildren). Children of former marriages of the parties are also within the consideration (*Attorney-General* v *Jacobs-Smith* [1895] 2 QB 341) because their interests are closely related to those of the children of the marriage. However, illegitimate children and others to whom the parties stand in loco parentis are outside the marriage consideration.

The operation of these rules is illustrated by *Pullan* v *Koe* [1913] 1 Ch 9. In the marriage settlement, the wife covenanted to put into the settlement any property having a value of £100 or more which she acquired after the marriage. She later received £285, which, in breach of covenant, she paid to her husband and which he invested. On the husband's death the trustees claimed the £285 in investments from his estate. They were entitled to do so, because as soon as the wife received the money, it was subject to her covenant to settle all after-acquired property, and thus impressed with the trust under the maxim 'equity looks on as done that which ought to be done', the wife had covenanted to settle the property and equity treated it as settled from the time of her promise. Anyone within the marriage consideration could enforce the promise.

Often in such settlements, there is a gift over to the next of kin in the event that those within the marriage consideration should fail to take the gift. It was held in *Re Plumptre's Marriage Settlement* [1910] 1 Ch 609 that the next of kin in such circumstances could not enforce the settlement, even though it had been validly created – they were not within the marriage consideration and were thus volunteers.

Where the beneficiaries are volunteers, the courts have consistently refused leave to the trustees to specifically enforce covenants to which they were themselves parties. There is conflict within the case law as to whether trustees have the common law right to sue in damages. The leading case is *Re Pryce* [1917] 1 Ch 234 in which leave to the trustees to sue on a covenant to settle after-acquired property was refused, on the ground that to permit such an action would enable the volunteers to sue on the covenant by indirect means. Eve J regarded the covenant as a mere voluntary contract to create a trust. This decision was followed in *Re Kay's Settlement* [1939] Ch 329 and subsequently in *Re Cook's Settlement Trusts* [1965] Ch 902 where Buckley J dealt with a similar case as one of contracts, not of trusts. In that case, the son had made a promise to pay the proceeds of sale of some valuable artefacts (including a Rembrandt painting) into trust for his children, should the artefacts ever be sold. However, this was not a marriage settlement and so the marriage consideration did not apply: the children/beneficiaries were mere volunteers. The trustees were refused leave to sue on their behalf, even though they themselves were parties to the settlement. Buckley J concluded that the court should positively direct the trustees not to take proceedings to enforce the covenant. Further, since the covenant did not create a debt enforceable at law, it did not give rise to a property right which was capable of being the subject matter of an immediate trust when the promise was made.

Buckley J distinguished this case from *Fletcher* v *Fletcher* (1844) 4 Hare 67 which concerned a trust of existing, not future, property (and which was decided at a time when the court was still prepared to uphold a trust created by precatory words). Buckley J also declined to follow *Re Cavendish-Browne's Settlement Trust* [1916] WN 341, where substantial damages at common law were awarded to the trustees, when, at the time of her death, the promisor had failed to settle into trust property already in her possession at the time the promise was made. Because the covenant related to specified property, there was a measurable loss. However, the question of assisting volunteers was not addressed in this case.

The principle 'equity will not assist a volunteer' might therefore be interpreted in the following way. The only way in which a volunteer can establish a right to the subject matter of a promise for which he or she has given no consideration is to show that the promisor made a valid declaration of trust, in which the three certainties are established and concerning which all the requisite formalities have been complied with. This will establish conclusively that it was the irrevocable intention of the promisor to create a trust and that no other form of gift was intended.

The justification for this principle is that 'equity looks to the substance rather than the form'. If the volunteer cannot enforce the covenant, the trustee can be in no better a position than the beneficiaries. If there is no clear declaration of trust (although informal words will suffice: *Paul* v *Constance* [1977] 1 WLR 527), or if the formalities for the passing of legal title to the property have not been completed, there is no certainty of a continuing intention. The court was able to establish such certainty, however, in the case of *Re Rose* [1949] Ch 78, where the settlor had done everything in his power to ensure that the transaction would be completed. In the case of after-acquired property, there is no certainty of subject matter and the trustees cannot enforce the trust or establish any right at common law to the promised property. If the promise concerns property already in existence, the promise to settle can itself constitute trust property and the trustees can claim the property in contract on behalf of the trust, whether or not the beneficiaries have given consideration. If the beneficiaries have given consideration, including marriage consideration, for the property, they can enforce the promise or call on the trustees to do so on their behalf. It is submitted that the rules relating to volunteers are justified and relatively consistent in that they relate back to the requirements for the constitution of a valid trust.

There are some exceptions to the maxim, however, when the court will assist the volunteer:

a) the rule in *Strong* v *Bird* (1874) LR 18 Eq 315 where the legal title passes to the trustees in another legal capacity, in this case as executor under a will, and the trust is thereby constituted by the completion of the formalities for passing legal title to the property;

b) donatio mortis causa where the settlor disposes of property by informal means in contemplation of death: the gift takes effect only if the donor dies;

c) the application of the doctrine of proprietary estoppel where a voluntary promise has been made to the donee, who then relies on the promise and acts to their detriment. This brings to an end the donor's right to claim their strict legal rights, because it would be inequitable to allow them to go back on their promise.

These exceptions are dependent on principles of equity which override the application of the maxim relating to volunteers.

The contractual rights of third parties who are not privy to a contract have now been addressed in the Contracts (Rights of Third Parties) Act 1999. Under this legislation, a third party can enforce rights granted to them if the contract so provides, or if the contract confers a benefit and there is no provision excluding the third party's right to enforce. If, following *Re Cooks Settlement Trusts* [1965] Ch 902, the rights of beneficiaries in these circumstances are founded in contract, this legislation appears to give volunteer beneficiaries new rights to sue. It is submitted that there can be no automatic right in equity for a volunteer to enforce a promise, since equitable remedies are discretionary. Further, it is only just that the equitable balance should favour the promisor when the promise is voluntary and has not been fulfilled. Such promises are often made in a family context, where the courts are traditionally reluctant to intervene. Thus, the new legislation satisfies the need for reform, and such equitable rights as are afforded to beneficiaries and trustees strike a fair balance between the promisor and one who has not given consideration for that promise.

QUESTION TWO

Consider whether a valid and enforceable trust has been created (and if so for whose benefit) in each of the following cases.

a) On returning from their honeymoon, A said to his new wife, B: 'Darling, from now on I will hold this house and everything in it upon trust for the two of us'.

b) Two years ago C covenanted with D to transfer to him investments worth £20,000 to be held in trust for E. C has recently died without having performed the covenant.

c) Last year F wrote to his nephew, G, enclosing a cheque for £30,000 payable to G, and stating in the letter: 'I am sending you this cheque so as to enable your daughter, H, to receive a Swiss education'. Shortly before leaving England to take up a place in a Swiss academy, H was fatally injured in a road accident.

d) By his will J, who has recently died, left £40,000 to K and directed that K should hold the same upon trust to distribute the capital 'amongst such one or more of J's good friends as K shall consider most deserving and (if more than one) in such shares as K shall think fit'.

University of London LLB Examination
(for External Students) Law of Trusts June 1993 Q1

General Comment

This question highlights the interaction of the three key areas of express trusts, namely (a) the 'three certainties', (b) 'formalities' and (c) 'constitution', and as such benefits from a brief resumé of each of the three. Thereafter the four scenarios can be properly considered.

Skeleton Solution

Three certainties: formalities; constitution – *Paul* v *Constance* and s53(1)(b) LPA 1925 – trust of a promise and *Fletcher* v *Fletcher* – resulting trusts, *Re Sanderson's Trusts* – discretionary trusts; *McPhail* v *Doulton*.

Suggested Solution

To establish a valid and enforceable trust it is necessary to comply with a number of fundamental requirements. Perhaps the three most important of these are conveniently referred to as (a) the 'three certainties'; (b) 'formalities' and (c) 'constitution'. Before turning to the four scenarios in question it is useful to briefly outline these three.

The three certainties are certainty of intention, subject matter and objects; that is, it must be clear that the settlor intended to create a trust with all of its ensuing rights and obligations. Whilst there is no set formula, or wording, to evidence such intention, generally mere precatory words (those expressing a wish or desire) are insufficient: *Re Adams and The Kensington Vestry* (1884) 27 Ch D 394). Similarly the subject matter, or trust property, must be clearly identifiable; this includes being able to identify any shares if more than one beneficiary is intended: *Sprange* v *Barnard* (1789) 2 Bro CC 585 and *Boyce* v *Boyce* (1849) 16 Sim 476). Finally the objects, or beneficiaries, of the intended trust must be ascertained or ascertainable; albeit that this test varies slightly according to the exact nature of the trust: *McPhail* v *Doulton* [1971] AC 424.

In addition to the three certainties the settlor must also comply with any formalities imposed in respect of the trust property on which he is trying to impose a trust. There are no formalities for personalty (money, chattels etc); however s53(1)(b) Law of Property Act (LPA) 1925 requires any declaration of trust in respect of land (either freehold or leasehold) to be evidenced in writing. Failure to comply is not fatal to the trust, for rather than being void the declaration of trust is unenforceable until evidenced in writing.

Finally there is the need to constitute the trust. This only arises if the trust property is to be transferred to a third party who is to act as a trustee and not if the settlor has declared himself trustee. However, if a third party is to be trustee the trust property must be transferred (according to any legal formalities by virtue of the property's nature) to the third party. Failing which the intended beneficiary will fall foul of the general equitable doctrine that 'equity will not assist a volunteer' (that is someone who has not given consideration, money or money's worth). Unless the beneficiary can show he is not a volunteer, or show that one of the exceptions to the general principle applies, failure to transfer the property will result in the trust being unenforceable.

It is now appropriate to consider the four scenarios to determine if a valid and enforceable trust has been created in each.

a) A's declaration of trust of 'this house and everything in it' probably complies with all of the three certainties. Namely there is sufficient certainty of intention: *Paul* v *Constance* [1977] 1 WLR 527; subject matter (albeit that an inventory of the house contents would be useful); and beneficiaries (A and B). Similarly A has declared himself as trustee therefore there are no problems of constitution. However, insofar as A has attempted to declare a trust in respect of the house, until this is evidenced in writing the trust in respect of the house (not the contents) will be unenforceable: s53(1)(b) LPA 1925.

b) Similarly C's covenant of £20,000 worth of investments to be transferred to D and to be held on trust for E probably satisfies the requirements of the three certainties. C's intention is clearly evidenced by the terms of the covenant itself; likewise the identity of the beneficiary, namely E, is clear. However, there could be a problem as regards the nature of the investments to be held on trust (especially as they have not been transferred and therefore identified). It is probable, however, that the court would not find this as fatal to finding a valid and enforceable trust so long as £20,000 worth of investments to which the trust could attach could be shown to exist.

Further, insofar as the trust property is personalty (not realty) there are no formalities to be complied with.

Despite this it is unlikely that C's covenant has created a valid and enforceable trust. The property has not been transferred to D. (We can only presume transfer has not taken place by virtue of D being C's executor or personal representative: *Strong* v *Bird* (1874) LR 18 Eq 315.) Similarly neither D nor E seem to have given any consideration for C's covenant (we are not advised if E is the 'issue of marriage' so as to qualify as having given consideration through marriage: *Pullan* v *Koe* [1913] 1 Ch 9). E therefore appears to be a volunteer (as does D) and is unlikely to be able to enforce the trust.

One possible exception is for D to sue C's estate for damages (not specific performance) on behalf of E (indeed at E's insistence) for C's alleged breach of promise: *Fletcher* v *Fletcher* (1844) 4 Hare 67. However this requires C to be shown to have intended not only to create a trust but to permit D to be able to sue to enforce the trust. Generally the court will only find this if a special relationship can be shown to exist between C and E (akin to a family link). This is doubtful on the facts.

c) F has attempted to create a trust in favour of H. There is certainty of subject matter, the £30,000, and certainty of objects, H. Further there are no formalities required in respect of money and F has constituted the trust by sending the money, by cheque, to G to hold as trustee. However, H has died before taking her place up in the Swiss academy, the apparent reason for F having established the trust.

In these circumstances there are three possible results. The first is that the trust has failed and the money results back to F, by resulting trust: *Re Abbott Fund (Trusts of the)* [1900] 2 Ch 326. Alternatively G will be held to have been given the money absolutely subject to the terms of the trust in favour of H. Therefore H's death enables G to take the money absolutely: *Re Andrew's Trust* [1905] 2 Ch 48. Finally it is possible for H to have received the money (albeit held on trust) absolutely subject to the general condition that she attend a Swiss school. The money (or the benefit of the trust) would pass to H's estate on her death. The most likely, and accepted view is that the gift is absolute and that G will take the money absolutely.

d) J has attempted to establish a trust in respect of a number of (unidentified) friends. There is certainty of intention and subject matter. There is also no problem with formalities; the trust property is £40,000 and similarly the property has been transferred to K as trustee thereby constituting the trust.

Having noted this, the objects of the trust 'such one or more of J's good friends as K shall consider most deserving and (if more than one) in such shares as K shall think fit' is more problematical. J has attempted to create a discretionary trust which requires the beneficiaries (or potential beneficiaries) to be conceptually certain: *McPhail* v *Doulton* [1971] AC 424. Whilst 'old friends' had previously been upheld as being sufficiently certain this is widely regarded as now being insufficient. The trust is therefore likely to fail and the money revert to J's estate.

QUESTION THREE

'The dictum "Equity will not assist a volunteer to perfect an imperfect gift" seems to be more honoured in the breach than in the observance.'

Discuss.

University of London LLB Examination
(for External Students) Law of Trusts June 1999 Q2

General Comment

This is a straightforward question, but its scope is narrower than that of Question One in this chapter: here the student must concentrate on the cases relating to imperfect gifts, and the answer requires a critical analysis of the application of the rule. There is a considerable overlap between the subject matter of the two questions, but the requirements of the examiner in each case are specific, and neither question will be answered at all well if they are addressed as 'write all you know' questions.

Skeleton Solution

Explain the maxim and its application – review cases: *Jones* v *Lock*; *Richards* v *Delbridge*; *Paul* v *Constance*; *Milroy* v *Lord*; *Re Fry*; *Re Rose*; *Mascell* v *Mascell* – explain the circumstances in which the rule has not been followed – conclusion: say whether you agree with the proposition in the question and why.

Suggested Solution

Where a gift fails for want of the formalities necessary to pass legal title, the court will not impose the burden of a trust on the donor in order to allow the gift to be made by other means. If the formalities have not been complied with fully, the court will look to the intention of the donor, and only where the words and circumstances indicate clearly that it was the donor's intention to make an irrevocable declaration of trust will the property pass to the beneficiary or trustee: equity will not assist a volunteer to perfect an imperfect gift.

In the nineteenth century cases this rule was applied strictly. For example, in *Jones* v *Lock* (1865) 1 Ch App 25 the court refused to impose a trust on the basis of a 'loose conversation' between a father and his family. The father was reprimanded for not bringing his baby son a present when he returned from a business trip. He took a cheque out of his pocket and gave it to the baby, then took the cheque back and locked it in a safe. The cheque was found at the time of the father's death. The cheque had not been endorsed in favour of the baby, and the court refused to construe the words of gift used by the father as a declaration of trust. Clear, unambiguous words are necessary, although the word 'trust' need not be used.

Similarly, in *Richards* v *Delbridge* (1874) LR 18 Eq 11, a grandfather's attempt to give his business to his grandson (who was a minor) failed for want of formality. The grandfather endorsed on the lease of the business premises a memorandum of the gift. This was not effective to pass title in the lease, and, in any event, a minor could not hold real property. The court held that there was no clear declaration of trust. Again, the rule was strictly applied.

In the case of *Paul* v *Constance* [1977] 1 WLR 527 the words used by the donor were held to be a sufficiently clear declaration of trust to defeat argument that the fund was a gift within the terms of *Jones* v *Lock*. The property was an account with Barclays Bank in the sole name of Constance, who was cohabiting with Mrs Paul in the days when living together was considered to be 'living in sin'. To spare Mrs Paul embarrassment, the bank manager suggested that the account be held in Mr Constance's sole name, but Mr Constance declared, with the bank manager as witness and on numerous other occasions, that the money he paid into the account 'is as much yours as it is mine' (meaning that it belonged to Mrs Paul as much as to him). This was held by Scarman

LJ to be a valid declaration of trust, showing a clear intention that the money be held thereafter for the benefit of both Mr Constance and Mrs Paul. The way in which the account was operated was consistent with this declaration, and there was also a previous course of dealing which established joint ownership in equity.

Another line of cases concern situations where the donor believes he has taken all the necessary steps to effect a gift. Here, the leading case is *Milroy v Lord* (1862) 4 De GF & J 264. In this case, the donor thought he had done everything he could to allow a gift of shares in a bank to proceed. He executed a deed, which did not itself constitute a valid transfer of the shares, but he also gave the trustee power of attorney to enable him to carry out all the formalities necessary for an effective transfer of the shares. The trustee neglected to use the power of attorney, and it ceased to have effect on the donor's subsequent death. Refusing to recognise the transaction as a valid transfer in favour of the beneficiary, the judge observed that in order for property in the shares to pass to the trustee, the settlor must have done everything which was necessary according to the nature of the property to transfer title in the property and to render the settlement binding. He suggested four ways in which a gift might be effected, and said that if the donor intended the gift to take effect in one way, the court could not allow it to operate in another way. The case suggests that the trust will not be properly constituted until the shares are registered in the name of the trustee.

This was followed in *Re Fry* [1946] Ch 312 where the transfer was not completed because the donor was unable to comply with Treasury regulations, which were in force at the time. The donor had completed all the necessary documentation, but Treasury consent to the transaction had not been obtained before he died.

However, in *Re Rose* [1952] Ch 499 the Court of Appeal departed from this strict approach. This was a tax case. Rose had executed share transfers, but the directors of the company had failed to register them until three months later. The question for the Court was when the transfer was effective, as estate duty would be payable if the date of registration was the relevant date, but not if the date on which the transfers were signed by Rose was the effective date. The Court held that the transfer was effective when the settlor had done everything in his power to effect the transfer, because the actual registration of the transfer was beyond his power. The Court followed an earlier, unconnected, case also called *Re Rose* [1949] Ch 78, which distinguished *Milroy v Lord* (1862) 4 De GF & J 264 and *Re Fry* on the grounds that the settlors in those cases had not done all in their power according to the nature of the property to transfer the shares: the settlor in *Milroy v Lord* had executed a power of attorney, which did not itself pass title to the property, and in *Re Fry* it was the testator's responsibility to obtain Treasury permission. By contrast, it was not Rose's responsibility to register the shares in the names of the trustees. He had fulfilled his role in signing the necessary papers, and thus divested himself of ownership of the shares.

Yet, until the shares were registered in the name of the new legal owner, Rose still retained legal title to the shares. There is no clear intention to declare himself trustee, and under the rule in *Milroy v Lord*, this should defeat the gift of the shares, as equity will not allow the gift to take effect by alternative means. Pending transfer of the legal title, Rose had done everything in his power to effect the transfer. An alternative interpretation is that he held the title under a constructive trust until the formalities were completed. Certainly Rose would have manifested the necessary intention, but it was still open to the directors to object to the transfer, and they could have required further action on the part of the transferor, Rose.

Re Rose [1952] Ch 499 was subsequently followed in *Mascell* v *Mascell* (1984) 81 LS Gaz 2218, where a transfer of registered land had been executed by the transferor, sent to the Inland Revenue for stamping and had been handed to his son (who had in fact given consideration) together with the Land Certificate. Before the son could send the documents to HM Land Registry for registration of his title to the property, the transferor and the son quarrelled and the transferor changed his mind. Following *Re Rose*, the court held that the gift was complete, as the transferor had done all in his power to effect the transfer of the property. In the case of a transfer of land, there is a statutory duty on the part of the Land Registry to register the new title, so it could truly be said that the transferor had done all in his power to effect the title, and at the point when he tried to revoke the transaction it had become irrevocable.

The later cases seem to show that equity will assist a volunteer to perfect an imperfect gift, but the evidence of the donor's intention is perhaps stronger in these later cases. In *Paul* v *Constance* [1977] 1 WLR 527, the person challenging Mrs Paul's entitlement to the money was Mr Constance's estranged wife, who was the beneficiary on his intestacy. The words used by Mr Constance were very clear, but Lord Scarman expressed some reservations: the case was only argued before him as one of express trust. He carefully reviewed the requirements of certainty and formality for a valid express trust and was satisfied that these requirements were fulfilled. Yet he pointed out that it was difficult to say exactly when the trust had been declared, and also noted that there was no argument as to whether this would be dealt with more appropriately as a case of constructive trust. Scarman LJ himself concluded that this was a borderline case.

By contrast with *Milroy* v *Lord* (1862) 4 De GF & J 264, in *Re Rose* Rose had followed the normal course of a transfer of shares, and the failure to register was beyond his control. His own actions clearly indicated his true intention. The son in *Mascell* had in any event given consideration, so there is scope for a future court to distinguish *Re Rose* in the case of a voluntary transaction, although it is suggested that this is unlikely in the case of a straightforward transfer of shares or of real property.

It is thus submitted that it cannot truly be said that the maxim 'equity will not assist a volunteer to perfect an imperfect gift' is always strictly applied. What the cases demonstrate is more of a willingness and desire for the court to give effect to the true intentions of the donor when these can be established beyond reasonable doubt.

Chapter 5
Secret Trusts and Mutual Wills

5.1   **Introduction**

5.2   **Key points**

5.3   **Key cases**

5.4   **Questions and suggested solutions**

	Communication		Acceptance		Changes	Attest will		Trustee beneficiary	
	When?	By sealed letter?	Implied?	More than one trustee?		By secret trust?	By secret beneficiary?	Sole beneficiary?	Other?
Secret	Before death – *Wallgrave v Tebbs* (1855)	OK – if trustee knows it contains terms of trust	Possible *Ottaway v Norman* (1972)	Effect depends on whether they hold as joint tenants or tenants in common	Each change must be communicated to and accepted by trustee *Re Colin Cooper* (1939)	Trust fails	Trust valid	Trustee cannot take any benefit	Trustee can take if can prove by evidence – *Re Rees* (1950)
Half-Secret	*Re Keen* (1937) Before or at date of will – *Blackwell v Blackwell* (1929)	OK – if will refers to it having been done		If one accepts (before or at date of will) all are bound They hold as joint tenants		Trust valid – *Cresswell v Cresswell* (1868)			

5.1 Introduction

Secret and half-secret trusts are out-of-date topics in that in reality they are now practically extinct. The rules remain, however, and are straightforward. More complicated are the arguments surrounding the nature of such trusts – express or constructive – and the various rationales which have been put forward on the doctrine. The only way for a student to gain sufficient understanding of these problems is to familiarise yourself fully with at least some of the many articles written about them. Cases and textbooks alone will not offer the answers.

5.2 Key points

Secret trusts

Background

Wills are public documents and thus any legacies made in them are open to public scrutiny. The doctrine of secret and half-secret trusts evolved to enable legacies to be made privately.

Secret trusts can arise in cases of inter vivos gifts: *Bannister* v *Bannister* [1948] 2 All ER 133, and in cases of intestacy: *McCormick* v *Grogan* (1869) LR 4 HL 82. However, the main area of their applicatioin is trusts created by will. In *Gold and Another* v *Hill* (1998) The Times 24 August a further method was allowed. It was decided that where a person is nominated as a beneficiary under a life assurance policy and the nominee is then told to hold the money for his family's benefit then this will cause that person to hold on constructive trust through the operation of secret trust principles.

SECRET	HALF-SECRET
Nature	
Where	Where a trust is created on the face of the will, but the beneficiaries are not named. The will must refer to communication having already taken place. If it refers to future communication the trust will be invalid under the 'best evidence rule'.
a) No sign of a trust on the face of the will; or	
b) Any words in the will attempting to create a half-secret trust fail the test for certainty of intention (see Chapter 2).	
Communication	
a) When	
Testator must communicate fact of trust to secret-trustee at any time during testator;'s lifetime (ie can be done after date of will): *Wallgrave* v *Tebbs* (1855) 2 K & J 313.	Communication must be before or contemporaneously with making of the will: *Blackwell* v *Blackwell* [1929] AC 318 and *Re Bateman* [1970] 3 All ER 817. If none, trustees hold on resulting trusts for the residuary beneficiary under the will (or, if none, those entitled on intestacy) and never take beneficially themselves.

SECRET	HALF-SECRET
If no communication, secret trustee takes absolutely if he knew nothing of any trust. If the person knew he was to take as trustee but did not know the terms of the trust, there is a resulting trust to the estate.	

b) Terms

All terms must be communicated (trust property, beneficiaries and how much each is to receive): *Re Boyes* (1884) 26 Ch D 531. If the fact of the trust, but not the terms, is communicated, the trustee holds on trust for the residuary beneficiary.	Same, except that the fact of the trust will always be communicated in the will.

c) By sealed letter

If trustee is handed a sealed envelope before death not to be opened until after testator's death, this will satisfy the communication requirement if the trustee knows the envelope contains the terms of trust: *Re Keen* [1937] Ch 236.	If trustee is handed an envelope before or contemporaneously with the date of the will and the will refers to this having already been done, this will satisfy the communication requirement: *Re Keen* [1937] Ch 236.

d) Nature

Communication must be of a legally binding obligation and not merely a moral obligation: *McCormick* v *Grogan* (1869) LR 4 HL 82. In other words, it must satisfy the test of certainty of intention. If no such certainty, trustee takes absolutely. If certainty, but trust fails on another ground, trustee holds on trust for residuary beneficiary.	Same. If words in the will are not sufficiently certain, the only possibility is a fully-secret trust.

Acceptance

a) General

Trustee must expressly or impliedly (*Ottaway* v *Norman* [1972] Ch 698) accept the trust. If the terms of the	Same. Acceptance must also be before or contemporaneously with the date of the will.

SECRET	HALF-SECRET
trust are communicated and the trustee rejects, he holds on trust for the residuary beneficiary. If only the fact of the trust is communicated, the trustee can take absolutely if he rejects: *Wallgrave* v *Tebbs* (1855) 2 K & J 313.	

b) Gift to more that one trustee

As tenants in common: if one accepts on behalf of all, only the one who actually accepts is bound.

As joint tenants: if one accepts before the date of the will, all are bound.

If one accepts after date of will, only he is bound and the others can take their share beneficially.

HALF-SECRET: Always take as joint tenants in equity, and thus all will always be bound, since if one accepts after the date of the will, the half-secret trust fails in any event.

Changes

Each change must be communicated to and accepted by the trustee: *Re Cooper (Colin)* [1939] Ch 811.

HALF-SECRET: Same.

Revocation

Following *Re Gardner (No 2)* [1923] 2 Ch 330 this does not appear to be possible as the beneficiary acquires an interest as soon as the trust is communicated and accepted. However, this case has been strongly criticised.

Attestation of the will

a) By secret beneficiary

By s15 Wills Act 1837 a witness or their spouse cannot benefit under a will. However, in equity, the beneficiary can take the benefit as the trust operates outside the will: *Re Young (Dec'd)* [1951] Ch 344.

HALF-SECRET: Same.

SECRET	HALF-SECRET
b) By trustee	
Legacy and trust fail as the trust has nothing to operate on.	Legacy succeeds because there is a trust on the face of the will following *Cresswell v Cresswell* (1868) LR 6 Eq 69.

Secret beneficiary predeceases testator

Following *Re Gardner (No 2)* [1923] 2 Ch 330 the trust is not defeated as the beneficiary receives his interest when the trust is created.	Same.

Secret trustee predeceases testator

Trust fails: *Re Maddock* [1902] 2 Ch 220.	Provided the purpose of the trust is known it should be enforced as equity will not allow trust to fail for want of a trustee.

Secret trustee is also a beneficiary

a) Sole beneficiary	
Cannot take under trust: *Re Pugh's Will Trusts* [1967] 1 WLR 1262.	Same.
b) Other	
Re Rees' Will Trust [1950] Ch 204 suggests that trustees can take if can prove evidence other than their own of existence of the gift. Possibly written evidence is required.	

Express or constructive trust?

Half-secret trust of land must be evidenced in writing under s53(1)(b) LPA: see *Re Baillie* (1886) 2 TLR 660, but in *Ottaway v Norman* [1972] Ch 698 a fully-secret trust or land was valid without written evidence. This suggests a fully-secret trust is constructive but a half-secret trust is express.

Rationales

a) Doctrine of incorporation (half-secret trusts).

b) Fraud. It is not necessary to comply with the Wills Act 1837 because equity will not allow it to be used as an instrument of fraud.

c) Inter-vivos trusts: *Re Gardner (No 2)* [1923] 2 Ch 330.

d) Operate outside the will: *Re Young (Dec'd)* [1951] Ch 344.

Mutual wills

Elements

Similar wills and intention that they should be irrevocable.

Husbands and wives may wish to try to ensure that their wealth is passed to their spouse upon their death and then on to their children after the death of the other spouse. If they both make wills in similar terms the problem is that the survivor may attempt to revoke his or her will. The doctrine of mutual wills provides a means to give effect to the original arrangement. The parties have to agree not to revoke their will; unless of course they agree to revoke or alter their wills. People other than husbands and wives may wish to make the same or similar arrangements. In the case of *Re Dale* [1994] Ch 31 parents wished to ensure that their son and daughter would have equal shares of their property upon the death of each parent. The father died and his property was duly shared between the children. Upon the death of the mother a problem arose because the mother had made a new will in which the daughter received much less than the son. The court enforced the original arrangement. In such cases an implied or constructive trust is held to arise. For a mutual will to operate there must be evidence of the intention of the parties that this is what they intended. In *Goodchild* v *Goodchild* (1997) The Times 12 May a husband and wife made identical wills, the wife died and the husband remarried. Wills are normally revoked upon marriage (s8 Wills Act 1837). A further problem was that the husband sought to leave property to his new wife by means of a new will whilst the original will had been in favour of his son. The court thought that the husband was bound by a trust that arose when his first wife had died.

Similar wills

a) Not necessarily identical: *Re Cleaver* [1981] 1 WLR 939.

b) Can be in a joint will: *Re Hagger* [1930] 2 Ch 190.

Irrevocable

a) Evidence can be found from the recitals in the wills: *Re Hagger* [1930] 2 Ch 190.

b) Very similar wills equals irrevocable intention: *Re Oldham* [1925] Ch 75.

Effect

a) Between parties during life equals a contract.

b) On the survivor – bound by trust: *Re Hagger* [1930] 2 Ch 190.

Subject matter of trust

a) Specific property or the whole of the deceased's estate: *Re Green* [1951] Ch 148.

b) Survivor's property – subject to trust: *Re Hagger* [1930] 2 Ch 190.

c) Survivor's ability to deal with property: *Birmingham* v *Renfrew* (1937) 57 CLR 666.

5.3 Key cases

* *Blackwell* v *Blackwell* [1929] AC 318
  Half-secret trust – communication – not after will

* *Re Dale* [1994] Ch 31
  Mutual wills – constructive trust – defeated new will

* *Wallgrave* v *Tebbs* (1855) 2 K & J 313
  Secret trust – communication – during lifetime

5.4 Questions and suggested solutions

QUESTION ONE

Ted prepares a will in which he leaves his car to Fran absolutely, his equitable interest in 1,000 shares of XYZ plc held under a bare trust by his broker to Joan 'on the trust which I have communicated to her', and his house to Robert 'on the trust which I have communicated to him'. Ted holds a meeting with Fran, Robert and Joan, at which he tells them that on his death: Fran is to give the car to his mistress, Kate; Joan is to hold the equitable interest in the shares on trust for Kate and her son Eric; and Robert is to hold the house on trust for his nephew, Paul. They all agree to carry out Ted's instructions. Two weeks later Ted writes out and signs a memorandum of the meeting, and then executes the will. Some time later, Ted has a falling out with Paul, and sends a written instruction to Robert to hold the house on trust for Kate instead of Paul. Hearing news of this from Robert, both Fran and Joan become very upset with Ted, and together write him telling him that they are no longer willing to carry out the trusts. Ted then dies without making any changes to his will.

Discuss.

> University of London LLB Examination
> (for External Students) Law of Trusts June 1998 Q4

General Comment

This is a fairly straightforward question on secret trusts, but it requires some specific answers and addresses the issue of whether a testator can validly revoke a secret trust when the bequest to the named beneficiary stands.

Skeleton Solution

Nature of secret trusts – Fran; fully-secret – Joan and Robert; half-secret – *Blackwell* v *Blackwell* criteria – time of communication of trusts – requirement of writing for trust of land (s53(1)(b) LPA) and of an equitable interest (s53(1)(c) LPA) – revocation of trust by Ted – revocation of trusts by Joan and Fran; *Re Maddock*; *Blackwell*.

Suggested Solution

Ted has used the device of a secret trust to make testamentary gifts without the need to disclose his wishes on the face of the will itself. The will mentions the dispositions to Fran, Joan and Robert, and provides specifically that those to Joan and Robert are to be held by them on trust. Thus, Fran will become the trustee of a fully-secret trust, where the very existence of the trust is kept off the face of the will but its terms are communicated secretly to the trustee.

In *Blackwell* v *Blackwell* [1929] AC 318 Lord Buckmaster laid down the criteria for a valid secret trust:

a) the testator must have intended that the beneficiary named in the will should take the property subject to the trusts;

b) that intention must be communicated to the trustee; and

c) the trustee must accept the obligation, either expressly or by acquiescence.

At the meeting, which takes place before the will is executed, Ted communicates the terms of the three trusts to the proposed trustees. This fulfils the requirements that the terms of secret trusts must be communicated and accepted before the will is executed, in the case of half-secret trusts, and before the testator dies in the case of fully-secret trusts.

The memorandum of the meeting complies with the requirement in s53(1)(b) Law of Property Act (LPA) 1925 that the declaration of a trust of land (the house left to Robert) should be evidenced in writing and signed by the settlor. Once that meeting is concluded and recorded and the will is signed, Lord Buckmaster's three requirements have been complied with and the trusts are constituted in respect of the car and the house.

However, the shares left to Joan are the subject of a bare trust, of which Ted's broker is trustee. Ted is thus declaring a trust of an equitable interest, which in the case of a normal express private trust must be effected in writing within the terms of s53(1)(c) LPA 1925. In *Ottaway* v *Norman* [1972] Ch 698, the court upheld a fully-secret trust of real property on an oral declaration of trust on the ground that it would be fraud on the part of the named beneficiary to accept the bequest and not comply with its terms; arguably, the court might uphold the secret trust despite the want of formality.

Ted then tries to revoke or vary the terms of the secret trust. It is said (see *Blackwell* v *Blackwell*) that secret trusts operate independently of the will and, on that basis, as with other express private trusts, the court may not entertain variations or revocations of secret trusts after the trust is constituted by the execution of the will. Yet the purpose of the secret trust is to give effect to the true intention of the testator, and Ted's express intention was that Paul should not receive the house under the terms of the secret trust. Where, as here, there is no question of fraud, the court could be invited to recognise the revocation, whereupon the house would fall into residue, since Robert did not accept the new terms of the trust, which in any event were communicated after execution of the will and thus inadmissible.

Can Fran and Joan revoke their appointments as trustees? According to dicta in *Re Maddock* [1902] 2 Ch 220 Fran's renunciation of the gift will defeat the trust, because the rights of the beneficiary are dependent upon whether or not the legatee accepts the legacy. Under a fully-secret trust, the time for communication and acceptance runs until the date of death, when the will takes effect and, by analogy, the time during which the legatee can renounce should also run until death. In the case of the half-secret trust, of which Joan is trustee, Lord Buckmaster suggested in *Blackwell* v *Blackwell* [1929] AC 318 that, since the trust was declared on the face of the will, the court might uphold it and step in to appoint someone else as trustee (assuming it is not in any event defeated by s53(1)(c)).

Thus, the house may pass to Paul under the half-secret trust, despite Ted's change of heart. The car is likely to fall into residue, as, following *Re Maddock*, Kate can only receive it if Fran accepts the terms of the trust. The shares, if Lord Buckmaster's dicta are followed, will pass to Kate provided the court appoints a new trustee and provided that s53(1)(c) does not apply.

QUESTION TWO

By his will made in 1988, Fred leaves all his personal property to Brian and Bertrand. The will also states that he leaves all his real property to Cyril 'on trust for such person or persons as I shall communicate to him'. Last year, Fred handed Brian an envelope with the instruction that it was not to be opened until after his (Fred's) death. Unknown to Brian, the letter states that Fred's personal property should be held by Brian and Bertrand on trust for Gloria, Fred's mistress. At the same time, Fred telephones Cyril and tells him that the property he will receive under Fred's will should be held by him on trust for Roger, Fred's illegitimate son. Cyril agrees that he will do this.

Fred has now died. Advise Gloria and Roger as to any interests they may have in Fred's estate.

University of London LLB Examination
(for External Students) Law of Trusts June 1995 Q5

General Comment

Problem questions of this nature require the student to address the issues raised and apply the appropriate legal rules to them. The advantage of this type of problem is that it provides its own framework for the answers.

Skeleton Solution

Take each bequest in turn – half-secret trust problem – fully-secret trust.

Suggested Solution

There is a distinction between the real property and the personal property left by Fred after his death. Fred's will states that his real property is to be left on trusts to be communicated by Fred to Cyril. Fred does communicate the terms of this trust to Cyril in a telephone conversation. The property is to be held on trust for Roger. Cyril agrees to be a trustee on this basis. There is an issue here therefore of a secret trust. It is required by s53(1)(b) Law of Property Act 1925 that trusts of land must be evidenced in writing. Similarly, the Wills Act 1837 requires that testamentary dispositions of this sort must be made in writing.

The issue arises whether the precise terms of the trust must be evidenced, or simply that there is such information as to enable the parties to find out the terms of the trust. The issue is, therefore, whether the oral trust should be enforced, or whether the legatee should be required to hold the property on resulting trust for Fred's estate. The general rule is that the trust will be enforced in favour of the beneficiary Roger: *Thynn* v *Thynn* (1684) 1 Vera 296. On these facts, the secret trust should be enforced because the testator validly declared an inter vivos trust during his lifetime, and the trust thereby became constituted by the vesting of the property on his death in Cyril, the legatee.

However, this theoretical underpinning has not been the approach which the courts have taken in seeking to enforce secret trusts in these circumstances. The approach taken in the courts was that it would be a fraud if the legatee, Cyril, were allowed to retain the property: *McCormick* v *Grogan* (1869) LR 4 HL 82. This theory eludes the argument that the Wills Act 1837 is not being enforced if the trust is given effect without the observance of the relevant formalities. In these circumstances, the fact that the will states that Cyril holds only as trustee means that the property can be validly held for Roger's benefit as sole beneficiary under the trust, as in *Blackwell* v *Blackwell* [1929] AC 318.

With reference to Gloria's interest, there is a problem revolving around the conflict between the terms of Fred's will and the purported instruction handed to Brian that Fred's personal property be held for Gloria's benefit by Brian and Bertrand after his death. The will, made in 1988, states quite clearly that all of Fred's personal property is to pass to Brian and Bertrand. The written instruction to Brian, the content of which is undisclosed at the time it is given to Brian, was created in 1994. The issue therefore is whether the subsequent written instruction will override the bequest in the will.

There is no issue here that there would be a fraud if the property were to be passed to Bertrand. However, Brian is informed that the instruction exists but he is ignorant of the terms of the letter. Therefore, it can be said that Brian is bound by the terms of such instruction. For Brian to deny to be bound by those terms after Fred's death would permit him to perpetrate a fraud on the trust, because it might be that, had Brian objected to being bound by any such instruction, Fred would have made alternative arrangements for that property.

The general rule is that the legatee will hold the property on resulting trust for the estate. In *Re Boyes* (1884) 26 Ch D 531, where a solicitor had undertaken to hold a property on trust according to instructions he was to receive by letter, Kay J explained that the legatee accepts property on the basis of a trust which it would be a fraud for him not to carry into effect. Here there is no communication of the terms of the trust, as with Roger's gift, before the time of death, and therefore the property must be held on resulting trust rather than being passed on to Gloria.

QUESTION THREE

In 1989, Jenny executed a will containing the following dispositions:

> 'I leave (a) my freehold house and its contents to my friends, Katie and Mandy, knowing that they will carry out my wishes concerning the same and (b) all my residuary estate to Nicholas.'

The will was witnessed by Mandy and her husband.

In 1990 Jenny informed Katie that on her death she wished Katie and Mandy to sell the house and contents and divide half the proceeds between themselves equally and distribute the other half amongst such worthy or charitable causes as they thought fit.

Last year Katie was killed in a road accident. Jenny has recently died.

Advise Mandy, the estate of Katie, and Nicholas.

University of London LLB Examination
(for External Students) Law of Trusts June 1992 Q2

General Comment

The question on secret trusts is usually a popular choice with students, and this one raised some familiar issues, although with some complicated twists.

Skeleton Solution

Is this a secret or half-secret trust? – certainty of intention on the face of the will – if half-secret trust fails for late communication – if fully-secret, what is effect of communication to one trustee only? – can M benefit when she witnessed the will? – does trust survive the death of K? – is the trust wholly and exclusively charitable?

Suggested Solution

The first issue to be resolved is whether on the face of the will there is an outright gift to Katie and Mandy or whether on the face of the will, Katie and Mandy take as trustees. This depends on whether the will discloses an intention to impose a legally binding obligation on Katie and Mandy (see *Re Adams and The Kensington Vestry* (1884) 27 Ch D 394). There is no need to use expressions such as 'to hold on trust' to impose a trust, but here the wording of the will is vague. Whilst the will relates that Katie and Mandy know the testatrix's wishes, there does not appear to be any intention to oblige them to carry out those wishes, although no doubt she would be surprised if they did not. Should the court hold that there is an intention on the face of the will to impose a trust, such a trust will be a half-secret trust as its terms are not disclosed on the face of the will. The terms of a half-secret trust must be communicated before or at the same time as the execution of the will – see *Blackwell v Blackwell* [1929] AC 318. Here there is no communication by Jenny until after the execution of the will and any half-secret trust will fail – the house and its contents will revert to the estate and pass to Nicholas.

Therefore, it is strongly suggested that the will should be construed to make an outright gift to Katie and Mandy so that any trust will be a fully-secret trust. The terms of a fully-secret trust may be communicated at any time during the testator's lifetime, though not after his death (see *Wallgrave v Tebbs* (1855) 2 K & J 313). Thus it does not affect the validity of the fully-secret trust that it was communicated after Jenny made the will. Communication of a fully-secret trust of land may be oral (see *Ottaway v Norman* [1972] Ch 698), despite LPA 1925 s53(1)(b) which requires written evidence of a trust of land, signed by the settlor, except for resulting and constructive trusts. The courts will recognise a fully-secret trust despite the apparent contradiction of the formality provisions of Wills Act 1837. It has been said that the trust operates outside the will.

The next problem is that Jenny communicated her intentions to Katie alone. In passing it should be said that the communication itself shows a clear intention that the property be used in a particular way only and thus is sufficient to impose a trust. The case law on communication to one of two trustees is difficult to follow on a logical basis but *Re Stead* [1990] 1 Ch 237 appears to hold that if communication is made to one of two joint tenants, all are bound if the communication takes place before the execution of the will, but only those who have accepted the trust are bound if the communication is after the execution of the will. If the two take as tenants in common, only those who are told are bound, regardless of when the communication takes place (*Tee v Ferris* (1856) 2 K & J 357). In this case it seems that Katie and Mandy take as joint tenants (there are no words of severance), but in any event, since the communication occurs after the making of the will, only Kate is bound by the terms of the secret trust.

A further problem then arises as Katie dies before Jenny. Although there is an equitable maxim that 'equity will not allow a trust to fail for lack of a trustee', *Re Maddock* [1902] 2 Ch 220 is authority for the view that a secret trust will fail if the legatee predeceases the testator. In general, a legacy under a will lapses if the beneficiary predeceases the testator, and in secret trusts it can be argued that if the legacy itself fails, the trust must also fail. In this case, if the gift is to Katie and Mandy as joint tenants, the gift would pass to Mandy alone if Katie predeceases Jenny and Mandy is apparently not bound by the terms of the secret trust.

As has been said, it appears that under the communication rules of *Re Stead*, Mandy is not bound by the terms of the secret trust and in the usual case, if there is no communication of a secret trust during the testator's lifetime, the 'trustee' takes absolutely, as his conscience is not affected by any knowledge of a trust and there is no trust on the face of the will (*Wallgrave* v *Tebbs* (1855) 2 K & J 313). Clearly Mandy could not take absolutely as beneficiary under the will as she witnessed it and Wills Act 1837 s15 would preclude her from benefitting. Supposing that the court would distinguish *Re Stead* [1900] 1 Ch 237 and hold Mandy bound by the terms of the secret trust, is the trust valid or will it fail as Mandy witnessed the will?

It is not completely clear whether a secret trust fails if the legatee witnesses the will. Dicta in *Re Maddock* suggest that it will fail on the basis that on the face of the will the legatee takes as beneficiary and if the legacy is not valid the trust must also fail. An express trust created by a will does not fail if the trustee witnesses the will (see *Cresswell* v *Cresswell* (1868) LR 6 Eq 69), and it could be argued that if a legatee is in trust a trustee, not a beneficiary, the situation is analogous to *Cresswell* v *Cresswell* and the secret trust should not fail. Certainly such a situation would be outside the policy of s15. There is no problem in a beneficiary under a secret trust witnessing the will as *Re Young (Dec'd)* [1951] Ch 344 shows that the beneficiary may take as the secret trust operates outside the will and s15 is inapplicable.

If the gift to Katie on secret trust fails because she dies before Jenny and the gift to Mandy fails because she witnesses the will, the secret trust fails absolutely and the property will pass to Nicholas. However, the validity of the terms of the secret trust will now be discussed to cover the possibility that the secret trust might be valid. Jenny has directed that one half of the property is to be divided between Katie and Mandy equally. On the basis that this trust is valid, Katie's share would normally fail as she died before Jenny and there would be a resulting trust to Jenny's estate and thus to Nicholas as residuary beneficiary. However, in the very surprising decision of *Re Gardner (No 2)* [1923] 2 Ch 330 it was held that a gift under a secret trust to a beneficiary who predeceased the testator did not lapse but passed to the beneficiary's estate. Hanbury writes 'no rational theory can be found which will justify [this] remarkable decision'. The decision has never been overruled although it has been heavily criticised. Thus Katie's share might pass to her estate, subject to the following.

There is a further problem which arises. The secret trust is in favour of Katie, a trustee. It is not clear whether a secret trustee may take a benefit, although in general, in trust law, there is nothing to preclude a trustee being also a beneficiary. In *Re Rees' Will Trusts* [1950] Ch 204, the Court of Appeal refused to allow the trustee of a half-secret trust to claim as a beneficiary and would not allow evidence to show that the testator intended his trustee to benefit. Half-secret trusts pose a particular problem as evidence that the trustee was intended to be a beneficiary would contradict the will. In this case the trust is fully-secret and there would be no contradiction of the will, but the court will be aware of the potential danger of fraud by the trustee. It is suggested that provided there is very clear evidence that the trustee was intended to benefit, he should be allowed to do so, but the position is not clear at present. Thus assuming the court follows *Re Gardner (No 2)* [1923] 2 Ch 330, Katie's estate may be allowed to benefit, if the court would then distinguish the decision in *Re Rees' Will Trusts* [1950] Ch 204.

The other part of the secret trust is a direction to distribute the property amongst such worthy or charitable causes as the trustees think fit. It is suggested that this direction will fail for lack of certainty of objects. Such a trust is not wholly and exclusively charitable as 'worthy' is not restricted to objects which are charitable in law – *Chichester Diocesan Fund and Board of Finance Inc* v *Simpson* [1944] AC 341 – and it is unlikely that the court could be persuaded to construe 'or' disjunctively so that objects were restricted to those which were worthy and were charitable in law. In this case the half of the property would be held on resulting trust for the estate and thus for Nicholas.

This question poses a number of problems and there is no single definitive answer. In practical terms, it may well be that as only Katie knew of the trust and she is dead, the gift to Katie and Mandy will fail as the former predeceased Jenny and the latter witnessed the will, and thus the whole estate will pass to Nicholas. If the terms of the trust are known, it becomes more complicated. The trust has a chance of success only if considered a fully-secret trust and even then, on present case law, it seems Mandy is not bound as there was no communication to her and the trust may fail with respect to Katie as she predeceased Jenny. Even if the trust is effective, the gift under the trust to the trustees may fail as in *Re Rees' Will Trusts* and the other gift seems to fail for lack of certainty. In conclusion, Nicholas has an excellent chance of inheriting the whole estate.

QUESTION FOUR

'A testator cannot reserve to himself a power of making future unwitnessed dispositions by merely naming a trustee and leaving the purposes to be supplied afterwards.' Per Viscount Sumner in *Blackwell* v *Blackwell* (1929).

Discuss in relation to both fully-secret and half-secret trusts.

University of London LLB Examination
(for External Students) Law of Trusts June 1996 Q1

General Comment

This is a standard essay-type question concerning fully-secret and half-secret trusts.

Skeleton Solution

It would be sensible to begin with a resumé of the relevant law on fully- and half-secret trusts – the quotation is true of half-secret trusts because the effect of the law is that the testator cannot by this means change his will after execution – it is not true of fully-secret trusts because there the testator can (effectively) alter his will after execution.

Suggested Solution

This quotation represents what is basically a correct, logical and justifiable statement of the law. Taken out of context, however, it is a little misleading.

A secret trust is where property is given by will on trust but without the beneficiary (or sometimes even the existence of the trust) being disclosed on the face of the will. There are two types of secret trust, fully-secret trusts and half-secret ones.

Under a fully-secret trust the testator leaves property apparently beneficially on the face of his will to someone other than the real intended beneficiary and without any mention of a trust (eg 'I give all my residuary estate to A'). The testator tells A that A is to hold the property which A has been left on trust for B. This A accepts. Equity enforces this secret trust (and admits parole evidence in order to do so) because A's conscience is affected. Where there is a fully-secret trust both the existence of the trust and the details of that trust must be communicated to the 'secret trustee' before the testator's death: *Wallgrave* v *Tebbs* (1855) 2 K & J 313. If the 'secret trustee' only discovers the existence of the trust after the testator's death (eg by stumbling upon something among the testator's papers), the trust is not binding: *Wallgrave* v *Tebbs*. But with that caveat, the trust can be communicated at any time either before or after the will is made: *Moss* v *Cooper* (1861) 1 J & H 352. If the 'secret trustee' is not prepared to accept the trust, the testator can change his will.

Under a half-secret trust, the property is expressly given on trust on the face of the will, but the identity of the beneficiary is unspecified (eg 'I give all my residuary estate to C on the trusts which I have already communicated to him'). A half-secret trust must be communicated either before or at the time the will is made, and the communication must appear on the face of the will: *Blackwell* v *Blackwell* [1929] AC 318. Notice the words 'which I have already communicated to him' in the above example. The communication is probably sufficient if the testator merely gives the 'secret trustee' an envelope which contains the details of the trust and is marked 'not to be opened until after my death': see *Re Keen* [1937] Ch 236. If this happens, the 'secret trustee' must know that the envelope contains the terms of the secret trust and must agree to carry them out: *Lomax* v *Ripley* (1855) 3 Sm & G 48.

If a fully-secret trust fails, the 'secret trustee' can take beneficially because there is no trust, unless the 'secret trustee' knew that he was to hold as a trustee but only learned the details of the trust after the testator's death, in which case he will hold for the residuary legatee or the next of kin – otherwise the testator would be able to alter his will from time to time by an unexecuted codicil: *Re Boyes* (1884) 26 Ch D 531.

Thus, the quotation posed by the question is true in respect of half-secret trusts. It is a fundamental rule of half-secret trusts that the details of the trust must be communicated before or at the time of the making of the will. The rationale behind this rule is that otherwise a testator would be able to alter his will by a document not executed as a will. The quotation also reflects the rule of will making that a will must be executed strictly in accordance with the requirements of the Wills Act 1837. As such the rule is a perfectly logical and rational application of that rule to a new situation. What is perhaps striking is that, although a secret trust operates outside the will (*Re Young (Dec'd)* [1951] Ch 344; *Cullen* v *Attorney-General for Ireland* (1866) LR 1 HL 190 per Lord Westbury), the strictures of the Wills Act 1837 are still extended into its domain.

Where the quotation breaks down, is with fully-secret trusts. For with this type of trust communication can be made after the will has been made. Arguably this is clearly an anomaly, but the big difference here is that there is no trust on the face of the will. With fully-secret trusts the fact that a secret trust operates outside the will is given free reign. This rule is completely consonant with the fact that the trust itself can be created after the will has been made, and with the fact that the trust is enforced on the basis of conscience. However, that fact of itself gives the lie to the quotation in the case of fully-secret trusts, since the testator is able here to change his will without executing any document at all. Indeed, though there is no authority directly in point, presumably he could tell the putative beneficiary that he is to hold as a secret trustee rather than as a beneficiary and then tell him what the trusts are some time later. There is a restriction in this in that the 'secret trustee' must learn of the terms of the secret trust (as well as its existence) before the testator's death: otherwise he will not take beneficially but will hold on trust for the residuary legatee or next of kin: *Re Boyes* (1884) 26 Ch D 531.

Finally, it is perhaps pertinent to note that *Blackwell* v *Blackwell* [1929] AC 318 is the leading case on half-secret trusts, and it is therefore perfectly logical to find its dicta out of step with the rules for fully-secret trusts: *Re Boyes*.

In conclusion, it is submitted that this is a perfectly accurate statement of the law, but it really only applies to half-secret trusts. That, however, is where it was intended to apply.

QUESTION FIVE

Graham has recently died. By his will, he left his house, Dalston Villas, to David 'on trust for such purposes as I have communicated to him in writing', and his collection of valuable coins to Edna. Before making his will, Graham telephoned David to tell him that he was leaving him Dalston Villas to hold on trust for Sarah. He also told Edna that she was to hold the coin collection on trust for Louise. The two witnesses to Graham's will were Sarah's husband, Nigel, and Louise.

Advise Graham's residuary legatee, Bert, as to the validity of these dispositions.

University of London LLB Examination
(for External Students) Law of Trusts June 1999 Q4

General Comment

This problem question raises some specific issues on secret trusts. The candidate must demonstrate a knowledge of the operation of fully-secret trusts and half-secret trusts, and their relationship to the will itself.

Skeleton Solution

Introduction; half-secret and secret trusts; criteria in *Blackwell* – rules for half-secret trusts – conflict of actual communication with what was said in will; *Re Keen* – trust will not fail for lack of writing; *Ottaway* v *Norman* – fully-secret trust – attestation; *Re Young* – conclusion.

Suggested Solution

Graham's intention was to create a half-secret trust of Dalston Villas in favour of Sarah and a fully-secret trust of the coin collection in favour of Louise. If the secret trusts are valid, Bert has no claim on the property which was put into trust during Graham's lifetime.

In order for a secret trust to be valid, there are three requirements, which were laid down by the House of Lords in *Blackwell* v *Blackwell* [1929] AC 318, that must be present:

a) the testator must intend to leave the property to the named beneficiary on trust for another;

b) that intention must be communicated to the named beneficiary; and

c) the named beneficiary must accept the obligation to hold the property on trust.

In the will, Graham expressed his intention to leave Dalston Villas to David on trust without disclosing the trust on the face of the will. This is a half-secret trust. This means that David cannot take the property beneficially, and if the trust fails, Dalston Villas will fall into residue, and as such Bert can claim it. It is necessary in the case of a half-secret trust for the terms of the trust to be notified to the named beneficiary before the will is made. It was stated by Viscount Sumner in *Blackwell* v *Blackwell* that the reason for this rule was to prevent the testator from making future dispositions without the need to comply with the Wills Act 1837.

However, the will provides that the property is left 'on trusts for such purposes as I have communicated to him in writing'. This is inconsistent with the oral communication of the trusts which David actually received. The dicta of Viscount Sumner were applied in *Re Keen* [1937] Ch 236, a case in which £10,000 was given on trusts to be notified to the trustees during the testator's lifetime. In fact, the testator had notified them in writing of the terms of the trusts before the will was made. Because of the inconsistency between the statement in the will that notification of the trusts would take place in the future, when in fact it had taken place in the past, the court declared the trusts invalid. Following *Re Keen*, it is likely that the inconsistency in the communication to David would invalidate the trusts. The half-secret trust of Dalston Villas will thus be invalid. In *Ottaway* v *Norman* [1972] Ch 698 the court enforced an oral secret trust of land, so that the lack of writing would not have invalidated the trust on that ground.

The coin collection is personalty. It is subject to a fully-secret trust, the terms of which were communicated orally to Edna during the testator's lifetime. Once the terms of the trust had been communicated to Edna, she would be bound by them unless she refused the bequest. It was held in *Ottaway* v *Norman* that the trust would be binding if the three *Blackwell* v *Blackwell* [1929] AC 318 criteria were met. The trust is enforceable either by making the named beneficiary a constructive trustee of the trust property, from which she was not intended to benefit, or on the basis that equity will not allow a statute (here s9 Wills Act 1837) to be used as an instrument of fraud.

The attestation of the will by Sarah's husband and by Louise would not invalidate the trusts of the property which operate outside the will itself. Since neither Sarah nor Louise are named as beneficiaries on the face of the will, neither Sarah's husband nor Louise would be in a position to exercise undue influence, since Graham's true intentions are not disclosed. Thus Bert cannot claim that the gifts to the intended recipient are invalidated by the attestation. This was established in *Re Young (Dec'd)* [1951] Ch 344 where it was held that s15 Wills Act 1837 did not apply when the beneficiary, under a half-secret trust, witnessed the will. The court found that the secret trusts operate outside the will because the recipient takes not from the will itself, but by virtue of the secret trusts which are imposed outside the will on the named beneficiary.

Thus Bert can be advised that he will receive Dalston Villas as part of the residue of Graham's estate, because the half-secret trust failed under the rule in *Re Keen* [1937] Ch 236, but he will not receive the coin collection since this is the subject of a properly constituted fully-secret trust. Furthermore, s15 Wills Act 1837 has been complied with and Sarah's husband and Louise could witness a will which makes no mention of the terms of the secret trusts.

Chapter 6

Implied and Resulting Trusts

6.1   **Introduction**

6.2   **Key points**

6.3   **Key cases and statute**

6.4   **Questions and suggested solutions**

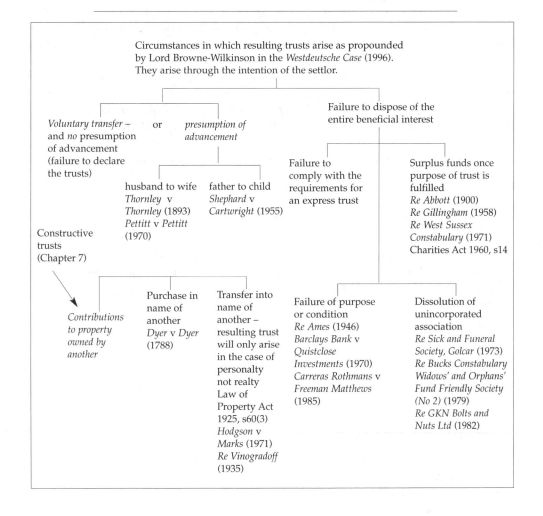

Circumstances in which resulting trusts arise as propounded by Lord Browne-Wilkinson in the *Westdeutsche Case* (1996). They arise through the intention of the settlor.

Voluntary transfer – and *no* presumption of advancement (failure to declare the trusts)

or   *presumption of advancement*

Failure to dispose of the entire beneficial interest

husband to wife
Thornley v *Thornley* (1893)
Pettitt v *Pettitt* (1970)

father to child
Shephard v *Cartwright* (1955)

Failure to comply with the requirements for an express trust

Surplus funds once purpose of trust is fulfilled
Re Abbott (1900)
Re Gillingham (1958)
Re West Sussex Constabulary (1971)
Charities Act 1960, s14

Constructive trusts (Chapter 7)

Contributions to property owned by another

Purchase in name of another
Dyer v *Dyer* (1788)

Transfer into name of another – resulting trust will only arise in the case of personalty not realty
Law of Property Act 1925, s60(3)
Hodgson v *Marks* (1971)
Re Vinogradoff (1935)

Failure of purpose or condition
Re Ames (1946)
Barclays Bank v *Quistclose Investments* (1970)
Carreras Rothmans v *Freeman Matthews* (1985)

Dissolution of unincorporated association
Re Sick and Funeral Society, Golcar (1973)
Re Bucks Constabulary Widows' and Orphans' Fund Friendly Society (No 2) (1979)
Re GKN Bolts and Nuts Ltd (1982)

6.1 Introduction

As the flowchart shows, this topic is a wide one. The main area of difficulty is that of matrimonial property which is considered in Chapter 7.

6.2 Key points

Analysis of this topic used to be based on the classification of resulting trusts made by Megarry J in *Re Vandervell's Trusts (No 2)* [1974] Ch 269. This has been replaced by the classification presented by Lord Browne-Wilkinson in *Westdeutsche Landesbank Girozentrale* v *Islington London Borough Council* [1996] 2 All ER 961. This depends on the idea that resulting trusts are based on the intention of the settlor and thus the notion of an automatic resulting trust has been abandoned. Lord Browne-Wilkinson identified two sets of circumstances when a resulting trust arises. First, where A makes a voluntary payment to B or pays (wholly or in part) for the purchase of property which is vested either in B alone or in the joint names of A and B. There is a presumption that A did not intend to make a gift to B: the money or property is held on trust for A (if he is a sole provider of the money) or, in the case of a joint purchase by A and B, in shares proportionate to their contributions. Second, where A transfers property to B on express trusts, but the trusts declared do not exhaust the whole beneficial interest. He added that 'where a settlor has expressly, or by necessary implication, abandoned any beneficial interest in the trust property, there is in my view no resulting trust: the undisposed of equitable interest vests in the Crown as bona vacantia'.

Voluntary transfer

If X voluntarily transfers property to Y, not on trust, and there is no presumption of advancement, Y holds the property on resulting trust for X.

There will be a presumption of advancement if X is a husband transferring to Y, his wife: *Thornley* v *Thornley* [1893] 2 Ch 229, or if X is a father transferring property to Y his child: *Shephard* v *Cartwright* [1955] AC 431. In the former situation, the presumption of advancement is now very weak and is easily rebutted: *Pettitt* v *Pettitt* [1970] AC 777.

A resulting trust may thus arise in the following situations.

Purchase in the name of another

A resulting trust arises in the absence of evidence to the contrary: *Dyer* v *Dyer* (1788) 2 Cox Eq 92.

Transfer into the name of another

No resulting trust in the case of land, due to s60(3) Law of Property Act 1925 (and see *Hodgson* v *Marks* [1971] Ch 892). There is, though, it seems, a resulting trust if the property is personalty: *Re Vinogradoff* [1935] WN 68.

Contributions to property owned by another

Whilst this is considered in Chapter 7, the case of *Abrahams v The Trustee of the Property of Anthony Abrahams (A Bankrupt)* (1999) The Times 26 July can be noted here. The case decided that a person who paid money to a lottery syndicate gained the right to have any winnings duly administered in accordance with the rules of the syndicate, and that right was 'property' which could be held on a resulting trust. Here a wife continued to pay into a syndicate after her husband had stopped doing so. The wife was entitled to the winnings on resulting trust principles, based on her contributions, there being no presumption of advancement to the husband. As a result the trustee in relation to her husband's bankruptcy would not be entitled to the money.

Failure to dispose

If X makes a disposition to Y on trusts which leave some or all of the beneficial interests undisposed of, Y will hold the undisposed of beneficial interests on resulting trust for X. There exist four main situations in which a resulting trust of this nature will arise.

Failure to comply with the requirements for an express trust

If this is the case, the settlor has failed to dispose of any of the beneficial interest which is held by the trustees on resulting trust for the settlor.

Failure of a purpose or a condition

If a trust is created for a specific purpose which fails or subject to a condition such as the attainment by the beneficiary of a particular age (as in *Re Ames's Settlement* [1946] Ch 217) which is not fulfilled, then the trustees will hold the property on resulting trust for the settlor. If the situation is one of failure of purpose, the nature of the trust imposed was considered in the two important cases of *Barclays Bank Ltd v Quistclose Investments Ltd* [1970] AC 567 and *Carreras Rothman Ltd v Freeman Matthews Treasure Ltd* [1985] 3 WLR 1016. In *Twinsectra Ltd v Yardley and Others* [1999] Lloyd's Rep Bank 145, a wider notion of a Quistclose type trust than had been allowed in earlier cases was accepted. Then in *R v Common Professional Board, ex parte Mealing-McCleod* (2000) The Times 2 May Sir Christopher Slade stated three requirements for a Quistclose trust in relation to a loan: that the money would never become part of the general assets of the borrower, that it was to be used only for a specified purpose and that except for the use for that purpose it was to be held on resulting trust for the lender. It should be noted that the House of Lords decided that there was no resulting trust in the circumstances of the case of *Westdeutsche Landesbank Girozentrale v Islington London Borough Council* [1996] 2 All ER 961. Here the council had received money from the bank with the council having no reason to think that it was not free to treat it as its own. The contract turned out to be void and the court thought that the money was recoverable at common law as money had and received. As a House of Lords decision it could now be mentioned in an answer to the question below. The point to make is that whilst the courts may not always be willing to find a trust they have much more reason to do so in the situation of Harry and Joe than in the *Westdeutsche* case.

Surplus funds once the purpose of a trust has been fulfilled

If the purpose is charitable and the donor is unascertainable, the funds will be applied cy-près following s14 Charities Act 1960. If the donor is ascertainable, then his contribution will be held on resulting trust for him unless he waives his right to it under s14. (See also Chapter 12.)

If the purpose is not charitable and the donor is ascertainable, his contribution will similarly be held on resulting trust for him: *Re Abbott Fund (Trusts of the)* [1900] 2 Ch 326, unless the donations were in the form of subscriptions under a contract. In the latter situation, it seems that the subscriptions would go to the Crown bona vacantia following *Re West Sussex Constabulary's Widows, Children and Benevolent (1930) Funds Trust* [1971] Ch 1. More problematic is when the donors are unascertainable. It was held in *Re Gillingham Bus Disaster Fund* [1958] Ch 300 that the donations would nevertheless be held on resulting trusts for the donors. However, a different conclusion was reached in the *Re West Sussex* case, in which it was held that the donors should be considered as parting with the money outright and thus it would go to the Crown bona vacantia.

Dissolution of unincorporated association

The courts avoid the application of resulting trusts as far as possible, and instead treat the matter as one of contract. In *Re Sick and Funeral Society, Golcar* [1973] Ch 51 it was said that equal division would be ordered in the absence of rules to the contrary. However, in *Re Buckinghamshire Constabulary Fund (No 2)* [1979] 1 WLR 936 it was held that the destination of the surplus funds would be governed exclusively by the contract between the members and this was reiterated in *Re GKN Bolts and Nuts Ltd* [1982] 2 All ER 855. A further possibility is to follow the cases concerning failure of purpose above so that a resulting trust would exist in favour of each member to the extent of his contribution or subscription.

6.3 Key cases and statute

- *Re Buckinghamshire Constabulary Fund (No 2)* [1979] 1 WLR 936
  Unincorporated association – surplus fund – contract

- *Re Gillingham Bus Disaster Fund* [1958] Ch 300
  Not charitable – donor unknown – resulting trust

- *Westdeutsche Landesbank Girozentrale* v *Islington London Borough Council* [1996] 2 All ER 961
  Resulting trust – Lord Browne-Wilkinson classification – based on intention

- Charities Act 1960, s14 – charitable; surplus funds; donor unascertainable; cy-près

6.4 Questions and suggested solutions

QUESTION ONE

What are resulting and constructive trusts, and how do they differ?

University of London LLB Examination
(for External Students) Law of Trusts June 1998 Q3

General Comment

This is an open-ended question requiring definitions of resulting and constructive trusts along with a clear note of the distinctions and why they are important. Mention should be made of the dicta of Lord Bridge in *Lloyds Bank plc v Rosset and Another* [1990] 2 WLR 867 and of Lord Browne-Wilkinson in *Westdeutsche Landesbank Girozentrale v Islington London Borough Council* [1996] 2 All ER 961. This question is far too wide in scope for a good student to do justice to it within the 45 minutes allowed under examination conditions.

Skeleton Solution

Dicta of Lord Bridge in *Rosset* – tests for resulting and constructive trusts – resulting trusts: presumed; rebuttal of presumption; automatic; automatic disapproved in *Westdeutsche* – constructive trusts: dicta in *Westdeutsche*; still no concept of remedial constructive trust; constructive trust of matrimonial home; new model constructive trust; *Gissing* v *Gissing*; *Eves* v *Eves*; *Grant* v *Edwards*; *Rosset*; *Midland Bank* v *Cooke* – summarise differences and note their importance.

Suggested Solution

Confusion between these two terms arose following the case *Lloyds Bank plc v Rosset and Another* [1990] 2 WLR 867 in which Lord Bridge recast the requirements for a constructive trust of the family home. He held that in order to establish an interest under such a constructive trust, in the absence of misrepresentation, the claimant must show that there had been an agreement with the legal owner (that the claimant should have a share in the property) upon which they had acted to their detriment. In the absence of an express agreement, only a direct contribution to the purchase price or the mortgage repayments would suffice to found such a claim. He thus applied the same test for the existence of a constructive trust of the family home as that which raises the presumption of a resulting trust. Yet the application and consequences of these two types of implied trust are very different.

A resulting trust arises when there is a question over the beneficial ownership of the property, either, in the case of a presumed resulting trust, because someone other than the legal owner has provided some or all of the purchase price, or, in the case of an automatic resulting trust, because the legal owner has failed to dispose of the entire beneficial interest in the property. In these circumstances the beneficial ownership 'results' (from the Latin *resultare* – to jump back) to someone other than the legal owner.

In the case of a family home bought in the sole name of one partner, but with a contribution from the other, there is a presumption that the partner who is not the legal owner is entitled to a share in the beneficial ownership of the property in proportion to their contribution. The presumption arises from the fact of the contribution. However, the presumption can be rebutted by evidence that there was no intention that the contribution should found a share in the property: for example, it could be shown that the money was intended as a gift or a loan.

Where a father contributes to the purchase of property for a child, or a husband for a wife (but not in any other close relationship), there is a further presumption of advancement. This overrides the presumption of resulting trust and in turn raises the presumption of a gift in favour of the legal owner. However, if the advance is made for the purposes of fraud, including fraud of creditors, no evidence can be adduced if it discloses the fraud to the court, and thus the presumption of resulting trust will prevail: see *Tinsley* v *Milligan* [1994] 1 AC 340 and *Tribe* v *Tribe* [1996] Ch 107.

In *Re Vandervell's Trusts (No 2)* [1974] Ch 269 Megarry J established a second category of resulting trust, the automatic resulting trust. This arises where the legal owner has failed to divest himself or herself of all interest in the property (as Mr Vandervell failed to do when he retained control of the share option granted to the Royal College of Surgeons). The property was held to revert automatically on resulting trust to the original owner. This analysis has now been disapproved by Lord Browne-Wilkinson in *Westdeutsche Landesbank Girozentrale* v *Islington London Borough Council* [1996] 2 All ER 961. He preferred the analysis in *Re West Sussex Constabulary's Widows, Children and Benevolent (1930) Funds Trust* [1971] Ch 1 which suggested that the interest which was not accounted for should go bona vacantia to the Crown as property which had been abandoned.

It is said (in *Westdeutsche*) that a resulting trust gives effect to the presumed common intention of the parties. By contrast, a constructive trust is imposed by the court where it is unconscionable for the legal owner to claim entitlement to full beneficial ownership of property. In English law, the concept of the remedial constructive trust, which is applied in other common law jurisdictions, is still resisted, despite obiter dicta of Lord Browne-Wilkinson which suggested that this may be the way forward in English law. His approach was not adopted by the Court of Appeal in the subsequent case of *Re Polly Peck International plc* [1998] 3 All ER 813, however.

Five distinct categories of constructive trust are recognised at English law:

a) constructive trusts of the family home;

b) a constructive trust arising from breach of fiduciary duty;

c) constructive trusts imposed on strangers to a trust under accessory liability and recipient liability;

d) constructive trusts imposed in cases of fraud;

e) the constructive trust which arises when a contract is specifically enforceable.

Although the court requires some element of unconscionable conduct on the part of the legal owner, a constructive trust, within the jurisdiction of England and Wales, is thus not an automatic remedy for unjust enrichment, although Lord Denning appeared to try to make it so with his 'new model constructive trust' in the 1970s. Lord Diplock had settled criteria for the imposition of a constructive trust in *Gissing* v *Gissing* [1971] AC 886: that it would be inequitable for the legal owner to claim the full beneficial interest because, by words or conduct, he has induced the claimant to act to his own detriment in the reasonable belief that by so acting, he is acquiring an interest in the property. By contrast in *Cooke* v *Head* [1972] 1 WLR 518 Lord Denning suggested that all jointly acquired property intended to be used for the joint benefit of the parties could be the subject of a constructive trust. Anticipating the reforms of the Matrimonial Causes Act 1973, Lord Denning attempted to establish the existence of an agreement to share the beneficial ownership where there had been no direct contribution to the purchase price from the claimant.

Nevertheless, Lord Bridge approved Lord Denning's decision in *Eves* v *Eves* [1975] 1 WLR 1338 where he awarded a 25 per cent share under a constructive trust where the man had deliberately misled the woman as to her legal entitlement to own the property jointly. In that case, she had made no contribution to the purchase price. Lord Bridge acknowledged that it would be unconscionable for the court to allow the man to claim the full entitlement in a case of fraud. *Eves* v *Eves* was followed in the slightly more recent case of *Grant* v *Edwards* [1986] Ch 638.

Where there has been no misrepresentation, however, the court has consistently drawn away from Lord Denning's approach. In *Burns* v *Burns* [1984] Ch 317, Lord Denning's 'community of property' approach was specifically disapproved in the case of a woman cohabitee who stayed at home to look after the children, but who made no direct contribution to the purchase price of the property. Instead *Gissing* was approved, and Fox LJ emphasised that the starting point was the intention of the parties at the time when the property was acquired. As we have seen, this strict approach was applied in *Lloyds Bank plc* v *Rosset and Another* [1990] 2 WLR 867, where the nature of the evidence of the agreement was clarified. Mrs Rosset had supervised the building works for the renovation of a derelict farmhouse, but had made no direct contribution to its purchase and thus failed to establish a beneficial interest. The building works undertaken by her were considered to be de minimis.

In *Midland Bank plc* v *Cooke* [1995] 4 All ER 562 Waite LJ, while taking Bridge LJ's requirements as a starting point, once he had established an initial contribution from the wife of 6.47 per cent, the judge went on to award her a 50 per cent share of the property. Both parties had given evidence that they had never even discussed the wife's entitlement. Waite LJ held that a common intention to share the property equally could be presumed from their dealings over a long marriage. This case did not go to the

House of Lords as expected, and has been criticised as a step backwards towards Lord Denning's 'new model constructive trust'.

Midland Bank plc v *Cooke* [1995] 4 All ER 562 illustrates the practical importance of the distinction between resulting and constructive trusts. If Mrs Cooke's entitlement rested simply on her direct contribution, she would have been awarded only 6.47 per cent of the value of the property. The Court's declaration of a constructive trust enabled them to give her what they considered to be an equitable settlement in the circumstances, half the value of the property in this case.

In a resulting trust, the fact of the contribution raises a presumption of entitlement to a fixed share in the property so that, in the absence of evidence to rebut the presumption, the court acknowledges an existing trust; by contrast, the court itself declares the constructive trust and brings it into existence.

In doing so, however, the court acknowledges the burdens of trusteeship, and will therefore not impose a constructive trust on an innocent volunteer. The only category of constructive trust which is imposed without fault on the part of a constructive trustee is that which applies to fiduciaries where liability to account is strict. In *Re Montague's Settlement Trusts* [1987] 2 WLR 1192 Sir Robert Megarry V-C said that the crucial question was whether the conscience of the recipient of property had been bound in a way which would justify equity imposing a constructive trust. He noted that the duties of trusteeship were very onerous, and refused such a remedy where money had been paid to the wrong beneficiaries under an innocent mistake. However, they were ordered to return the property to the rightful recipients.

Constructive trustees are placed under the same duties as trustees appointed under an express trust and this facilitates the following:

a) the recovery of trust property;

b) tracing of the trust property if the constructive trustee has disposed of it; and

c) a personal remedy against the trustee, including the liability to account for profit and losses.

The facts which give rise to a resulting trust are much easier to prove than those which establish constructive trusteeship. Both Lord Bridge in *Lloyds Bank plc* v *Rosset and Another* [1990] 2 WLR 867 and Lord Browne-Wilkinson in *Westdeutsche Landesbank Girozentrale* v *Islington London Borough Council* [1996] 2 All ER 961 have tried to limit the imposition of the constructive trust, Lord Bridge in relation to the family home and Lord Browne-Wilkinson in relation to commercial matters. However, the true owner of the beneficial interest is afforded much greater protection under a constructive trust. The beneficiary under a resulting trust is entitled to a defined share of the value of the property claimed, but under a constructive trust the court can award whatever is equitable and order an account of the property, which may include enhanced value of the assets claimed. Furthermore, although since *Rosset* the tests applied for entitlement to benefit from these implied trusts are similar, the remedies available differ very significantly, as can be seen from *Midland Bank plc v Cooke* [1995] 4 All ER 562.

QUESTION TWO

At his death in 1988, Sherman left £1 million in his will to the trustees of the All England Handgun Club, of which he was a devoted member, to be held on trust to support activities promoting the sport of pistol-shooting and to improve facilities of the club. In 1997, legislation was passed prohibiting the private ownership or possession of handguns and the club is to be wound up. The trustees have always held the money from Sherman's bequest in a special account, and £375,000 remains. The residuary beneficiary under Sherman's will is now demanding the immediate transfer of these funds.

Advise the trustees.

University of London LLB Examination
(for External Students) Law of Trusts June 1997 Q2

General Comment

This is a problem question, concerning resulting trusts and unincorporated associations.

Skeleton Solution

Whether the property goes on resulting trust and back to Sherman's estate (in which case his residuary beneficiaries would take it) or goes to the members of the Club, because it is club property – it is submitted that the latter is the better view.

Suggested Solution

Sherman's gift to the All England Handgun Club ('the Club') was a gift to an unincorporated association. Though this is not specifically stated, it seems fairly obvious that the Association did not have charitable status.

The question in this case is whether there is a resulting trust to Sherman's estate (in which case Sherman's residuary beneficiary would indeed take the gift), or whether the money belongs to the Club (in which case it would presumably be distributed amongst all the members).

There are three classic situations where there is a resulting trust to the settlor or grantor (or his estate). These are outlined below.

a) Where the trusts themselves are not exhaustive, eg where property is granted 'to A for life with remainder to his children' and A dies a bachelor: *Re West, George v Grose* [1900] 1 Ch 84. Plainly this scenario does not apply to the instant case, since there are no beneficiaries who were expected to materialise and who have not. When the gift was made the Club (presumably) had members and still does have. The problem is caused by the fact that the Club has had to be wound up.

b) Where the trusts are only partly expressed, eg where property was granted 'to A for life'. This scenario would only apply here if it could be argued that the gift should be construed so that it only lasted as long as the Club survived. It is difficult to be sure of this since the exact words of the gift are not set out in the question, but on the information available there seems no basis for construing the gift in this way.

c) Failure of a beneficiary's interest. This does not seem to apply here.

It is interesting to compare the case of *Re Buckinghamshire Constabulary Fund (No 2)* [1979] 1 WLR 936 (Walton J). This is an example of where the surplus assets of (in this case) a friendly society did not pass as bona vacantia to the Crown, because there were members in existence at the time of dissolution. It is also an example of where the property was divided equally, because the contract between the members provided for no other method of distribution. This case suggests that the property would pass to the members of the Club, rather than to Sherman's residuary beneficiary.

There is an alternative line of approach to this problem because this is a gift to an unincorporated association. Such gifts used to cause a legion of problems to the courts, but over the years they have evolved seven constructions which in the majority of cases enable the courts to validate such gifts. It is not entirely clear which of these constructions applies in the instant case. Very likely it is the fourth construction (which is probably the most commonly used) – there is no trust, and the gift is valid as an out and out gift to the present members beneficially as an accretion to the Club's funds to be dealt with in accordance with the rules of the association by which the members are contractually bound: eg *Re Lipinski's Will Trusts* [1976] Ch 235.

Whichever of the first four constructions is used, it does not matter greatly, because they all involve a gift to the membership of the association in some form. Once there is a gift to the membership, it ipso facto creates an absolute gift, which thus leaves little room for any resulting trust to the settlor (or to the settlor's estate). Therefore in this case the members of the Club would take on whatever basis is appropriate.

The fifth, sixth and seventh constructions are a little more complicated, but do not seem to apply here.

Construction five is that there is a trust for non-charitable purposes which directly or indirectly benefits those who have locus standi to enforce it, though they have no right to claim the trust fund: *Re Denley's Trust Deed* [1969] 1 Ch 373. This construction does not apply here as the gift is apparently one to the Club and not merely for its purposes. The gift is apparently expressly to the trustees of the Club.

Construction six is that there is a trust for abstract or impersonal non-charitable purposes. Here the trust has to fall within one of the anomalous categories to be valid. In other words it has to be a valid purpose trust. This gift might fall within the miscellaneous category of purpose trusts: *In Re Thompson* [1934] Ch 342 (where a trust for the furtherance of fox hunting was held a valid purpose trust, provided it was limited within the perpetuity period). However, this construction seems unlikely to apply here for the same reason, that the gift is apparently one to the Club and not for its purposes.

The seventh construction is that there is a charitable trust. As already mentioned, plainly this is not the answer here.

Finally there are a couple of possibly complicating factors. We do not know what the rules of the Club say about winding-up. Clearly this could have an important effect on the outcome of the case. Presumably Sherman's estate would be bound by these, since he was a member and presumably the gift would have been accepted on the basis of the Club's rules.

Secondly, it seems a little unusual that the gift was kept in a separate account. Plainly this would facilitate its return to Sherman's estate in the event (which has now happened) of winding-up. One wonders whether this is evidence that (for whatever reason) this is what was intended. A lot would depend on why the money was paid into and then retained in a separate account, but there is nothing in the question to say why this is so.

The trustees should be advised accordingly.

QUESTION THREE

a) Explain the operation of the presumption of resulting trust and the presumption of advancement.

b) How are these presumptions relevant in the context of property placed on trust for the illegal purpose of defeating creditors?

c) 'The presumption of resulting trust should be abolished.'

   What reasons support this view, and what reasons detract from it?

University of London LLB Examination
(for External Students) Law of Trusts June 1999 Q8

General Comment

This is a very straightforward question on resulting trusts. The first part of your answer should explain how the presumption of resulting trust can be rebutted, and note the limitations to the presumption of advancement. The second part requires a detailed discussion of *Tinsley* v *Milligan* [1994] 1 AC 340 and *Tribe* v *Tribe* [1996] Ch 107. In the final part you must express a reasoned opinion on whether resulting trusts are now outmoded.

Please note that the three sections to the question will carry equal marks.

Skeleton Solution

a) Resulting trust – define and explain – advancement: define and explain; relationship of the two presumptions.

b) Illegality: *Tinsley* v *Milligan*; *Tribe* v *Tribe* – consequences of failure of illegal purpose.

c) Reasons for and against abolition – conclusion.

Suggested Solution

a) The presumption of resulting trust is raised when someone, other than the legal owner of property, has contributed to its purchase in whole or in part. In those circumstances, the court will presume that the person making the contribution is intended to receive a proportionate share of the property, but this presumption can be rebutted by evidence to show that a gift, loan or some other financial arrangement was intended. In the leading case of *Hodgson* v *Marks* [1971] Ch 892 Mrs Hodgson transferred her house into the sole name of her lodger, Evans. It was agreed between them orally that the house would remain hers, but this agreement was ineffective because it was not evidenced in writing: s53(1)(b) Law of Property Act 1925. The Court of Appeal held that there was a resulting trust in Mrs Hodgson's favour. In *Re Vinogradoff* [1935] WN 68 a grandmother bought war-loan stock in the joint names of herself and her granddaughter. On the death of the grandmother the court held that the presumption of resulting trust applied, and the granddaughter held the stock on resulting trust for her grandmother's estate.

When the contribution is made by a husband to his wife or a father to his legitimate child another presumption comes into play: the presumption of advancement. The starting point for the court in these cases is that the contribution was intended as a gift, because of the special relationship of moral responsibility of the man to the wife or children. Lord Diplock said in *Pettitt* v *Pettitt* [1970] AC 777 that the presumption of advancement was outdated, because it was based on values more appropriate to a bygone era. Its application has never been extended in English law, so that there is no such presumption when a contribution is made by the wife to the husband or the mother to her children; nor does the presumption of advancement apply in favour of illegitimate children. However, in the Australian case of *Nelson* v *Nelson* (1995) 312 ALR 133 the presumption of advancement was recognised between a mother and daughter.

The presumption of advancement will rebut the presumption of resulting trust, so that a husband or father will be presumed to have intended a gift, but both presumptions are rules of evidence and starting points in deciding the beneficial ownership of the property. It is open to the parties to bring evidence to show their true intention.

b) Problems arise when the intention of one of the parties is an illegal or fraudulent one. For example, in *Gascoigne* v *Gascoigne* [1918] 1 KB 223 a husband put his property into the name of his wife in order to defeat his creditors. Under the principle that he who comes to equity must come with clean hands, he could not plead this improper purpose in order to rebut the presumption of advancement. But in *Tinsley* v *Milligan* [1994] 1 AC 340 this approach, taken in the Court of Appeal, was rejected when the case came to the House of Lords. The majority in the House of Lords were of the opinion that the claimant would be successful if she could establish her claim without pleading the illegality. Tinsley and Milligan were a lesbian couple who had purchased property jointly. It was bought in Tinsley's sole name, so that they could make a fraudulent claim for housing benefit for Milligan from the DSS. When they subsequently quarrelled, Milligan claimed to be entitled to a share of the property by virtue of her contribution. Tinsley claimed successfully in the Court of Appeal that the claim was barred because of the illegal purpose. The House of Lords, by a majority of three to two allowed the appeal, on the basis that Milligan only had to raise a presumption of resulting trust, so that the only person who had to plead the illegality was Tinsley if she wished to defeat the claim. Milligan's case could be argued solely on the presumption of resulting trust. It was acknowledged that, if the case rested on the presumption of advancement rather than that of resulting trust, Milligan would have been unsuccessful, because evidence of the illegality would be required in order to show a contrary intention. By the time the case came to court, Milligan had repaid to the DSS all sums which had been received as a result of the deception.

Tinsley v *Milligan* [1994] 1 AC 340 was applied by the Court of Appeal in *Tribe* v *Tribe* [1996] Ch 107. In this case a father had to rebut the presumption of advancement when he had transferred shares into the name of his son in order to defeat his creditors. It had been agreed by the father and son that the shares were held on trust for the father, pending settlement of the creditors' claims. A settlement was reached with the creditors without the need to put the illegal purpose into effect. Millett LJ said that it was established that no party could rely on his own illegality to found a claim or rebut a presumption, but that equity would assist him if he had no need to rely on the fraud or illegality: *Tinsley* v *Milligan*. It was also established that the property could be recovered if the claimant withdrew from the illegal scheme and, since the settlement with the creditors was achieved without recourse to the use of the disputed shares, this was effectively the situation here. Thus, the courts appear to offer an incentive to claimants to change their minds and resolve their problems within the law. Millett LJ went on to question whether these principles were co-extensive, and concluded that they were, which enabled the father to establish an entitlement under a resulting trust.

c) Before one can determine whether or not the presumption of resulting trust should be abolished, it is necessary to consider what purpose it continues to serve. Its primary purpose is to protect those who have made a financial contribution to the acquisition of property. The presumption allocates to the recipient the burden of proof that an outright gift was intended to the recipient.

In cases such as *Hodgson* v *Marks* [1971] Ch 892 it affords protection to the weaker party who has effectively been defrauded of their rights. It is plain common sense that the person who pays may intend to benefit in some way. Where the donor was not intended to benefit, any such claim can be defeated by evidence that a gift or loan was intended.

The presumption has particular relevance where a couple cohabit in a home which is bought in the name of one of them, and to which the other has contributed. It enables the court to allocate a share of the property to the other party, when cohabiting couples still do not benefit from rules of community of property or a regime under which property is divided between them, as on divorce. With better public education and equality of earning power in recent times, perhaps this is of less relevance, but again the balance is struck under a resulting trust so that the weaker party is afforded protection, and until the law is changed to give unmarried couples rights equivalent to married couples on divorce and separation, the presumption of resulting trust still has efficacy and relevance.

A stronger case could be made for the abolition of the presumption of advancement. Where this was effective in an age when women and children could not hold real property, and where the father was the provider for his wife and children, the presumption applied in most cases where money or property were advanced. In modern times wives tend to work and acquire their own assets, and children are encouraged to be independent of their parents. With an ageing population, a case could be made for an extension of the presumption of advancement to cover advances to aged parents from their children, but it is submitted that this presumption is outmoded for the twenty-first century.

In the fraud cases, the courts take the view that the existing policy of allowing parties to recover property, if it can be done so without pleading the illegality, has the function of encouraging them to repent of their illegal and unethical conduct. With a recent House of Lords decision to this effect, this particular change in the law would require litigation.

Chapter 7

Matrimonial Property (Including that Owned by Co-habitees)

7.1   Introduction

7.2   Key points

7.3   Key cases

7.4   Questions and suggested solutions

7.1 Introduction

It has been established at least since *Pettitt* v *Pettitt* [1970] AC 777 that beneficial interests in property owned by one or both parties to a marriage or other similar relationship will be determined by the law of trusts. The judges in the relevant cases, however, seem confused as to the nature of such trusts – resulting and/or constructive? In addition, it is generally accepted that the concept of proprietary estoppel may come to the aid of a party who cannot establish a beneficial interest in the form of a resulting or constructive trust.

Due to the resulting complexity of the topic and the fact that the topic encompasses several rather than a single area of the law of trusts, it seemed appropriate to devote a separate chapter to the problem.

The topic has been the subject of dramatic developments in recent years; indeed, the idea that constructive trusts are of any relevance in this area is a new one introduced by Lord Denning in the period around 1970.

7.2 Key points

It has been established since *Pettitt* v *Pettitt* [1970] AC 777 that the question as to whether a party has a beneficial interest in property is to be determined by the law of trusts.

If the parties are married, many of the questions can be answered by reference to the matrimonial statutes which deal with declaration of beneficial interests and adjustment of such interests. In addition the presumption of advancement from husband to wife may be relevant. The law of trusts is also important.

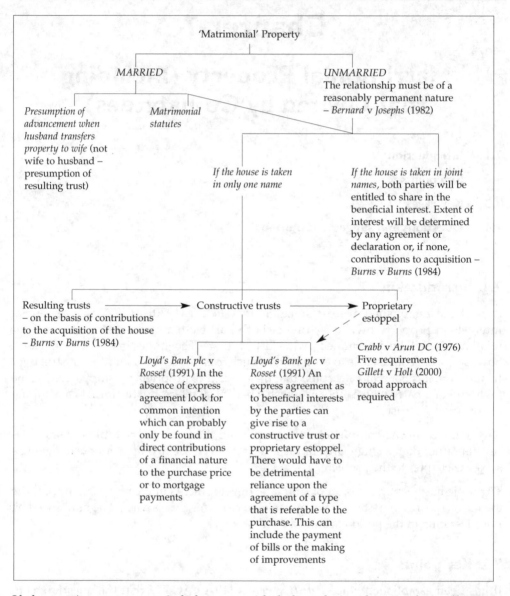

If the parties are unmarried then, provided the relationship is of a sufficiently permanent nature – *Bernard* v *Josephs* [1982] Ch 391 – the question of beneficial interests will be determined by the law of trusts:

If the house is taken in joint names

Prima facie, both parties will be entitled to a share in the beneficial interest. The extent of that interest will be decided in the same way that the question of whether a party has a beneficial interest at all, in the case of a house taken in one name only, is decided (see below): *Burns* v *Burns* [1984] Ch 317.

If the house is taken in only one name

Resulting trusts

The 'non-owning' party will have a beneficial interest under a resulting trust if (s)he has contributed to the acquisition of the house, and the extent of such interest will be the amount of the contribution: *Burns* v *Burns* [1984] Ch 317.

Constructive trusts

It is a new idea that constructive trusts should cover the area of jointly-owned property. It is now, however, well established that they do and if a claimant fails to establish a beneficial interest under a resulting trust they may nevertheless be able to do so under a constructive trust.

In *Grant* v *Edwards* [1986] Ch 638 it was held that a constructive trust would be imposed if it would be unequitable for the legal owner to claim beneficial ownership. This will be the case if the claimant ('non-owning' party) can show that there existed a common intention that s/he should have a beneficial interest and that s/he acted to her/his detriment on the basis of that common intention.

The leading case in this area is the decision of the House of Lords in *Lloyds Bank plc* v *Rosset and Another* [1990] 2 WLR 867. The judgment of Lord Bridge figures strongly. The facts of the case were that a married couple decided to buy a house and to renovate it. The purchase money came from a trust fund of which the husband was the beneficiary. The trustees insisted that the property was bought in his name. The husband used the property as security for an overdraft without the knowledge of his wife. She provided some assistance with the renovations. Later the husband moved out of the property after a split up. The bank sought possession of the property as the loan had not been repayed.

For the wife to have rights in the property Lord Bridge stated that there were two possibilities. Firstly, that there had been an express agreement between the parties, normally prior to acquisition of the property, as to beneficial interests. If there was such an agreement then a constructive trust or proprietary estoppel would be possible where there had been detrimental reliance upon the agreement. The reliance would have to be referable to the purchase price but the payment of bills or the making of improvements could count for this purpose. You would get whatever had been agreed upon. In the case an agreement was alleged but not proved.

The second possibility in the absence of agreement is that common intention can be found which can act as the basis for a constructive trust. The behaviour that would suffice for this is direct contributions of a financial nature such as helping with the purchase price or mortgage payments. Lord Bridge thought that it was extremely doubtful that any thing else would do. The size of the interest would relate to the size of the contributions. This is of limited help as the same would be achieved through the use of a resulting trust. In the case there was no evidence of such contributions. The wife had no interest in the property.

This is very unfair on working wives who make contributions to the family budget with the husband funding the mortgage. Equally, it is unrealistic to expect couples to sit down and discuss beneficial interests when they are deciding to live together.

The view taken by Lord Bridge is very different to the concept of a new model constuctive trust as championed by Lord Denning and others in cases such as *Hussey* v *Palmer* [1972] 1 WLR 1286. This offered much greater possibilities for helping co-habitees. Note the support for the remedial constructive trust to be found in the view of Lord Browne-Wilkinson in *Westdeutsche Landesbank Girozentrale* v *Islington London Borough Council* [1996] 2 All ER 961. He stated that 'the remedial constructive trust, if introduced into English law, may provide a more satisfactory road forward ... However, whether English law should follow the United States and Canada in adopting the remedial constructive trust will have to be decided in some future case where the point is directly in issue'.

Proprietary estoppel

This offers a further means by which a party could hope to acquire rights. Note in particular that it does not require agreement, which is a difficulty if a constructive trust is being sought.

The case of *Crabb* v *Arun District Council* [1976] Ch 179 laid down five requirements which must be fulfilled in order to establish a case of proprietary estoppel. In *Gillett* v *Holt* [2000] 2 All ER 289 proprietary estoppel was presented as being a general means to prevent unconscionable conduct rather than being restricted to a limited number of pre-determined circumstances. In *Yaxley* v *Gotts* [1999] 3 WLR 1217 it was stated that proprietary estoppel is very similar to constuctive trusts – particularly the common intention constructive trust.

7.3 Key cases

- *Burns* v *Burns* [1984] Ch 317
  Joint names – provides a share

- *Crabb* v *Arun District Council* [1976] Ch 179
  Five requirements stated here – provides a guideline – a more flexible approach likely

- *Gillett* v *Holt* [2000] 2 All ER 289
  Proprietary estoppel – general means to prevent unconscionable conduct

- *Grant* v *Edwards* [1986] Ch 638
  Constructive trust – where inequitible to deny

- *Lloyds Bank plc* v *Rosset and Another* [1990] 2 WLR 867
  Lord Bridge – agreement – common intention

- *Yaxley* v *Gotts* [1999] 3 WLR 1217
  Proprietary estoppel – very similar to the common intention constructive trust

7.4 Questions and suggested solutions

QUESTION ONE

In 1965 Jane, who was divorced, went to live with Peter, who had left his wife. A year later a house was bought in Peter's name, the purchase money coming from his savings and by way of mortgage. At this time Jane gave up her job when a child was born to them, and in addition to looking after their child, Jane performed all the usual domestic duties in the house. In 1977, Jane went back to work and used her earnings to contribute towards the housekeeping expenses, and to pay for decorations to the house. In 1978 Peter built an extension to the rear of the house and he told his neighbour, Ned, that if it had not been for the fact that both he and Jane were working he would not have been able to afford to build the extension.

Last year Jane, taking the child with her, left Peter and she now wishes to claim a beneficial interest in the house. Peter and Jane have never been married.

Advise Jane.

University of London LLB Examination
(for External Students) Law of Trusts June 1984 Q2(b)

General Comment

The length and depth of the answer presuppose that this is a whole, rather than half of a question. As half of a question in an examination, the answer would have to be modified (shortened) accordingly.

Skeleton Solution

Resulting trust – direct/indirect contribution – constructive trust – common intention – proprietary estoppel.

Suggested Solution

This situation concerns an unmarried couple and thus the matrimonial statutes are of no assistance. Consequently, whether Jane has a beneficial interest in the house is to be determined by the law of trusts: *Pettitt* v *Pettitt* [1970] AC 777. Although Peter is the sole legal owner of the house, he may nevertheless be trustee of part of the beneficial interest in the house for Jane, if it can be shown that she does in fact have such an interest under either a resulting or a constructive trust or, as a last resort, under the doctrine of proprietary estoppel.

For Jane to establish an interest in the house under a resulting trust, she must show that she made a contribution – either direct or indirect – to the acquisition of the house: *Burns* v *Burns* [1984] Ch 317. A direct contribution would be a contribution to the purchase money or the mortgage instalments, which Jane has not made. An indirect contribution must be financial and must be 'referable to the acquisition of an interest in the house': *Gissing* v *Gissing* [1971] AC 886, and more recently *Winkworth* v *Edward Baron Development Co Ltd* [1988] 1 FLR 237. This means that the indirect contribution must have enabled the other party to meet the mortgage payments. The time Jane spent bringing up their child and performing domestic duties would not qualify as an indirect contribution as it is not financial (although it could be argued that it enabled Peter to work and, therefore, to pay the mortgage instalments and thus should, logically, so qualify). As regards the payments by her for decorations, although it was suggested in *Pettitt* v *Pettitt* [1970] AC 777 that home improvements should qualify as indirect contributions, subsequent cases suggest that this is not the case and it is submitted that any interest created as a result is better explained in terms of constructive trusts (see below). Finally, Jane's contributions to household expenses will give rise to a resulting trust in her favour if Peter would not have continued to meet the mortgage instalments otherwise. Peter's comments to Ned suggest that although this is probably not the case (Peter had previously been paying the mortgage instalments and supporting himself Jane and the child), Jane's contribution did enable him to build the extension and thus a resulting trust will operate to give Jane a beneficial interest in the increase in the value of the house due to the extension, the value of which will be the value of her contributions to household expenses up until the extension was completed.

It is possible that Jane has a further interest in the house as a result of her other financial and non-financial contributions via the machinery of a constructive trust. The use of constructive trusts in this area is a recent idea. However, it now well established that a constructive trust will be imposed if Jane can show that a common intention existed that she would have a beneficial interest in the house and that she acted to her detriment on the basis of this common intention: *Grant* v *Edwards* [1986] Ch 638. Although the contribution to decoration would clearly constitute sufficient detriment, it is doubtful whether the time spent bringing up the child and carrying out domestic duties would. Lord Denning in *Hall* v *Hall* [1981] 3 FLR 379 suggested that it would, and although his views have been strongly criticised in recent cases, in the recent decision of *Lloyds Bank plc* v *Rossett and Another* [1990] 2 WLR 867 it was held that it may constitute sufficient detriment. Browne-Wilkinson V-C's comments in *Grant* v *Edwards* were applied – that once a common intention had been established any act done by the party 'to her detriment relating to the joint lives of the parties is … sufficient detriment to qualify'. However, on the facts there is no evidence of a common intention that Jane should have a beneficial interest in the house, and without this no constructive trust will arise. More information is needed from Jane as to whether the question of whether she was to have an interest in the house was ever discussed by Peter and herself.

A final possibility is that Jane has an interest of some description as a result of the application of proprietary estoppel. For this to be of assistance Jane must have believed that she had an interest in the house and must have acted to her detriment on the basis of this belief; Peter must have known of her belief: *Crabb* v *Arun District Council* [1976] Ch 179. In *Gillett* v *Holt* [2000] 2 All ER 289 proprietary estoppel was presented as being a general means to prevent unconscionable conduct rather than being restricted to a limited number of pre-determined circumstances. If there is no common intention between the parties of Jane's beneficial interest, it is unlikely that a court would find that the requirements of belief concerning proprietary estoppel were present as the two ideas are similar, as are, in fact, the concepts of constructive trusts and proprietary estoppel as a whole. In *Yaxley* v *Gotts* [1999] 3 WLR 1217 it was stated that proprietary estoppel is very similar to constuctive trusts- particularly the common intention constructive trust. As a result, if Jane fails to establish an interest via a constructive trust, she is unlikely to do so using proprietary estoppel.

QUESTION TWO

a) Are there any real grounds for distinguishing between the doctrines of:

    i)   constructive trust; and

    ii) resulting trust; and

    iii) proprietary estoppel?

b) Five years ago, at Vicky's suggestion, Thomas gave up his protected tenancy of a flat in order to move into Vicky's house of which she was (and remains) the freehold owner subject to a mortgage. Since then Thomas has spent £3,000 of his own money on improvements to the house and has met all the household expenses other than mortgage interest and repayments.

    Vicky has now fallen in love with another man and has asked Thomas to leave, offering him the £3,000 he spent on improvements but nothing more. The house (as improved) has a market value of £60,000 and the outstanding mortgage loan is £20,000, £5,000 having been paid off by Vicky in instalments over the past five years.

    Advise Thomas whether he has any beneficial interest in the property.

University of London LLB Examination
(for External Students) Law of Trusts June 1992 Q6

General Comment

Whilst constructive trust and estoppel are areas which students usually find interesting, they are complex areas which should not be attempted by those who do not have a sound knowledge of case law.

Skeleton Solution

a) Give main examples of other types of constructive trust, resulting trust and proprietary estoppel – similarities: Denning in *Hussey* v *Palmer*; Browne-Wilkinson in *Grant* v *Edwards*; *Yaxley* v *Gotts* – constructive trust: *Lloyds Bank plc* v *Rosset* formulation – resulting trust: purchase money, contributions – *Re Densham*: significance of contribution – estoppel: is any contribution required? – how important is the distinction?

b) Legal title in Vicky alone – does Thomas have a share in equity? – improvements MPPA 1970, s37 – household expenses: referable to the acquisition of the house? – was there any agreement between Thomas and Vicky? – did Thomas act to his detriment in reliance? – *Eves* v *Eves* – did Vicky make a representation to Thomas? – if any equity arises, which is the most appropriate way to satisfy it?

Suggested Solution

a) A constructive trust is a trust imposed by the courts regardless of intention but its exact scope has been a matter of debate for years. The term covers trusts as diverse as a trust imposed to prevent a fiduciary obtaining a benefit from his position, as in *Keech* v *Sandford* (1726) Sel Cas t King 61, trusts imposed on exchange of contracts on a sale of land, probably fully secret trusts, as well as the so-called new model constructive trust. Resulting trusts can be broadly divided into two types, the so-called automatic resulting trust which arises on failure of a beneficial interest, and the presumed resulting trust. It is in the area covered by the new model constructive trust and the presumed resulting trust that the overlap arises where legal title to property is vested in one person but another claims to be entitled in equity to the property or to a share in it. Increasingly the doctrines of proprietary estoppel have started to overlap with those of constructive trust and this overlap was recognised judicially in both *Grant* v *Edwards* [1986] Ch 638 and *Lloyds Bank plc* v *Rosset and Another* [1990] 2 WLR 867.

In a claim under a resulting trust, the plaintiff is claiming a share in the property proportionate to the contribution which he has made. Thus in *Re Densham* [1975] 1 WLR 1519 where the wife had contributed one-ninth of the total purchase price, she was entitled to a one-ninth share in equity and the fact that both parties had intended she should have a one half share was not relevant to the resulting trust claim. It seems that intention is not important in a resulting trust claim as there will be a presumption of resulting trust in favour of the person making the contribution. The contributions, however, must according to Hanbury be in money or money's worth.

In a claim under a constructive trust, the plaintiff may claim a share which is greater than the amount of his or her contribution. Thus in *Re Densham* the wife was able to claim a one half share under a constructive trust since the partner had agreed that they would share equally. The basis of a constructive trust claim was set out by the

House of Lords in *Lloyds Bank plc v Rosset and Another*. According to Lord Bridge there are broadly two types of case in which a constructive trust will be imposed. The first is where there has been an agreement between the parties that the property will be shared beneficially and that the non-legal owner then acted to his or her detriment in reliance on this understanding. *Eves v Eves* [1975] 1 WLR 1338 was cited as an example of this type of constrictive trust. The second case is where, although there is no evidence of any express agreement between the parties, a common intention to share the property can be inferred since the non-legal owner has made direct contributions to the purchase price. Lord Bridge doubted that in the latter case anything less than payment of mortgage instalments or an actual contribution to the price would suffice.

In the old case of *Willmott v Barber* (1880) 15 Ch D 96 Fry LJ considered that five requirements had to be satisfied before a claim based on what is now called proprietary estoppel could be made. The plaintiff must make a mistake as to his legal right, he must act in reliance on that mistaken belief and the defendant must be aware of his own rights and the plaintiff's mistaken belief. Finally, the defendant must have encouraged the plaintiff's actions in reliance on his mistaken belief. In most modern cases the courts have adopted a more flexible approach and the doctrine has been used in a wide variety of situations. The court will determine the appropriate remedy which may be a transfer of the legal estate, as in *Pascoe v Turner* [1979] 1 WLR 431, a grant of an easement, as in *Crabb v Arun District Council* [1976] Ch 179 or an entitlement to live in a house for life as in *Greasely v Cooke* [1980] 1 WLR 1306.

There is clearly a considerable overlap between the three different doctrines and as long ago as 1972 in *Hussey v Palmer* [1972] 1 WLR 1286 Lord Denning asserted that there was no real difference between resulting and constructive trust. It is suggested though that there is still a real distinction. Resulting trusts depend on contributions and the share is proportional to the size of the contribution. Constructive trusts depend on express or implied agreement of the parties and contributions are only one way of proving the existence of such an agreement. The amount of any contributions made may be relevant in determining the size of the share but it is not the only factor. It is suggested that the type of family case is better handled under constructive rather than resulting trusts.

The overlap between constructive trust and proprietary estoppel has become apparent more recently. In *Grant v Edwards* [1986] Ch 638 the Court of Appeal stated that principles from proprietary estoppel might be relevant in establishing whether the plaintiff had acted on reliance on the agreement. In *Lloyds Bank plc v Rosset and Another* [1990] 2 WLR 867 Lord Bridge talked about conduct 'sufficient to give rise to a constructive trust on proprietary estoppel'. In *Re Basham* [1987] 1 All ER 405 the court held that the plaintiff succeeded in a claim based on proprietary estoppel and that this gave rise to a constructive trust. Many writers have doubted whether it is helpful to impose a constructive trust in case of estoppel as this would seem to detract from the flexibility which is one of the characteristics of estoppel. In *Yaxley* v *Gotts* [1999] 3 WLR 1217 it was stated that proprietary estoppel is very similar to constuctive trusts – particularly the common intention constructive trust. In *Gillett* v *Holt* [2000] 2 All ER 289 proprietary estoppel was presented as being a general means to prevent unconscionable conduct rather than being restricted to a limited number of pre-determined circumstances.

One can distinguish between the doctrine in theory but it is clear from the case law that in the cases the distinctions become blurred. It may well be that in the future the doctrines become less distinct. But the theoretical basis of each is still distinct. Resulting trusts depend on contributions and the size of the share depends on the size of the contribution. It is likely that only direct contributions in money are relevant. Constructive trusts depend on express or implied agreement and contributions are one way of proving the existence of the agreement. They are relevant but not decisive in determining the size of the share. Proprietary estoppel depends on acting to one's detriment in reliance on representations. The remedy given depends on the representation made and will not necessarily be a share of the property. The distinctions are less clear than formerly and may become less clear in the future.

b) Clearly Vicky has the sole legal title to the house and the issue is whether Thomas is entitled to any equitable interest under a resulting or constructive trust, or whether the court would grant him any remedy under the doctrine of proprietary estoppel. Thomas has paid £3,000 for improvements to the house and he may argue that this should give him an interest in the equity. Since the couple are not married, Matrimonial Proceedings and Property Act (MPPA) 1970, s37 does not apply, but Thomas can still argue that his contribution shows evidence of a common intention that he should have a share. Vicky may well argue in reply that the contribution was simply a loan which she is now willing to repay, or that the contribution was in exchange for rent-free accommodation as in *Thomas* v *Fuller Brown* [1988] 1 FLR 237.

It is not clear from the question whether there was any express agreement between Thomas and Vicky that he should have a share in the house. If there was such an express agreement it is suggested that Thomas will be able to claim a share as it seems clear that he has acted to his detriment in reliance on such an agreement. He has given up his secure tenancy, spent money on improvements and contributed to the housekeeping expenses. In *Lloyds Bank plc* v *Rosset and Another* [1990] 2 WLR 867 it was said that where there was an express common intention that each would have a share, detrimental reliance would be sufficient. This was the proper explanation of *Eves* v *Eves* [1975] 1 WLR 1338.

If there was no express agreement, Thomas is in a more difficult situation as he has not made any direct contribution to the purchase price. Lord Bridge indicated that if there was no evidence of any express agreement, he thought that an agreement could be inferred if there were direct contributions to the acquisition, but was doubtful if anything else would suffice. Thomas may be able to argue that the £3,000 he spent on improvements was a type of direct contribution, equivalent to paying the mortgage instalments. It would probably be easier to establish this if his £3,000 was used to pay for some major capital improvement such as installation of central heating. Improvements which just amounted to interior redecoration would not be regarded as referable to the acquisition of the property. It may also be possible for Thomas to establish that there was an agreement between him and Vicky that both would contribute to the acquisition, but that for convenience, she would pay the mortgage and he would meet the other payments. In this case, he could argue that his contribution was equivalent to payment of the mortgage.

Assuming that he could establish he was entitled to a share under a constructive trust, the next problem for Thomas would be to establish the size of the share. There is no indication that there was any agreement he would have a particular share. If there is no agreement, it seems from *Grant* v *Edwards* [1986] Ch 638 that the amount of the contributions made by him would be taken into account in assessing his share. It is suggested that the amount of his payments would be compared to the payments made by Vicky and it would also be relevant that he has only contributed for five years. It is suggested that unless there was an agreement that he should have a certain share, a small share such as one quarter might be all Thomas could expect.

Finally if there was no express agreement that Thomas would have a share and his contributions were not regarded as sufficiently direct, could he claim under the doctrine of estoppel? In this case he would need to show that Vicky made some representation to him about his position. He has certainly acted to his detriment in giving up his protected tenancy but there must be a reliance on a representation by Vicky. In *Tanner* v *Tanner* [1975] 1 WLR 1346 a woman gave up her protected tenancy to move in with a man and the Court of Appeal would clearly have permitted her to stay on the basis that she had a contractual licence to remain. But in *Coombes* v *Smith* [1986] 1 WLR 808 the plaintiff moved into the defendant's house and was assured that he would provide for her and it was held that a claim based on proprietary estoppel failed. She had no mistaken belief that the defendant would provide for her indefinitely. It seems unlikely that Vicky could have assured Thomas he could stay in the house without time limit and an estoppel claim seems doubtful. Even if it were successful, what remedy would the court give? It would surely be inequitable to allow Thomas to stay for ever and more likely that he might simply be granted a licence to stay until Vicky repaid him the £3,000 spent on improvements as in *Dodsworth* v *Dodsworth* [1973] 228 EG 115. Vicky is in any event willing to pay the money.

Thus unless he can prove an express agreement between them that he would have a share in the house, Thomas does not seem to be in a strong position. If he can establish such an agreement a claim based on constructive trust should succeed as he has then clearly acted to his detriment. It is difficult to assess the size of his share but perhaps a quarter of the equity might be appropriate – certainly no more and quite possibly less. If there was no agreement, a trust claim is doubtful in the light of Lord Bridge's dicta in *Lloyds Bank plc* v *Rosset and Another* [1990] 2 WLR 867 as the contributions were not to the mortgage. An estoppel claim might succeed if he can show an assurance by Vicky but it is doubtful that she promised him accommodation for life and he might only be granted some form of licence to stay for a limited time or until his £3,000 is repaid.

QUESTION THREE

a) 'In the context of the family home, the boundaries between the doctrines of constructive trust, resulting trust and proprietary estoppel have become blurred.'

Discuss.

b) Paul bought a house to live in with Samantha and their three children. The legal title was vested in Paul's sole name and he paid the purchase price by taking out a 90 per cent mortgage. The other 10 per cent of the purchase price was paid by Paul's parents as a 'moving-in present to you both'. Over the years the mortgage was always paid out of Paul's salary whilst Sam paid all the other running costs of the home out of her income as a novelist. Paul has now been declared bankrupt. According to both his evidence and that of Sam they both assumed that the house was jointly owned although the matter was never actually discussed.

Advise Sam.

University of London LLB Examination
(for External Students) Law of Trusts June 1996 Q2

General Comment

Part (a) is a typical essay-type question involving a comparison of constructive and resulting trusts and proprietary estoppel. Part (b) is a problem question on co-ownership and joint contributions to the purchase price.

Skeleton Solution

a) Suggest definitions of the various terms – consider judicial definitions of the same – draw the conclusions to which you come.

b) This is a question of co-ownership and who owns what share in the house – apparently Paul and Samantha own 10 per cent of the equity of redemption in equal shares, while Paul has acquired the remainder – Samantha's payment of the outgoings is unlikely to give her an interest – her chances of resisting a sale seem poor.

Suggested Solution

a) This quotation concerns the line of cases beginning with *Bull* v *Bull* [1955] 1 QB 234 and the doctrine of proprietary estoppel which was particularly enunciated in *Inwards* v *Baker* [1965] 2 QB 29.

The result which is desired and which is achieved is clear. The broad principle is that an individual should not be allowed to act to their detriment in respect of land when they have been led to believe that they will receive a corresponding benefit and they should not be allowed to contribute towards the purchase price of property without receiving a corresponding share in the equity, unless they agree otherwise. The difficulty is how one classifies the trusts and other rules of equity which are imposed.

It is submitted that the best definition of a resulting trust is as a type of implied trust where there is a lacuna in the beneficial interest: eg 'To A for life'. In such an example the resulting trust supplies the remainder which is missing from the express limitation by providing that the property will result (from the Latin resultare 'to jump back') to the settlor or (if the settlor is dead) to the settlor's estate. A constructive trust, on the other hand, is, it is submitted, better defined as a trust which equity imposes ab extra where conscience requires, rather than where equity needs to imply something to fill a lacuna. This view is entirely consonant with the dictum: 'A constructive trust is the formula through which the conscience of equity finds expression' per Judge Cardozo in *Beatty* v *Guggenheim Exploration Co* (1919) 225 NY 380. Under this approach, the trusts imposed by equity on a home which has been paid for jointly are likely to be constructive trusts rather than resulting ones. Clearly, in co-ownership cases there is no lacuna in the beneficial interest of the sort envisaged in the above example. One might argue that the court is implying what the parties must be taken to have intended. However, that would create an implied trust rather than a resulting one and, in any event, in most cases one party will be claiming to be entitled to the whole equitable interest as well as the whole legal estate, so that really the court is imposing a trust on the situation ab extra.

Though the above principles are mostly of general application, it is in the context of the family home that particular problems occur. The difficulty with the above analysis arises in that there are judicial dicta referring to this situation both as a constructive trust and a resulting trust. Perhaps the most striking example is *Hussey* v *Palmer* [1972] 1 WLR 1286, in which Phillimore LJ held that there was a resulting trust, while Lord Denning MR held that there was a constructive trust. In the recent case of *Drake* v *Whipp* [1996] 1 FLR 826, the Court of Appeal styled trusts where the parties contribute to the purchase price jointly as resulting trusts, and those where the doctrine of equitable estoppel applied as constructive trusts. While one can see the logic of this, it is submitted that 'implied trusts' would have been a more felicitous term than 'resulting trusts'.

While there are similarities with the doctrine of equitable estoppel, it is submitted that this is a rather different animal, since it is a rule of evidence and operates on a totally different basis from constructive trusts. The difficulty with this argument is that the result is much the same. By the nature of the animal, though, the doctrine of equitable estoppel tends to affect family homes rather than being of general application. A good example of this is *Inwards* v *Baker* [1965] 2 QB 29, the leading case on proprietary estoppel. Here Baker wanted to build a bungalow. His father suggested that Baker build the bungalow on land which the father owned. Baker did this and lived in the bungalow. After the father's death his trustees claimed the bungalow. The Court of Appeal held that the father had induced Baker to build his bungalow on the father's land and Baker had spent money on the bungalow in the expectation that he would be allowed to remain there. Consequently, the father was estopped from defeating that expectation. The trustees could be in no better position.

Finally, it is submitted that the fundamental difference between equitable estoppel and the co-ownership cases is that the latter concern the payment of money towards the purchase price simpliciter, while the former is concerned with a situation where there is normally no such payment, but someone who does not own the property acts to their detriment on the basis of and encouraged by a representation by the true owner. It is therefore submitted that there is a clear distinction between proprietary estoppel and the co-ownership cases and that it is perfectly possible to maintain a meaningful and realistic distinction between resulting and constructive trusts (both in co-ownership cases and elsewhere), but that some blurring in the way in which these terms are used exists and has indeed been encouraged by judicial usage. In *Yaxley* v *Gotts* [1999] 3 WLR 1217 it was stated that proprietary estoppel is very similar to constructive trusts – particularly the common intention constructive trust.

b) The basic principle is that whoever pays the purchase price owns a proportionate share in the equity: eg *Bull* v *Bull* [1955] 1 QB 234. Contributions to the mortgage repayments constitute payments of the purchase price: *Winkworth* v *Edward Baron Development Co Ltd* [1988] 1 FLR 237. In this case the mortgagee takes priority over everyone else and on different legal principles. The sole issue here is, therefore, the initial 10 per cent of the beneficial ownership in the house which constitutes the equity of redemption, which has now grown to an unspecified percentage. As the initial 10 per cent was paid for by Paul's parents, prima facie it belongs to them. However, they expressly made a gift of this 'to you both'. This in turn suggests that the equity is owned jointly and in equal shares. There might be a slight technical problem under s53(1)(c) Law of Property Act 1925 with whether this might constitute a gift of an equitable interest which is not in writing, but it is submitted that the better analysis is that it is a gift of money (which, not being land, need not be in writing) and that Paul and Samantha acquired the equity of redemption in the house directly from the vendor rather than via Paul's parents. If this analysis is correct, there is no problem.

Since payments of the mortgage instalments constitute a contribution to the purchase price, prima facie Paul has acquired all the equity of redemption subsequently bought by the mortgage repayments. The question is whether

Samantha's paying the outgoings of the house gives her any share in that equity of redemption. This is a difficult question and one on which the view of the courts has varied. There have been decisions in the past which suggest the contrary: eg *Burns* v *Burns* [1984] Ch 317; and *Grant* v *Edwards* [1986] Ch 638. However, it is submitted that the present view of the judiciary is not to give Samantha any share in the equity of redemption: *Lloyds Bank plc* v *Rosset and Another* [1990] 2 WLR 867. It is also arguable that Samantha was paying income items which did not go to acquiring a capital asset and thus she did not acquire any interest in the equity of the house: *Savage* v *Dunningham* [1974] Ch 181.

The only way out of this difficulty seems to be to argue that whatever the parties' rights in equity would otherwise have been, they agreed that the house would be jointly owned and that overrides the presumptions of equity. Had there been a deed or a clause in a deed to that effect, Samantha's position would have been unassailable: *Goodman* v *Gallant* [1986] Fam 106. Given that this is not so, the law is more doubtful. There are authorities which suggest that Samantha has a case: eg *Hammond* v *Mitchell* [1991] 1 WLR 1127 (though here there was an element of detriment); *Bristol and West Building Society* v *Henning* [1985] 1 WLR 778. However, her case is not as strong as it might be.

Even assuming that Samantha is able to establish that she owns part of the equity, she may still not be able to resist a sale. Paul's trustee in bankruptcy may still be able to force a sale under s30 Law of Property Act 1925, though she will receive a proportionately larger share of the proceeds of sale with which to buy another property. The question is 'Whose voice should be heard in equity?': *Re Turner (A Bankrupt)* [1974] 1 WLR 1556. If her three children are still young, she will probably be allowed to stay there until they grow up, but if not and if she could buy a smaller but perfectly adequate property with ease, then the court will give priority to Paul's creditors and order a sale of the house: *Re Holliday (A Bankrupt)* [1981] Ch 405; and contrast *Re Lowrie (A Bankrupt)* [1981] 3 All ER 353.

Chapter 8

Constructive Trusts

8.1   Introduction

8.2   Key points

8.3   Key cases

8.4   Questions and suggested solutions

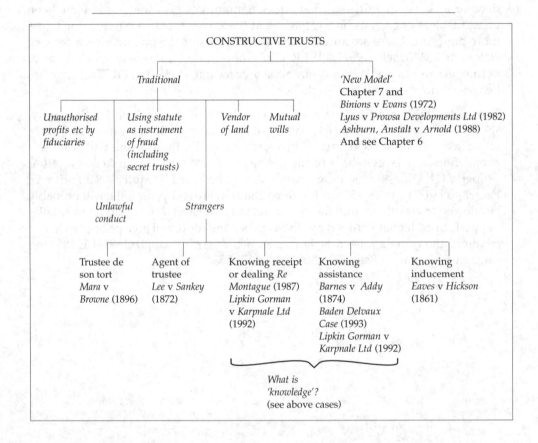

8.1 Introduction

Constructive trusts arise in various situations. The relevance of the concept in 'matrimonial' property is considered in Chapter 7, and the rules relating to when a constructive trust will arise as a result of a breach by the trustees of their fiduciary duty is dealt with in Chapter 14. Whether secret trusts are a breed of constructive trust is addressed in Chapter 5. The degree of difficulty to be found varies between the different aspects of the topic. You must be aware of the quite considerable number of decisions in this area.

8.2 Key points

Until the 1970s it was accepted that the operation of the constructive trust in English law was limited to defined situations, in contrast to the far more flexible approach employed by American courts. Whilst there was a period in which a broader approach was attempted, the idea of a new model constructive trust has been largely abandoned in favour of traditional categories.

Unauthorised profits, etc by fiduciaries

If a fiduciary benefits from his position, he will hold such benefits as constructive trustee for the person(s) in relation to who he is fiduciary. Trustees are clearly fiduciaries – their duties as such are examined in Chapter 14. In addition, a director is in a fiduciary relationship to his company: *Regal (Hastings) Ltd* v *Gulliver* [1942] 1 All ER 378, an agent to his principal and partners to each other. Indeed, a fiduciary relationship can exist in any situation if circumstances suggest that it should.

Using statute as an instrument of fraud (including secret trusts)

If this is attempted, equity will intervene to impose a constructive trust as in *Bannister* v *Bannister* [1948] 2 All ER 133 and, arguably, in the case of secret trusts (see Chapter 5).

Mutual wills

If a party to a mutual will alters it after the other party's death, the executors under the will will hold the estate on a constructive trust on the terms originally agreed.

Unlawful conduct

If a person benefits as a result of unlawful conduct, a constructive trust will be imposed on him of the benefit as in *Re Giles* [1972] Ch 544.

Vendor of land

Between exchange of contracts and completion, the vendor holds land on constructive trust for the purchaser in 'a modified sense': per Kekewich J in *Royal Bristol Permanent Building Society* v *Bomash* (1887) 35 Ch 390.

Strangers

A stranger will only be liable as a constructive trustee of trust property in five circumstances.

Trustee de son tort

If a person who is not a trustee and who has no authority from a trustee intermeddles with trust matters or acts as trustee: *Mara v Browne* [1896] 1 Ch 199.

Knowing receipt or dealing

If a person:

a) receives trust property with either actual or constructive knowledge that the transfer to him was in breach of trust; or

b) receives trust property and deals with it in a manner which he knows to be inconsistent with the trusts.

See *Re Montague's Settlement Trusts* [1987] 2 WLR 1192; *Cowan de Groot v Eagle Trust plc* [1992] 4 All ER 700.

Knowing assistance

If a person has knowingly assisted in a dishonest and fraudulent design on the part of trustees: *Barnes v Addy* (1874) 9 Ch App 244, whether or not the stranger in fact receives the trust property: *Baden Delvaux v Société Général* [1993] 1 WLR 509.

'Knowledge' in 'knowing receipt or dealing' and 'knowing assistance' above, has been the subject of much discussion. In the *Baden Delvaux* case, five types of knowledge were identified from actual knowledge to knowledge of circumstances which would put an honest and reasonable man on inquiry. In *Re Montague's Settlement Trusts* it was suggested that the latter type of negligence would not be sufficient and this was reiterated in *AGIP (Africa) Ltd v Jackson and Others* [1991] Ch 547. A lower standard was used in the cases of *Lipkin Gorman v Karpnale Ltd* [1991] 3 WLR 10 and *Royal Brunei Airlines Sdn Bhd v Tan (Philip Kok Ming)* [1995] 3 All ER 97. The cases of *Brinks Ltd v Abu Saleh and Others (No 3)* [1996] CLC 133, *Baden Delvaux v Société Générale*, *Attorney-General of Hong Kong v Reid* [1994] 1 AC 324 and *Westdeutsche Landesbank Girozentrale v Islington London Borough Council* [1996] 2 All ER 961 are further more recent attempts to deal with this difficult area of law. In the *Brinks* case, which was concerned with knowing assistance, it was decided that a wife who travelled with her husband on a money laundering trip was not a constructive trustee. She knew of the reason for the trip but she did not assist. In the *Baden* case, it was made clear that there are limits to the investigations that should be undertaken where a person is a stranger to a trust. In the *Reid* case where money was accepted as a bribe any investment of it that produced profit would lead to a constructive trust of the profit as well. In *Westdeutsche Landesbank Girozentrale v Islington London Borough Council* [1996] 2 All ER 961 case there was no constructive trust where a council received money from a bank, for purposes that the council was not legally authorised to undertake. The approach taken seems to be that an innocent volunteer who has received trust property is not a constructive trustee of that property. It can also be noted that in the *Westdeutsche* case Lord Browne-Wilkinson put the view that the remedial constructive trust could be used to provide a means to develop proprietary restitutionary remedies. You should also note *Halifax Building Society* v *Thomas* [1996] 2 WLR 63, a case in which there was no fiduciary relationship. A mortgagee who has sold property under a mortgage, the mortgage having been obtained fraudulently, is entitled to retain a surplus from the sale. There was no authority in English law establishing that a victim or intended victim of wrongdoing, who has suffered no loss, is entitled to retain or recover a profit arising from such a fraud.

Knowing inducement

If a person knowingly induces the trustees to commit a breach of trust he will be liable as a constructive trustee regardless of whether he actually receives trust property *Eaves* v *Hickson* (1861) 30 Beav 136.

Possession by an agent of the trustee

The agent is a stranger who, if he deals with the trust property 'in a manner inconsistent with the performance of trusts of which he is cognisant, is personally liable for the consequences which may ensue upon his so dealing' – per Bacon V-C in *Lee* v *Sankey* (1873) LR 15 Eq 204.

'New model' constructive trusts

Chapter 7 deals with the 'matrimonial' aspects of this species of trust. However, the key to these trusts is their flexible nature and thus their operation has not been limited to 'matrimonial' property.

In *Binions* v *Evans* [1972] Ch 359, vendors sold a house expressly subject to an agreement with the defendant that she could live there rent free for the rest of her life, at an accordingly reduced price. The plaintiffs brought proceedings for possession and it was held that they could not. Lord Denning thought that the defendant had a licence conferring an equitable interest. It was held in *Ashburn, Anstalt* v *Arnold* [1988] 2 All ER 147 that this is incorrect and that in fact the nature of her interest was that of a beneficiary under a constructive trust, a principle which had already been applied in *Lyus* v *Prowsa Developments Ltd* [1982] 2 All ER 953, on the basis that the plaintiffs' behaviour meant that it would be inequitable to deny the defendant an interest.

In matrimonial matters, as elsewhere, the new model approach has been largely abandoned in favour of traditional and narrow concepts as in the case of *Lloyds Bank plc* v *Rosset and Another* [1990] 2 WLR 867.

However, the dicta of Lord Browne-Wilkinson in *Westdeutsche Landesbank Girozentrale* v

Islington London Borough Council [1996] 2 All ER 961 offers some support for it. He stated that '… the remedial constructive trust, if introduced into English law, may provide a more satisfactory road forward … However, whether English law should follow the United States and Canada in adopting the remedial constructive trust will have to be decided in some future case where the point is directly in issue'.

8.3 Key cases

- *Baden Delvaux* v *Société Général* [1993] 1 WLR 509
  Knowing asistance – knowledge – five types

- *Lloyds Bank plc* v *Rosset and Another* [1990] 2 WLR 867
  Matrimonial – traditional rather than new model approach

- *Re Montague's Settlement Trusts* [1987] 2 WLR 1192
  Knowing receipt

- *Westdeutsche Landesbank Girozentrale* v *Islington London Borough Council* [1996] 2 All ER 961
  Matrimonial – Lord Browne-Wilkinson – some support for a new model approach

8.4 Questions and suggested solutions

QUESTION ONE

'Recent developments in the field of constructive trusts demonstrate beyond peradventure that Equity is by no means beyond the age of child-bearing.' Discuss.

University of London LLB Examination
(for External Students) Law of Trusts June 1986 Q5

General Comment

This is a common type of question which requires a detailed knowledge of both any developments and a discussion of the cases.

Skeleton Solution

Introduction: the traditional approach of English law compared to that of American law – summary of recent developments and introduction of 'new model' constructive trusts by the courts – consideration of the cases and developments in detail – development of the law since Lord Denning's retirement – conclusion.

Suggested Solution

The traditional approach of English law to the constructive trust is that it is a substantive institution only imposed in certain well-defined situations, for example, breach of fiduciary duty. Thus provided the facts of a case came within the bounds of one of these well-defined situations, a constructive trust could be imposed: see *English v Dedham Vale Properties Ltd* [1978] 1 WLR 93; *Re Sharpe* [1980] 1 WLR 219. This approach should be contrasted with the American approach to constructive trusts, where they are treated as a remedial institution. No clearly defined principles are laid down for the imposition of such trusts, instead they are imposed to prevent unjust enrichment, ie cases where the holder of the legal title may not in good conscience retain the beneficial interest: see *Beatty* v *Guggenheim Exploration Co* (1919) 225 NY 380.

The American concept of the constructive trust has been creeping into English law in relatively recent years, particularly in the area concerned with informal family arrangements as to the ownership of property. Many cases in this area, if and when decided on the lines of resulting trusts, produced what were considered to be unjust results. Accordingly, recourse was made to 'new model constructive trusts' as a means of providing a plaintiff with a remedy where established principles would not provide him with one and it was considered that he ought to win. Lord Denning MR was, before his retirement, prominent in adopting this approach as many of his decisions illustrate. Since his departure from the Court of Appeal, this approach would appear to have been adopted in some more recent decisions.

The idea of the new model constructive trust is traced back to Lord Diplock in *Gissing* v *Gissing* [1971] AC 886 by Lord Denning MR in *Eves* v *Eves* [1975] 1 WLR 1338, where he said: 'Equity is not past the age of child-bearing. One of her latest progeny is a constructive trust of a new model. Lord Diplock brought it into the world and we have nourished it'. Previously, in 1972 Lord Denning MR had shown enthusiasm for this new-found concept by applying it in three cases. In *Cooke* v *Head* [1972] 1 WLR 518 he overturned a decision of Plowman J that a mistress was entitled to one twelfth of the proceeds of sale of a bungalow she had helped to build and awarded her one third. He added that in cases where two parties by their joint efforts acquired property for their joint benefit a constructive or resulting trust would be imposed whereby the legal owner holds the property on trust for both. Some attention appears to have been paid in this case to what the mistress might have been entitled if she had been a spouse claiming benefits under matrimonial legislation. In *Hussey* v *Palmer* [1972] 1 WLR 1286 he seems to have imposed a constructive trust in favour of the plaintiff who gave her son-in-law £607 to build an extra bedroom to her house for her use. The plaintiff fell out with the son-in-law, hence the claim. The decisions of the other judges in this case are based on the idea that there was a loan or resulting trust. Lord Denning MR did not make his classification very clear but he did make clear the basis upon which he was imposing the trust, namely on the grounds of justice and good conscience where the defendant cannot conscientiously keep the property for himself alone. In *Binions* v *Evans* [1972] Ch 359, the new model constructive trust was imposed on a purchaser of a cottage in favour of the occupant by reason of an agreement between the vendor and occupant that the occupant could reside there rent free for the rest of her life. The price paid by the purchaser was reduced to take this matter into account. Lord Denning MR considered that the occupant had a licence giving an equitable interest but added if he were wrong on this a constructive trust would nevertheless be imposed on the purchaser as it would be wrong to allow him to remove the occupant contrary to the basis on which he took the property.

In *Lyus* v *Prowsa Developments Ltd* [1982] 2 All ER 953 a constructive trust was imposed on purchasers of a building plot who purchased it from a company who had agreed to build a house thereon for the plaintiff. The company went into liquidation and the plot was sold subject to the plaintiff's agreement. The Court of Appeal headed by Lord Denning MR concluded that the sale 'subject to' the agreement imposed a constructive trust. In the recent case of *Ashburn Anstalt* v *Arnold* [1988] 2 All ER 147, it was held that Lord Denning's licence explanation in *Binions* v *Evans* [1972] Ch 359 was incorrect and that, in fact, the correct interpretation of a similar situation was that employed by the court in *Lyus* v *Prowsa Developments Ltd*. It was underlined, however, that a prerequisite for a constructive trust to be imposed was that the plaintiff's behaviour must be such that it would be inequitable to deny the defendant an interest in the property; a slightly, stricter approach than that preferred by Lord Denning.

In *Eves* v *Eves* [1975] 1 WLR 1338, a constructive trust was imposed by Lord Denning MR but not by the other members of the Court of Appeal. This case concerned an unmarried couple living together, the man purchased a house in his name and told the plaintiff it was their house but would have to be in his name alone as she was under 21. This was merely an excuse by the man to avoid a conveyance into joint names. The woman did not contribute to the purchase of the house but she brought up two children she had to the man and did much work in the house and garden. Lord Denning MR imposed a constructive trust in these circumstances on the ground that it would be inequitable to deny the woman a share in the house. But it is notable that the other two judges in the case found in favour of the woman on the basis that there was an enforceable agreement between the parties that the woman shall have a share in the house by reason of her labour in repairing and improving it.

Since Lord Denning MR's departure from the Court of Appeal, decisions have both supported and ignored his approach. In support is the decision in *Grant* v *Edwards* [1986] Ch 638, this case concerned an unmarried couple. A house was purchased and conveyed into the name of the defendant and his brother. The plaintiff was told that she could not be on the title because this might affect her claims against her husband in divorce proceedings. In fact this was an excuse to keep her name off the title, the defendant did not intend her name to be on the title at all. The plaintiff made substantial indirect contributions to repaying the mortgage, to the housekeeping and to household expenses and bringing up the children. A constructive trust was imposed on the defendant on the ground that it would be inequitable for him to claim sole beneficial ownership because he had led her to believe she had an interest in the property. On the faith of this the plaintiff had made her contributions. Sir Nicholas Browne-Wilkinson V-C added that in cases such as this guidance might in future be obtained from the principles underlying the law of proprietary estoppel. The concept of new model constructive trusts was, however, not applied in *Burns* v *Burns* [1984] Ch 317. In this case the plaintiff made no contributions to the purchase of the house which was in the defendant's sole name. The parties were unmarried. These were no misleading statements from the defendant as to ownership. The Court of Appeal refused to give the plaintiff any share in the property on the basis only that she looked after their children and the home. It might be added that as there were no grounds for imposing a constructive trust a resulting trust only could benefit the plaintiff and she was unable to prove an interest in the property for herself.

More recently, in *Lloyds Bank plc* v *Rosset and Another* [1990] 2 WLR 867, the House of Lords has attempted to restrict the circumstances in which a constructive trust will be imposed. If there was an agreement between the parties that the property is to be shared beneficially, it would only be necessary for the non-legal owner to show that he had acted to his detriment or significantly altered his position in reliance. But if there was no agreement reached between the parties, a common intention to share will be readily inferred if the non-legal owner has made direct contributions to the acquisition, but it is douttful if anything less will do. The court will not impose a trust merely because it would be reasonable that the beneficial interest be shared and Lord Bridge doubted that the conduct of the female partner in *Eves* v *Eves* [1975] 1 WLR 1338 and *Grant* v *Edwards* [1986] Ch 638 would have been sufficient to justify the imposition of a trust hat there not been an express agreement to share the beneficial interest.

From all the cases discussed it would appear that there is further development of the constructive trust to bridge the gap between resulting and constructive trusts and provide a solution in those cases which do not, on their facts, fall neatly into either camp.

QUESTION TWO

a) 'Constructive trusts show the conscience of equity at work.'

Discuss.

b) Jack and Jill have for the last two years been living together in a flat. Jill had been the tenant of the flat for several years when, last year, the landlord offered to grant a 99-year lease to Jill at a nominal rent for £20,000, a price that was low by reason of the fact that Jill was a protected sitting tenant. Jill agreed but at her request the 99-year lease was granted to Jack who provided the whole of the £20,000. On the open market and with vacant possession, the leasehold flat would fetch £40,000 and Jack, having become disenchanted with Jill, is talking of selling and keeping the entire proceeds.

Advise Jill as to her interest, if any, in the flat or its future proceeds, on the assumption that her tenancy came to an end when Jack purchased.

University of London LLB Examination
(for External Students) Law of Trusts June 1991 Q3

General Comment

This is a question that invites in part (a) a general description of the meaning and scope of constructive trusts. A good question to begin with and which lends itself to a second class mark. Part (b) is straightforward case law.

Skeleton Solution

Trust or remedy – America versus England – standard categories of constructive trust – *Pettitt* v *Pettitt* – *Lloyds Bank plc* v *Rosset and Another* – relationship to resulting trusts.

Suggested Solution

a) Constructive trusts are often said to be at the cutting edge of a court's equitable jurisdiction. It is true that the 'constructive trust' is perceived by many to be an all-embracing remedy which the courts may use at their discretion to remedy 'inequitable' conduct by an individual, and this is indeed reinforced by the fact that constructive trusts are exempt from the normal formalities relating to the creation and operation of trusts: see s53(2) Law of Property Act 1925.

However, it is also clear that there is no set meaning to the term 'constructive trust' and that the many and various situations in which they can arise may defy definition. Some jurists argue that one feature common to all cases of constructive trust is that no person can be a constructive trustee (and hence there can be no constructive trust) unless he or she is the legal owner of property at the time the court imposes the trust. Such a 'definition' would seem to rule out 'knowing assistance' cases as examples of constructive trusts (because the person knowingly assisting does not have and does not acquire legal title). Another purported distinction is between the 'English' and 'American' constructive trusts, and herein lies the heart of the issue whether 'constructive trusts show the conscience of equity at work'.

The so-called 'English' approach sees constructive trusts as substantive trusts; that is, there are beneficiaries, trustees and those trustees have substantive duties of holding and administering the trust property just as if they had been constituted trustees under an express settlement. The consequence of this theoretical approach is that the court can impose a constructive trust only in certain reasonably defined situations. This does not mean that constructive trusts are not concerned with 'conscience', but rather that equity will remedy unconscionable behaviour only if certain conditions are satisfied. Examples of such constructive trusts are the rule that a trustee must not make a profit from his trust: *Keech* v *Sandford* (1726) Sel Cas t King 61; the rules of knowing receipt and assistance: *Lipkin Gorman* v *Karpnale Ltd* [1991] 3 WLR 10; *AGIP (Africa) Ltd* v *Jackson and Others* [1991] Ch 547; the rule that equity will not allow a statute to be an instrument of fraud: *Rochefoucauld* v *Boustead* [1897] 1 Ch 196; the law of secret trusts (possibly – see *Ottaway* v *Norman* [1972] Ch 698); the rule that a person cannot retain the benefit of a criminal act: *Davitt* v

Titcumb [1990] Ch 110; the law of mutual wills: *Re Cleaver* [1981] 1 WLR 939; and the rule that a vendor holds property on constructive trusts for a purchaser under a constructive trust, even before transfer of the property, if the contract for sale is specifically enforceable: *Lysaght* v *Edwards* (1876) 2 Ch D 499. All of these are cases where the court has imposed a trust to prevent inequity, but where the law has developed a reasonable certain set of rules to establish when this has occurred.

The 'American' view, on the other hand, sees the constructive trust as a flexible 'weapon' or 'remedy' which the court may use to prevent or redress inequitable conduct in any situation at any time. It is often known as the 'remedial constructive trust'. Furthermore, not only are there little restrictions on the circumstances in which such a trust can be imposed, but also the nature of this type of constructive trust is quite different. This constructive trust is clearly not substantive; the only duty which the constructive trustee will be under will be to return the trust property to its 'rightful' owner, ie the person to whom the court thinks in all fairness it should belong. It is a method of compelling a person to return property when they have been unjustly enriched. A good example in English law is *Chase Manhattan Bank* v *Israel-British Bank (London) Ltd* [1981] Ch 105, a case often considered under the law of tracing, but more properly regarded as one of unjust enrichment or remedial constructive trust because of the absence of any recognisable fiduciary relationship between the parties. This was how the case was viewed by Lord Browne-Wilkinson in *Westdeutsche Landesbank Girozentrale* v *Islington London Borough Council* [1996] 2 All ER 961. A similar approach was gaining ground in the law of matrimonial or quasi-matrimonial property where, under the guidance of *Grant* v *Edwards* [1986] Ch 638, the court adopted a flexible, result-oriented approach to ownership of property on the break-up of a stable relationship. This has been somewhat restricted by *Lloyds Bank plc* v *Rosset and Another* [1990] 2 WLR 867 which preferred the more defined 'English view'.

All in all then, it is true on one level to say that constructive trusts are the conscience of equity at work. Their purpose is to ensure that the legal owner of property should not unlawfully deprive another of his or her property. However, the more interesting question is how flexible this jurisdiction really is. In recent years, the courts of this country have been moving towards a more relaxed attitude to the use of constructive trusts and, in this sense, we can agree with the quotation in the question.

b) There are a number of possible answers to the question whether Jill has an interest in the flat or the proceeds of sale thereof. The first, most obvious, and clearly incorrect view is that Jill has no interest in the leasehold of the flat because legal title to the flat is in Jack's name alone. This is the presumption at law but, of course, it can be rebutted by showing that Jill has an interest by virtue of a resulting or constructive trust on the *Pettitt* v *Pettitt* [1970] AC 777, *Lloyds Bank plc* v *Rosset and Another* [1990] 2 WLR 867 model. It is clear, however, that no resulting trust can arise in Jill's favour because she has not contributed to the purchase price of the flat – it is purchased entirely with Jack's money. Indeed, the fact that Jack has legal title and that he alone provided the purchase money could go a long way to proving his sole ownership. However, this is unlikely because it appears that Jack is behaving inequitably and may be subject to a constructive trust in Jill's favour.

There are, perhaps two ways in which Jill could establish an interest – either of the whole or part – to the flat by virtue of a constructive trust. First, she could seek to show that there was a common intention between herself and Jack that she should have an interest in the flat plus some act of detriment by her in reliance on that promise: *Lloyds Bank plc* v *Rosset and Another* [1990] 2 WLR 867. On the facts, it may be possible to deduce such a common intention from the fact that she was offered the tenancy but insisted that it be given formally to Jack. Unless this was tantamount to a gift, there is little to explain such action unless Jill did have such intention. Her detriment would be similar to that in *Tanner* v *Tanner* [1975] 1 WLR 1346 in that she has given up the sure protection of a protected tenancy under the Rent Acts, as well as the chance of the leasehold at a low price. If this is the case, the extent of Jill's interest would be commensurate with the terms of the common intention – which could be that she have all the property (subject to repayment to Jack of his money) or some proportion thereof. However, this may be a rather complicated way of looking at the situation and the second angle of approach may be more helpful. Simply, Jack is now seeking to take advantage of the fact that he has an absolute conveyance in his favour and that there is no trust in writing as there should under s53(1)(b) Law of Property Act (LPA) 1925. He is, in essence, attempting to use a statute (s53 LPA) as an instrument of fraud: *Rochefoucauld* v *Boustead* [1897] 1 Ch 196. This is established as above viz, the flat was offered to Jill because she was a sitting tenant and at a low price because that tenancy was protected. This is clearly a case for equitable intervention and Jack will hold the flat on constructive trust for Jill, quite possibly as sole owner subject to Jack's right of repayment; *Hussey* v *Palmer* [1972] 1 WLR 1286.

QUESTION THREE

'When property has been acquired in such circumstances that the holder of the legal title may not in good conscience retain the beneficial interest, equity converts him into a trustee.' (Per Cardozo J in *Beatty* v *Guddenheim Exploration Co* (1919) 225 NY 380.)

Consider whether the circumstances in which English law imposes a constructive trust can be said to give rise to any similar principle of general application.

University of London LLB Examination
(for External Students) Law of Trusts June 1993 Q4

General Comment

Cardozo J's dicta in *Beatty* v *Guggenheim Exploration Co* (1919) 225 NY 380 represents the almost classic definition for the ill-fated 'new model constructive trust'. As such the question cries out for a brief review of constructive trusts then leading on to an exposé of the new model constructive trust and Lord Denning's use of it as an equitable remedy to rectify perceived injustice.

Skeleton Solution

Brief review of constructive trusts – 'no golden thread' – fiduciaries – strangers to the trust – new model constructive trust, *Hussey* v *Palmer* – *Gissing* v *Gissing* – *Lloyds Bank plc* v *Rosset and Another*.

Suggested Solution

It is often stated that constructive trusts lack an essential core of identifying principles; they lack a 'golden thread'. Practically the only real common feature to these trusts is that they are imposed by operation of law and, in sharp contrast to express trusts, are not dependent on the initial intention of the settlor. The result has been the emergence of certain identifiable types of constructive trusts that have emerged through developments in caselaw.

On that basis it is not strictly correct to suggest that a trust is imposed in all cases where the holder of the property has not acquired the property in circumstances so as to hold it in good faith (per Cardozo J, *Beatty* v *Guggenheim Exploration Co* (1919) 225 NY 380). This is usefully highlighted through citing examples of certain types of constructive trusts.

Perhaps the commonest form of constructive trust is one imposed when a fiduciary (for example a trustee, agent, professional adviser etc) has made a secret profit from their position: *Boardman* v *Phipps* [1967] 2 AC 46. To that extent it is true that equity has imposed a trust in a situation where the trustee (or fiduciary) has acquired the property with less than a good conscience.

However this type of constructive trust is first dependent on a fiduciary relationship being established. Therefore, whilst the definition of a fiduciary is not closed: *English* v *Dedham Vale Properties Ltd* [1978] 1 WLR 93, there are instances where such a relationship does not arise. For example it would not, normally, arise between business associates. Similarly it does not arise where property has been stolen: *Lister & Co* v *Stubbs* (1890) 45 Ch D 1. In both cases the property can have been acquired in bad faith but the trust will not arise.

A further peculiar example is the decision in *Boardman* v *Phipps*. In brief this matter involved Mr Boardman, a solicitor, assisting trustees of a minority shareholding in a private company in using knowledge gained in that capacity to reorganise the company and realise substantial increased share values. Specifically this was brought about through the purchase of shares by Boardman and one of the trust's beneficiaries so as to gain a majority holding. Whilst Boardman was held to be a constructive trustee of the profit made by him the House of Lords, nevertheless, ordered that he be paid compensation from the trust for his work and expertise!

Other forms of constructive trusts include those imposed when a stranger deals with trust property; mutual wills; property gained through unlawful conduct and possibly secret trusts. In each instance equity has devised a well established body of caselaw to determine when, or if, a constructive trust arises.

In contrast to this apparent morass of seemingly unconnected principles it is notable that in the past there was considerable support for the American view of constructive trusts (as espoused by Cardozo J). That support came to a head when Lord Denning ruled that in future a constructive trust could be 'imposed by law whenever justice and good conscience required it': *Hussey* v *Palmer* [1972] 1 WLR 1286. In turn Lord Denning had relied on the, albeit superficial, supporting dicta found in the earlier decision in *Gissing* v *Gissing* [1971] AC 886. Specifically Lord Denning noted Lord Diplock's comment that equity imposed a trust whenever the constructive trustee had so conducted himself as to demand that a trust to be imposed.

A line of subsequent case law in fields as diverse as matrimonial law: *Eves* v *Eves* [1975] 1 WLR 1338, registered land: *Peffer* v *Rigg* [1977] 1 WLR 285 and contractual licences: *Binions* v *Evans* [1972] Ch 359, in which Lord Denning cited Cardozo J, were quick to harness this new proprietary/remedial role for constructive trusts.

However this 'outbreak' (identified by the phrase the 'new model constructive trust') was fundamentally flawed insofar as Lord Diplock's statement (the bedrock of the line of cases) had been seriously misquoted. Whilst Lord Diplock had commented on the actions of the trustee as being important he added an important caveat that the trustee's conduct should be such as to have caused the beneficiary to have acted to his own detriment in the reasonable belief that they were thereby obtaining a beneficial interest. Suddenly the emphasis has changed from the good conscience, or otherwise, of the trustee to the reliance (required to be reasonable) of the beneficiary.

Whilst it took a while for Lord Diplock's caveat to be recognised it is notable that the new model constructive trust (through a series of damning decisions culminating in *Lloyds Bank plc* v *Rosset and Another* [1990] 2 WLR 867) has effectively been condemned to the archives. Arguably this was by far the best outcome for the Court of Appeal's vain attempt to catapult the constructive trust into the realm of injunctions and other purely remedial (rather than substantive) devices. From the outset concern was expressed at the creation of this vague, ad hoc, principle; not least of all because it deprived the law of much needed certainty. In addition its format, based on the use of dubious precedents, gave scant regard to its consequences. Third party rights, especially in relation to property law, were momentarily brushed aside in favour of short-term benefits. This was as compared to the tried, and well tested, older doctrines of constructive trusts. Not surprising then that the courts have reverted to the older doctrines thereby returning to a position where constructive trusts as a body lack a core, but individually do have recognisable principles.

Chapter 9
Setting Trusts Aside

9.1 **Introduction**

9.2 **Key points**

9.3 **Key statute**

9.4 **Question and suggested solution**

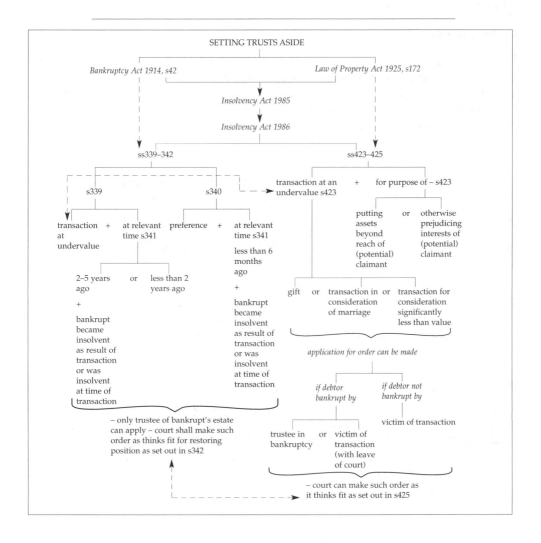

9.1 Introduction

Since the Insolvency Act 1986 most difficulties raised by the topic have disappeared. The law is now wholly contained in the statute which must simply be digested and learnt. The previous law is now only relevant in as much as the student should formulate an opinion as to whether and how the Act has ironed out previous problems and improved the law.

9.2 Key points

Until the Insolvency Act 1986 (replacing the Insolvency Act 1985), the law concerning whether a trust could be set aside in the event of the settlor's bankruptcy was contained in two statutory provisions.

Bankruptcy Act 1914, s42

The main defects in this provision as noted in the Cork Report on Insolvency Law and Practice (1982) Cmnd 8558 were that the section only covered settlements, so that gifts fell outside its provisions. In addition, it did not cover all transactions at an undervalue; only those for merely nominal consideration or less. The section has now been replaced by ss339–342 Insolvency Act 1986.

Law of Property Act 1925, s172

This provision contained many defects as outlined in the Cork Report. Notably, the section required an intention to defraud creditors, the meaning of which was unclear.

The section has now been replaced by ss423– 425 Insolvency Act 1986.

The Insolvency Act 1985 and then the Insolvency Act 1986 replaced the above provisions.

Sections 339–342

These sections allow the court to make an order regarding a transaction at an undervalue or a preference by a bankrupt provided that certain conditions are fulfilled. Only the trustee of the bankrupt's estate can apply for such an order.

Transaction at undervalue

By s339 this is either a gift, a transaction in consideration of marriage or a transaction for consideration 'significantly less' than the value. Such a transaction must have been entered into 'at a relevant time', which by s341 means within five years of the presentation of the individual's bankruptcy petition. If it is more than two years before that date, then the individual must also have been insolvent at that time – as defined by s341(3) – or must have become insolvent as a result of such transaction. In working out whether or not an individual is insolvent, account must be taken of contingent debts. Two cases on undervalue that can be referred to are *Re Kumar (A Bankrupt)* [1993] 2 All ER 700 and *Agricultural Mortgage Corporation plc* v *Woodward* [1995] 1 BCLC 1.

Preference

By s340 an individual gives a preference if he puts one of his creditors (etc – as defined in s340(3)) into a position which, on the event of the individual's bankruptcy, is a better position than he would otherwise have been in. The preference must have been exercised 'at a relevant time' within s341 – that is to say, within six months of the presentation of the individual's bankruptcy petition. In addition the requirements of the individual's insolvency apply as above.

Sections 423– 425

These sections will be resorted to in the case of a transaction at an undervalue which does not fall within the requisite time limits above. The main difference between the previous and present sets of sections is that for the court to make an order regarding a transaction of an undervalue under s423 it must be satisfied that the transaction was entered into in order to prejudice a potential claimant against him. The advantage of these sections is that there exist no time limits. In addition the power to apply is not restricted to the trustee in bankruptcy; any victim of the transaction can apply although if the individual has been adjudged bankrupt, the victim needs the leave of the court.

9.3 Key statute

*   Insolvency Act 1986

    *   ss339 to 342 – transaction at an undervalue – preferences

    *   ss423 to 425 – transaction at an undervalue – time limit – intention to prejudice

9.4 Question and suggested solution

QUESTION ONE

In 1986, Charles, a married man with children and who had made a small fortune in a computer programming business, decided to diversify and to embark upon business in the field of biotechnology.

In 1987, he obtained a divorce from his wife and later in that year married Jane. Shortly before his re-marriage he:

a) executed a marriage settlement whereby, in consideration of his intended marriage to Jane, he settled £200,000 upon trust for Jane for life remainder to any children he might have by Jane;

b) made an outright gift of £100,000 to his son by his first marriage, Dan;

c) gave £100,000 to the trustees of the golf club of which he was a member, to be held upon trust to apply the income in awarding trophies and cash prizes to the winners of club golfing tournaments which were held monthly;

d) settled his house upon trust for himself for life upon protective trusts and subject thereto upon trust for Jane absolutely.

After making these dispositions, he had enough resources left to meet his ordinary liabilities but proceedings had been commenced against him, which he was vigorously and optimistically defending, for breach of copyright.

In 1989, judgment was given against him in the copyright proceedings (which related to a computer programme) and at the same time his biotechnology business failed. He has now been adjudicated a bankrupt.

Advise his trustee in bankruptcy (with reasons) whether he (the trustee) can have recourse to any of the funds and assets disposed of under (a) to (d) above.

Adapted from University of London LLB Examination
(for External Students) Law of Trusts June 1986 Q4

General Comment

The statutory rules in this area require close attention and some familiarity with them. This is a question demanding, above all, statutory interpretation.

Skeleton Solution

Transaction at an undervalue (s339(3)(b)); s339(1) order to set the trust aside; s341(1): relevant time; assets and liabilities (s341(3)) – transaction at an undervalue – associates: s341(2)): purpose trust or people trust? – transaction at an undervalue: remedy under s423.

Suggested Solution

The trustee in bankruptcy may only have recourse to the funds and assets disposed of by Charles shortly before his re-marriage in 1987 if he can make a claim for setting the trusts aside under the Insolvency Act 1986.

a) The marriage settlement falls within the definition of a transaction of an undervalue under s339(3)(b) of the Act. Under s339(1) the trustee in bankruptcy can apply for an order to set the trust aside provided the transaction was entered into at 'a relevant time'. The relevant date for determining whether this requirement is satisfied is the date of the presentation of Charles' bankruptcy petition – 1989. He therefore entered into the transaction two years before this date. It is not clear whether this was more or less than two years before the bankruptcy. If less than two years the marriage settlement may be set aside. This will qualify as 'a relevant time' under s341(1) provided that Charles was either insolvent at the time or became insolvent as a result of the marriage settlement: s341(2). Section 341(2) goes on to provide that this 'insolvency requirement' will be presumed to be satisfied unless the contrary is shown if the transaction is entered into with a person who is an associate. Jane is clearly an associate, and so the presumption is raised. However, the facts suggest that the contrary can be shown; Charles was not insolvent at the time of the transaction and did not become insolvent in consequence of the transaction. His insolvency was rather as a consequence of a judgment against him in 1989 and of the failure of his business at the same time. This approach, though, does not take into account the definition of insolvency for this purpose in s341(3)(b) – that 'the value of his assets is less than the amount of his liabilities – taking into account his contingent and prospective liabilities'. The proceedings against him in 1987 would probably qualify as 'contingent and prospective liabilities' and, thus, it seems likely that the court would make an order to set the trust aside under s339(2).

In the unlikely event that the requirements of s341(2) are not satisfied, the trustee in bankruptcy may apply to have the trust set aside under s423. The court will make an order under this section if it is satisfied that Charles executed the settlement for the purpose of putting the assets beyond the reach of a person who is making, or may at some time make, a claim against him or of otherwise prejudicing the interests of such a person in relation to the claim which he is making or may make: s423(3). In view of the proceedings against him and of the fact that the settlement was made soon after a risky business diversification it is at least arguable that Charles executed the settlement for one of these purposes. If this can be proved, the court will make an order setting the trust aside under s423(2).

b) The gift to Dan is a transaction at an undervalue under s339(3)(a) and the same considerations apply as in (a) in deciding whether an application by the trustee in bankruptcy for the trust to be set aside will be successful.

c) As (a) except that no presumption will be raised under s341(2) as the other members of the golf club are unlikely to be considered 'associates'. Should proceedings for the trust to be set aside fail, another possibility is for the trustee in bankruptcy to argue that the gift is, in any event, void as offending the rule against purpose trusts, as stated in *Morice v Bishop of Durham* (1805) 10 Ves 522. The gift is one to the trustees of the golf club for specific purposes. Even if it were held to be prima facie valid under the principle in *Re Denley's Trust Deed* [1969] 1 Ch 373, the fact that the income alone is to be used and the gift is not limited to the perpetuity period indicates that it would probably – in any event, fail for this reason.

d) This settlement clearly qualifies as a transaction at an undervalue under s339(3)(a). The same considerations apply as in (a). In addition, if the trustee in bankruptcy is forced to resort to a remedy under s423, the fact that the life tenant of the settlement is to be Charles himself provides strong evidence that the purpose of the trust was an ulterior one under s423(3). The usual rule is that on the bankruptcy of a life tenant under a protective trust, the life interest comes to an end and there are discretionary trusts for the benefit of the life tenant, spouse and issue, or the life tenant and the person next entitled: Trustee Act 1925, s33. However, if the life tenant is also the settlor, his bankruptcy will not determine his interest: *Re Burroughs-Fowler* [1916] 2 Ch 251. Therefore, even if the trust itself cannot be set aside, the trustee in bankruptcy will be entitled to Charles' life interest.

Chapter 10

Trusts of Imperfect Obligation (Purpose Trusts)

10.1   Introduction

10.2   Key points

10.3   Key cases

10.4   Questions and suggested solutions

10.1 Introduction

The issue here is whether a trust will be void because it contravenes the rules against perpetuities. The general rule is that, if it is for a non-charitable purpose or does not directly benefit individuals, it will be void. This topic divides itself into two parts: firstly, gifts to unincorporated associations and, secondly, the other exceptions to the rule against purpose trusts. The latter part is straightforward and requires knowledge of the case law involved and of the rule against perpetuities. The former part, however, is a controversial and complex area of the law. The student must formulate an opinion on the state of the law based on a thorough knowledge and understanding of the relevant authorities.

10.2 Key points

As a general rule, trusts for non-charitable purposes are void for want of ascertainable beneficiaries: *Morice* v *Bishop of Durham* (1805) 10 Ves 522.

Limited exceptions to this rule do exist, although they are anomalous and exceptional: *Re Astor's Settlement Trust* [1952] Ch 534. In *Re Endacott* [1960] Ch 232, the classification of exceptions by Morris and Leach in *The Rule Against Perpetuities* was approved:

a) erection and maintenance of monuments and graves;

b) saying of masses;

c) maintenance and benefit of specific animals;

d) gifts to unincorporated associations;

e) miscellaneous cases.

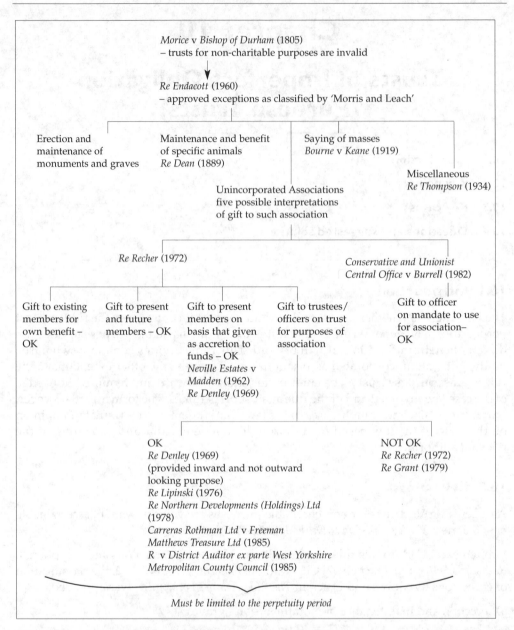

Morice v *Bishop of Durham* (1805)
– trusts for non-charitable purposes are invalid

Re Endacott (1960)
– approved exceptions as classified by 'Morris and Leach'

Erection and maintenance of monuments and graves

Maintenance and benefit of specific animals
Re Dean (1889)

Saying of masses
Bourne v *Keane* (1919)

Miscellaneous
Re Thompson (1934)

Unincorporated Associations
five possible interpretations
of gift to such association

Re Recher (1972)

Conservative and Unionist Central Office v *Burrell* (1982)

Gift to existing members for own benefit – OK

Gift to present and future members – OK

Gift to present members on basis that given as accretion to funds – OK
Neville Estates v *Madden* (1962)
Re Denley (1969)

Gift to trustees/officers on trust for purposes of association

Gift to officer on mandate to use for association– OK

OK
Re Denley (1969)
(provided inward and not outward looking purpose)
Re Lipinski (1976)
Re Northern Developments (Holdings) Ltd (1978)
Carreras Rothman Ltd v *Freeman Matthews Treasure Ltd* (1985)
R v *District Auditor ex parte West Yorkshire Metropolitan County Council* (1985)

NOT OK
Re Recher (1972)
Re Grant (1979)

Must be limited to the perpetuity period

Even if a purpose trust falls within one of the exceptions, it must be limited to the perpetuity period. This is lives in being plus 21 years and is unaffected by s15(4) Perpetuities and Accumulations Act 1964.

In addition, the trustees must be willing to carry out the trust.

(a)–(c) and (d) above

a) Will be valid provided it is not wasteful and of benefit to no-one: *McCaig* v *University of Glasgow* (1907) SC 231. The monument or grave need not be erected on church ground: *Re Dean* (1889) 41 Ch D 552.

b) *Bourne* v *Keane* [1919] AC 815.

c) *Re Dean* (1889) 41 Ch D 552.

d) *Re Thompson* [1934] Ch 342.

In some situations, trusts falling within these exceptions will also be charitable in which case they will be valid as such and it is unnecessary to consider whether they fall within the exceptions to the rule against purpose trusts (see Chapter 11).

An invalid purpose trust will not be upheld as a valid power: *IRC* v *Broadway Cottages Trust* [1955] Ch 20.

In *Re Denley's Trust Deed* [1969] 1 Ch 373 it was held that a distinction should be drawn between abstract and impersonal purpose trusts which are void and trusts which though expressed as purpose trusts are directly or indirectly for the benefit of individuals. The latter are valid. However, in *Re Grant's Will Trusts* [1980] 1 WLR 360 it was said that these trusts should be analysed not as purpose trusts at all, but rather as discretionary trusts for individuals.

Unincorporated associations (d)

For definition, see *Conservative and Unionist Central Office* v *Burrell* [1982] 2 All ER 1.

Re Recher's Will Trusts [1972] Ch 526 states four possible interpretations of a gift to an unincorporated association.

a) As a gift to existing members for their own benefit as joint tenants or tenants in common so that they could agree to divide it and so that any member can claim their share.

   Such a gift is valid as an absolute gift (provided the rules do not disallow such a division). As a result, this is not a purpose trust as the members are ascertainable beneficiaries and there are no perpetuity problems.

b) As a gift to present and future members.

   This is prima facie valid and since the Perpetuities and Accumulation Act 1964, it will not fail for perpetuity. Instead, it will operate in favour of those members who are ascertained within the perpetuity period: s15(4) of the Act does not apply as this is not a purpose trust.

c) As a gift to the existing members beneficially but on the basis that it is given as an accretion to funds and should be dealt with according to the rules of the association by which the members are contractually found inter se.

Such a gift is valid and the gifts in *Re Recher's Will Trusts* [1972] Ch 526 and *Neville Estates Ltd* v *Madden* [1962] Ch 832 were construed in this way.

There is no perpetuity problem as the gift vests immediately.

d) As a gift to the trustees or other proper officers of the association on trust to carry into effect the purposes of the association.

The gift will fail for lack of a beneficiary: see *Morice* v *Bishop of Durham* (1805) 10 Ves 522.

Conservative and Unionist Central Office v *Burrell* [1982] 2 All ER 1, offers a fifth interpretation of a gift to an unincorporated association.

e) As a gift to an officer of the association on mandate to use it for the association.

This is not possible if the gift is by will.

10.3 Key cases

- *Morice* v *Bishop of Durham* (1805) 10 Ves 522
  Beneficiary principle – non-charitable purposes – void

- *Re Denley's Trust Deed* [1969] 1 Ch 373
  Distinguish – trusts for individuals – abstract trusts

- *Re Endacott* [1960] Ch 232
  Anomalous and exceptional exceptions – Morris and Leach list

- *Re Recher's Will Trusts* [1972] Ch 526
  Existing members – present and future members – members beneficially but added to funds – trustees or officers for the association purposes

10.4 Questions and suggested solutions

QUESTION ONE

Tom died recently and his will contained the following bequest:

'£50,000 to the Trumpton Social Club to be used solely in the work of constructing the new bar and games room for the club and improving the facilities of the club house.'

The Trumpton Cricket Club is an unincorporated association whose rules freely allow the members to make resolutions and change the rules as they wish.

Advise the executors as to the validity of the bequest.

Written by the Author

General Comment

The unincorporated association questions require analysis of the form of gift made and some reconciling of case law that is often predicated on the uneasy conflict of different equitable principles.

Skeleton Solution

Analysis of the gift for it to be valid: gift to members for own benefit – gift to present and future members – gift to members as an accretion to funds – *Re Recher's Will Trusts*: gift to the officers of the association on trust for its purposes.

Suggested Solution

Whether a gift to an unincorporated association such as this is valid depends on the construction of the gift and on the interpretation of the case law in this area.

It is well settled that a gift to an unincorporated association will be valid as an express private trust if it can be construed in one of three of the four ways laid down in *Re Recher's Will Trusts* [1972] Ch 526. Firstly, as a gift to existing members for their own benefit as joint tenants or tenants in common; secondly, as a gift to present and future members who are ascertained within the perpetuity period; thirdly, as a gift to the existing members beneficially but on the basis that it is given as an accretion to funds and thus should be dealt with according to the rules of the association by which the members are contractually bound inter se – the gifts in *Re Recher's Will Trusts* and *Neville Estates Ltd* v *Madden* [1962] Ch 832 were valid by being construed in this way. The gift is clearly not intended to be for the members beneficially and thus, the only possible construction above is the third one. However, in view of the fact that the purpose has been stated, the gift is in fact unlikely to fall within this construction. Rather, it should be properly interpreted in the fourth way under *Re Recher's Will Trusts*.

The fourth classification by the court in *Re Recher's Will Trusts* of a gift to an unincorporated association is to the officers of the association on trust for the purposes of the association.

If the gift is interpreted in this way, then it was held in *Re Recher's Will Trusts* that it would be invalid as offending the rule against purpose trusts as stated in *Morice* v *Bishop of Durham* (1805) 10 Ves 522. This proposition was supported in *Re Grant's Will Trusts* [1980] 1 WLR 360 although other cases suggest that such a gift may in fact be valid following the decision in *Re Denley's Trust Deed* [1969] 1 Ch 373.

In *Re Denley's Trust Deed* a gift to an unincorporated association for a named purpose was held to be valid. A distinction was drawn by the court between a gift for an 'inward-looking' purpose (one which was for the benefit of the members) and an 'outward-looking' purpose (one which is not directly). A gift for the former type of purpose is, it was said, valid as it is, in fact, a private trust for the benefit of the members expressed differently to but being the same as a gift of the third construction in *Re Recher's Will Trusts* above. This contention was supported in *Re Lipinski's Will Trusts* [1976] Ch 235 where a similar gift was upheld, and either expressly or by implication in subsequent cases as recently as *R v District Auditor, ex parte West Yorkshire Metropolitan County Council* (1986) 26 RVR 24.

In *Re Grant's Will Trusts* [1980] 1 WLR 360 however, *Re Denley's Trust Deed* [1969] 1 Ch 373 was criticised and a gift for what seemed to be 'inward-looking' purposes of the association was held to be invalid as a purpose trust. At first sight, therefore, it seems that the gift to the Trumpton Social Club will be valid if *Re Denley's Trust Deed* is correct and invalid if *Re Grant's Will Trusts* is correct. It is submitted however, that despite Vinelott J's comments in *Re Grant's Will Trusts*, there is in fact no necessary conflict between the two cases, that the cases can be read together and that, therefore, the gift in question is undoubtedly valid.

An important fact in *Re Grant's Will Trusts* was that the rules of the donee association did not allow the members to control the property given to it. It is well established, in *Neville Estates Ltd v Madden* [1962] Ch 832, that a gift construed in the third way above as a gift to present members on the basis that it is given as an accretion to funds will only be valid if nothing in the rules prevents the members controlling how the association's property should be used. The same requirement will exist, therefore, in an application of *Re Denley's Trust Deed*. Following this line of reasoning, the gift in *Re Grant's Will Trusts* could not have been applied in the same way as the gift in *Re Denley's Trust Deed* as the associations rules were too restrictive. The two cases can be distinguished in this way and there is no necessary conflict between them.

The gift to the Trumpton Social Club will, therefore, be valid following *Re Denley's Trust Deed* as the rules of the association allow the members to control the use of property donated to it. Despite the wording, it is not a purpose trust but rather a trust for the members beneficially subject to the rules.

It would then follow that the gift need not be used by the members solely for the purposes specified. In *Re Lipinski's Will Trusts* [1976] Ch 235 it was held that a gift in similar terms could still take effect as a gift to the members beneficially as accretion to the funds and not as a trust for the specified purposes. In that case there was evidence that the testator was fully aware that it might not be possible to carry out the specified purpose and therefore must have intended that the gift could be used in other ways. If Tom knew that the purpose he specified might not be possible to carry out, there would be a strong argument that the decision in *Re Lipinski's Will Trusts* should be followed. If not it is possible that the court might hold that his words do attempt to impose a trust on the money so that it may be used in a particular way only, and the gift cannot then be construed as a gift to the members beneficially and the trust will fail as a private purpose trust.

QUESTION TWO

Consider the validity and enforceability of each of the following testamentary gifts:

a) '£50,000 to my executors upon trust to apply the income in maintaining my captive lions and tigers for the remainder of their natural lives';

b) '£100,000 to the George Bernard Shaw Society (an identifiable body) upon trust to apply the capital and income in promoting the adoption of a 40 letter alphabet';

c) '£200,000 to the British Coal Corporation upon trust to apply the capital and income in assisting needy ex-miners';

d) '£250,000 to the Archbishop of Canterbury upon trust to provide scholarships for the children of the clergy'.

> University of London LLB Examination
> (for External Students) Law of Trusts June 1993 Q7

General Comment

This question is relatively straightforward insofar as it involves the consideration of trusts for imperfect obligations and charities. However, it is essential that the actual facts are not forgotten and alternatives to charities (for example a discretionary trust) are not forgotten. Similarly the question should not be used as an excuse for a diatribe on charities; deal with the facts outlined and no more.

Skeleton Solution

a) Charitable trusts: *Commissioners of Income Tax* v *Pemsel* – *Re Grove-Grady* – trusts for imperfect obligations: *Re Astor's Settlement Trust* – perpetuities.

b) Educational trusts: *Re Shaw*; *Re Delius*.

c) Discretionary trusts: *McPhail* v *Doulton* – charitable trust for relief of poverty – public benefit: *Dingle* v *Turner*.

d) Discretionary trusts – *McPhail* v *Doulton* – educational trusts – public benefit – *Oppenheim* v *Tobacco Securities Trust Co Ltd*.

Suggested Solution

a) As the gift of £50,000 is to non-human beneficiaries (the lions and tigers) it will only be valid if it is a permitted form of charitable trust or a trust for imperfect obligation. It is necessary to consider each in turn.

There are four 'heads' of charity: *Commissioners of Income Tax* v *Pemsel* [1891] AC 531. These are charitable trusts for the relief of poverty; advancement of religion; advancement of education; and for other purposes beneficial to the community. Obviously the gift in question cannot fall under the first two of these four heads. It is less clear as to whether the gift falls under either the head of advancement of education or 'other purposes'. On balance, and for the following reasons, this is doubtful.

Trusts for the advancement of education requires some form of 'improvement to a useful branch of human knowledge': *Incorporated Council of Law Reporting for England and Wales* v *Attorney-General* [1972] Ch 73. The gift to the lions seems only to maintain them and has no underlying educational aim. Similarly trusts for 'other purposes' require some form of general public benefit. Therefore if the animals are to be kept in isolation there will probably be no public benefit and the gift will fail: *Re Grove-Grady* [1929] 1 Ch 557. However, if the intention is to promote human understanding of the animals and to permit access (for example in a zoo) then this will probably suffice: *Re Foveaux* [1895] 2 Ch 501.

If the gift fails as a charitable trust it is possible that it will succeed as a trust for imperfect (non-human) obligations: *Re Astor's Settlement Trust* [1952] Ch 534. Historically the courts have permitted testators to bequeath money for the upkeep and care of their animals: *Re Douglas* (1887) 35 Ch D 472, the key being that this tends to check man's tendency of cruelty towards animals. Having noted this, such trusts are still subject to the normal rules of vesting (the perpetuities rules). Therefore unless the gift can be shown to vest within 21 years (ie the animals die within 21 years for the capital to fall into residue) the gift will fail: *Re Dean* (1889) 41 Ch D 552. However the courts are free to take judicial notice of the longevity of the animals, *Re Haines* (1952) The Times 7 November, in an attempt to save the gift.

b) As previously noted there are four heads of charity, one of which is the advancement of education. Therefore gifts for the maintenance and support of schools are charitable. Further, the term 'education' has now been extended to more than academic based activities and can cover artistic and aesthetic purposes: *Royal Choral Society* v *IRC* [1943] 2 All ER 101. Similarly research can also be charitable: *Re Hopkins' Will Trusts* [1965] Ch 669.

However, as noted in *Incorporated Council of Law Reporting for England and Wales* v *Attorney-General* [1972] Ch 73 an educational trust requires, as its purpose, some form of 'improvement to a useful branch of human knowledge'. Mere education for education's sake is insufficient. On that basis it is extremely unlikely that the gift of £100,000 to the George Bernard Shaw Society for the purposes stated will be charitable: *Re Shaw* [1957] 1 WLR 729. The problem is that the usefulness (or otherwise) of the purpose is gauged subjectively by the courts, albeit they are notionally applying an objective test: *Re Delius* [1957] Ch 299 and *Re Pinion* [1965] Ch 85. Insofar as there has already been a decision on virtually identical facts ruling that this is not a charitable purpose the courts are unlikely to find it so now. The gift will fail and revert to the donor's estate (the society will not take it absolutely as they are clearly meant to take it as trustees for a failed purpose: *Briggs* v *Penny* (1851) 3 Mac & G 546.

c) In bequeathing £200,000 to the British Coal Corporation the testator has arguably established either a discretionary trust or a trust for charitable purposes (either under the head of relief of poverty or for other purposes beneficial to the community). Taking each in turn will determine if a valid and enforceable testamentary gift has been made.

Discretionary trusts are essentially trusts where the trustees are given a discretion as to who should receive the income and/or capital of the trust subject to the trust's terms. However, as with all express trusts, for it to be enforceable and therefore valid there must be certainty of objects. For discretionary trusts this requires the class of potential beneficiaries to be such that any given individual can be identified as either falling inside or outside of the class to be considered: *McPhail* v *Doulton* [1971] AC 424. In addition because discretionary trusts impose a fiduciary duty on trustees to consider the scope of potential beneficiaries the class itself must not be so wide as to make this impossible ie there must be administrational workability. Given the extremely wide class of potential beneficiaries and also the potential uncertainty of the term 'ex-miners' (are they only to be ex-British coal miners?) it is probable that this will not be upheld as a valid discretionary trust.

In contrast it is probable that the gift will be upheld as a charitable trust in favour of needy ex-miners. This is especially so in that such trusts need not have certain objects (unlike private trusts); rather they must be clearly charitable in nature. Therefore the gift of £200,000 would be viewed as being a trust for the relief of poverty and hence charitable: *Re Coulthurst* [1951] Ch 661. Further, unlike other forms of charitable trusts, charitable trusts for the relief of poverty are not required to satisfy any test of public benefit (representing a long accepted anomaly in this regard): *Dingle* v *Turner* [1972] AC 601.

d) As with (c) above it is arguable that the testator has either established a discretionary trust, or alternatively, a charitable trust albeit this time for the advancement of education. Again with reference to the points raised in (c) above, a discretionary trust requires certainty of objects. Therefore not only must the class enable any individual to be determined as either falling inside or outside of the class, it must also be of a size to be administratively workable: *McPhail* v *Doulton* [1971] AC 424. It is probable that the term clergy is too wide, especially if all forms of clergy (that is, not merely Church of England) are accepted within that definition. Therefore the discretionary trust will fail. If the term is not too wide the discretionary trust will, obviously, succeed.

Having noted the above it is possible that the testator actually intended to create a charitable trust for the advancement of education (thereby gaining the ancillary fiscal advantages). Certainly it is perfectly acceptable for an educational trust to involve the granting of scholarships. However, not only must the purpose be charitable it must also have sufficient public benefit. Essentially this requires, for trusts for the advancement of education, that the community or an appreciably important class of the community should benefit: *Verge* v *Somerville* [1924] AC 496. Further, any personal nexus used to limit the range of potential beneficiaries (by way of necessary qualification) will invariably cause the charitable trust to fail. This is so regardless of the actual number of potential beneficiaries falling within the personal nexus: *Oppenheim v Tobacco Securities Trust Co Ltd* [1951] AC 297. However, for these purposes the mere fact that the beneficiaries come from children of a particular profession (as in the case here) is not enough to show personal nexus. This charitable gift will therefore be upheld.

QUESTION THREE

a) 'It is unclear what role the beneficiary principle now plays in modern trusts law.'

   Discuss.

b) William wishes to leave £1,000,000 to provide the 'Cambridge and Oxford Club' with new premises. The membership of the club is made up entirely of graduates from Oxford and Cambridge Universities and it has no charitable aims. William seeks your advice on how to draft a valid bequest which best reflects his wishes.

University of London LLB Examination
(for External Students) Law of Trusts June 1996 Q3

General Comment

Part (a) is a typical essay-type question on trusts of imperfect obligation, while part (b) is a question on unincorporated associations.

Skeleton Solution

a) State the beneficiary principle – give its rationale – discuss the exceptions to the rule – come to a conclusion on the rule's present role.

b) The answer to this question requires a discussion of the law relating to unincorporated associations and some suggestions on drafting.

Suggested Solution

a) The beneficiary principle may briefly be stated as follows: 'there must be someone in whose favour the court can decree performance': per Grant MR in *Morice v Bishop of Durham* (1805) 10 Ves 522. Alternative formulations are 'A trust to be valid must be for the benefit of individuals': per Lord Parker in *Bowman v Secular Society Ltd* [1917] AC 406; 'A gift on trust must have a cestui que trust': per Harman J in *Re Wood* [1949] Ch 498; 'A gift can be made to persons (including a corporation) but it cannot be made to a purpose or to an object; so also, a trust may be created for the benefit of persons as cestuis que trust but not for a purpose or object unless the purpose or object be charitable': per Viscount Simonds in *Leahy v Attorney-General for New South Wales* [1959] AC 457.

Thus, the general rule is that there must be a human beneficiary who can enforce the trust before it can be valid.

The rationale behind this (and a perfectly logical rationale) is that 'a court of equity does not recognise as valid a trust which it cannot both enforce and control': per Roxburgh J in *Re Astor's Settlement Trust* [1952] Ch 534.

It is submitted that this principle is as valid in English trust law today as it always has been, though it does admit of a number of exceptions.

The first of these exceptions is where the gift is a charity. This is a well-recognised exception and an example of it is *Re Koeppler* [1985] 2 All ER 869 (which concerned a gift to 'the Warden and the Chairman of the Academic Advisory Council ... of the institution known as Wilton Park ... for the benefit at their discretion of the said institution as long as Wilton Park remains a British contribution to the formulation of an informed international, public opinion and to the promotion of greater cooperation in Europe and the West in general ...').

Another exception is where the gift is in fact outside the beneficiary principle. A distinction is drawn between 'purpose of object trusts which are abstract or impersonal' and which are void under the beneficiary principle, and a trust which 'though expressed as a purpose, is directly or indirectly for the benefit of an individual or individuals': *Re Denley's Trust Deed* [1969] 1 Ch 373 (which concerned a gift for a recreational sports ground for an ascertainable class which was held valid). Really this is not so much an exception as an apparent exception, since these gifts are outside the principle: *Re Grant's Will Trusts* [1980] 1 WLR 360 (where Vinelott J held that such gifts fell entirely outside the scope of gifts to unincorporated associations and other purpose trusts).

A further and similar exception is that the gift may be construed as a matter of contract, rather than as a trust: *Conservative and Unionist Central Office* v *Burrell* [1982] 2 All ER 1 (where funds which were given to the treasurer of a political party were held to be subject to a requirement to use them in a particular way, without any trust arising, except a fiduciary relationship as between principal and agent).

The major exception to the principle, however, is the five anomalous categories of purpose trust: (i) gifts for tombs and monuments (eg *Re Hooper* [1932] 1 Ch 38; *Parker* v *Ward* [1932] Ch 38); (ii) gifts for saying masses (eg *Bourne* v *Keane* [1919] AC 815); (iii) gifts for single animals (eg *Pettingall* v *Pettingall* (1842) 11 LJ Ch 176); (iv) gifts to unincorporated associations; and (v) miscellaneous cases.

It has been said that these are 'properly [to] be regarded as anomalous and exceptional': per Roxburgh J in *Re Astor's Settlement Trust* [1952] Ch 534; per Lord Evershed MR in *Re Endacott* [1960] Ch 232. They have also been described as 'concessions to human weakness or sentiment'; and 'merely occasions when Homer has nodded': per Harman LJ in *Re Endacott*.

It is submitted, therefore, that the role of the beneficiary principle is quite clear, and still fully functional, although it does admit of some clearly defined exceptions.

b) As the Cambridge and Oxford Club is not a charity, at first blush William's intended gift contravenes the beneficiary principle. However, this is in fact not so. Gifts to unincorporated associations form one of the anomalous categories of purpose trusts, and as such are prima facie valid.

It is assumed that the Oxford and Cambridge Club is a members' club rather than a proprietary club and that it is not incorporated.

Gifts to unincorporated associations used to cause a large number of problems for lawyers, but the courts have now developed seven different constructions which normally enable them to validate such gifts.

As the gift here is an absolute one, there should be no problems with the rule against perpetuities and the rule against inalienability. Probably, therefore, the best construction to seek to use is the fourth, which is that there is no trust, and the gift is validated as an out and out gift to the present members of the Club beneficially as an accretion to the Club's funds which must be dealt with in accordance with the Club's rules by which the members are contractually bound: eg *Re Lipinski's Will Trusts* [1976] Ch 235; *Neville Estates Ltd v Madden* [1962] Ch 832; *Conservative and Unionist Central Office v Burrell* [1982] 2 All ER 1. Land is vested in the trustees under a bare trust for the members according to the Club's rules: *Re Buckinghamshire Constabulary Fund (No 2)* [1979] 1 WLR 936.

William could simply leave his gift to the Club, or he could spell out in his will that it is to be an absolute one and an accretion to the Club's funds. It would, however, be prudent to provide that the receipt of the treasurer for the time being of the Cambridge and Oxford Club is a good receipt for his executors: *Leahy v Attorney-General for New South Wales* [1959] AC 457.

QUESTION FOUR

In 1997 Sam died, and his will contained the following provision:

'My leasehold property situate at 128 Oxford Street London and £100,000 to my trustees on trust for a period of 21 years, to convert the said premises into a facility suitable for fitness training, and to maintain such premises in a suitable condition as a facility for fitness training, and to make such facility available to the members of the Samco plc Social Club.'

The Samco plc Social Club is an unincorporated association of the employees and retired employees of the company Sam founded, who pay no membership fees and raise money for particular events by charging participating members for their share of the cost. In January 1998, the trustees began tendering contracts for the conversion of the property, a valuable commercial site. In March 1998, the Chairman of the association wrote to the trustees, demanding that the conversion of the property be stopped, that the site be rented out upon a commercial basis, and that the trustees hold the rental income on trust for the Samco plc Social Club to be used as the membership of the club should decide.

Advise the trustees.

University of London LLB Examination
(for External Students) Law of Trusts June 1998 Q2

General Comment

This is a complex question on the nature of a gift for a purpose. If there are ascertainable beneficiaries, will they be able to use the rule in *Saunders* v *Vautier* (1841) 4 Beav 115 to defeat the settlor's intention?

Skeleton Solution

Purpose trusts and unincorporated associations: *Re Denley*; *Re Lipinski* – perpetuity – does the rule in *Saunders* v *Vautier* apply – can it be used to further the wishes of the Samco Chairman – *Stephenson* v *Barclays Bank*; *Re Brocklebank*.

Suggested Solution

Although the trust is expressed as a trust for a purpose, there are ascertainable beneficiaries, since the facilities are to be provided for the benefit of the employees of Samco plc. They would have locus standi to enforce the trust in the event of a breach of trust. The trust cannot be charitable, because there is a personal nexus between the beneficiaries in that they are all employees of one company: see *Oppenheimer* v *Tobacco Securities Trust Co Ltd* [1951] AC 297.

This situation is similar to the case of *Re Denley's Trust Deed* [1969] 1 Ch 373 where land was given for the purpose of providing a sports ground for employees. Goff J observed that, although the *Denley* trust was expressed as a purpose, it was directly or indirectly for the benefit of individuals and thus outside the mischief at which the beneficiary principle was aimed. However, *Re Denley's Trust Deed* did not concern a gift to an association, simply a gift to employees as individuals.

In *Re Lipinski's Will Trusts* [1976] Ch 235 a gift to the Hull Judeans Association to construct new buildings for the association could not be interpreted as a trust for the present members of the association. However, the court was able to hold the gift valid, because the interests of the membership were determined on the basis of the contract between the members, drawn up in the rules of the association. Thus, the application of the gift was governed by the law of contract.

One problem which can prevent the validation of gifts on the basis of the contract between members is that of perpetuity. If the gift is to present and future members, as in *Re Lipinski's Will Trusts*, it may not vest within the perpetuity period. For a *Lipinski*-type trust to succeed, the rules must provide for the distribution of the property to its members. In the Samco plc scenario, the trust is expressed to run for a period of 21 years, so that, in any event, Sam and his professional advisers have foreseen this problem and made appropriate provision to overcome it.

It would appear, therefore, that Sam has been successful in setting up a trust for the present and future members of the Samco plc Social Club. This is a fixed trust which will require the trustees to be able to draw up a complete list of the beneficiaries, which can be done, presumably, from the company's employment records.

If this is construed as a trust for present employees, and all the beneficiaries are over the age of 18 years and of sound mind, and if they all consent, under the rule in *Saunders* v *Vautier* (1841) 4 Beav 115 they can call on the trustees to transfer the property to them, provided that they are entitled to the whole of the interest with immediate effect. If Samco plc had any employees who were aged under 18, the beneficiaries could apply to the court to ask it to supply consent on their behalf.

If there were provisions as to the acquisition and disposal of property, these might supply the consent necessary for the rule in *Saunders* v *Vautier* (1841) 4 Beav 115 to apply. However, *Stephenson* v *Barclays Bank Co Ltd* [1975] 1 All ER 625 established that the application of the rule in *Saunders* v *Vautier* entitled each individual member to an aliquot share of the trust property. This may or may not be what the Chairman had in mind. The case also established that the trustees cannot be compelled to act on trusts other than those provided for in the trust deed.

The rule in *Saunders* v *Vautier* can only be applied to bring the trust to an end, not to force the trustees to act in accordance with the wishes of the beneficiaries, or to vary the terms of their trust: *Re Brocklebank* [1948] Ch 206.

A more appropriate course of action might therefore be for the beneficiaries to apply to the court for an order under the Variation of Trusts Act 1958 for the terms of the trust to be varied in accordance with their wishes. The court will only grant such a variation if it considers that the new proposed terms will be for the benefit of all those on whose behalf the variation is being sought.

QUESTION FIVE

What are the effects of the following dispositions in Fred's will:

a) '£100,000 to my trustees for the education of my daughter Amy to the age of 18';

b) '£100,000 to the Sisters of Charity (a contemplative order of nuns)';

c) '£100,000 to the London University Squash Club (an unincorporated association) for the sole purpose of building new squash courts';

d) '£100,000 to my trustees to promote pigeon-racing'?

University of London LLB Examination
(for External Students) Law of Trusts June 2000 Q4

General Comment

For all four scenarios it is important to realise that the dispositions are not charitable: the issues to be considered are purpose trusts and unincorporated associations rather than charities.

Skeleton Solution

a) Consider the possibility of charitable status – briefly discuss resulting trust or absolute gift?

b) Consider the possibility of charitable status – briefly discuss beneficiary principle – gift to the members – gift to the association.

c) Consider the possibility of charitable status – briefly discuss gift for a particular purpose – gift to the members without restriction.

d) Consider the possibility of charitable status – briefly discuss beneficiary principle – miscellaneous cases.

Suggested Solution

a) The educational purpose cannot be charitable as it is restricted to one person and would fail the public benefit test. The issue is whether the money is intended to be for the purpose mentioned or for the person. This becomes important where there is a surplus after the educational needs have been met. Does the surplus go on resulting trust to the estate of the testator, or will Amy be regarded as absolutely entitled? This is a question of intention on the part of the testator. Did he intend to make an out-and-out gift on trust for Amy, his motive being to provide for her education, or did he intend that the money should be used only for her education? In *Re Abbott Fund (Trusts of the)* [1900] 2 Ch 326, money was collected to be used for the maintenance of two deaf and dumb ladies. It was held that the surplus remaining on the death of both ladies should return to the subscribers on resulting trust. In contrast, in *Re Osoba* [1979] 1 WLR 347, where there was a gift to the widow on trust 'for her maintenance and for the training of my daughter up to University grade and for the maintenance of my aged mother ...', it was held that the intention had been to make absolute gifts, and the surplus remaining after the death of the widow and mother, and the completion of the daughter's education, belonged to the surviving beneficiary, the daughter, absolutely. It is difficult to distinguish between gifts made for a particular purpose and gifts made out-and-out but from a particular motive, but on balance it is suggested that in relation to Amy she should take absolutely – it seems more likely that Fred intended to make an outright transfer of the money.

b) The religious purpose cannot be charitable as it is in favour of a contemplative order and would thus fail the public benefit test. A case with similar facts is *Leahy v Attorney-General for New South Wales* [1959] AC 457, which involved property that was to be held on trust for 'such order of nuns of the Catholic Church or the Christian brothers as my executors and trustees shall select'. Viscount Simonds in the Privy Council thought that it fell foul of the beneficiary principle in that, even though the individual members had an interest in enforcing the trust, they were not granted a full beneficial interest. The difficulty would be in finding someone to enforce the trust. A gift can be made to persons (including a corporation) but it cannot be made to a purpose or to an object; so, a trust may be created for the benefit of persons as cestui que trust, but not for a purpose or object unless the purpose or object be charitable. The contemplative order of nuns would seem to be viewable as a non-charitable purpose trust. There are devices that may operate to make such a gift effective. Some hope is offered by the dicta in *Re Denley's Trust Deed* [1969] 1 Ch 373. There may be a purpose or object trust, the carrying out of which would benefit an individual or individuals, that could be saved. These can be contrasted with cases where the benefit is so indirect that they are abstract or impersonal purpose trusts. The case of *Re Recher's Will Trusts* [1972] Ch 526 also offers possibilities where the gift is to an unincorporated association. Could the gift to the nuns be seen as a gift to existing members? If so, this would be effective and there would be no perpetuity problems. Similarly a gift to present and future members could be effective. Finally, if the gift could be seen as to the members beneficially, operating as an addition to the funds of the order, under their rule system, and this also could be effective. The beneficiary principle and the perpetuity rules are the problems for the disposition; the present state of the law offers possibilities but the outcome is uncertain.

c) Whilst a University could be a charitable body in terms of its educational role, the restriction to sport causes difficulties. The case of *IRC v McMullen* [1981] AC 1 saw a trust for the promotion of football in schools and universities approved as charitable – the present scenario is more restricted. It is best viewed as a gift to an unincorporated association for a particular purpose. The case of *Re Lipinski's Will Trusts* [1976] Ch 235, is instructive. There was a gift by will to a body for a purpose that was within its powers and its members were the beneficiaries. The gift was to be used solely for building work. This was viewed as a gift to the members without restriction. Following that case it is possible that the members could be viewed as absolutely entitled and not subject to the restriction as to its use for building new squash courts.

d) It is not plausible to view this as an animal charity; it is much more in the nature of sport or recreation and as such would not be charitable. There are no ascertainable beneficiaries and no particular body is mentioned. An attempt can be made to fit the facts into the anomalous class of trusts of imperfect obligation that are exceptions to the beneficiary principle. In *Re Endacott* [1960] Ch 232, they were listed as follows: trusts for the erection or maintenance of monuments or graves; trusts for the saying of masses in jurisdictions where such trusts are not regarded as charitable; trusts for the maintenance of particular animals; trusts for the benefit of unincorporated associations; and miscellaneous cases (a few further cases which do not fit into any of the other categories). The decisions which have established these anomalous exceptions have been described as concessions to human weakness or sentiment and will not now be extended. There are no particular animals in issue and it is the miscellaneous cases that need to be explored. *Re Thompson* [1934] Ch 342 concerned a gift of £1,000 to be applied towards the promotion and furtherance of fox-hunting. The residuary legatee, Trinity Hall Cambridge, wished to carry out the testator's wishes insofar as this was legally possible but, as a charity, felt obliged to object to the enforcement of this trust. The gift, which complied with the rule against inalienability, was upheld. Whilst this is close to the facts in the problem, it may not be close enough, as there is no enthusiasm at all for extending the miscellaneous cases.

Chapter 11

Charitable Trusts

11.1   Introduction

11.2   Key points

11.3   Key cases

11.4   Questions and suggested solutions

11.1   Introduction

Charitable trusts is a very wide topic and one which students generally find interesting. Much of the material comprises of numerous cases which simply decide whether a particular object is charitable and which raise no real difficulties. This is not true, however, of the requirement of public benefit – a complicated area involving theoretical concepts which many students find difficult to grasp. It cannot, unfortunately, be avoided as questions on charitable trusts invariably require the student to consider the problems raised by the cases in this area which must, therefore, be digested and fully understood.

11.2   Key points

The status of 'charitable trust' has several advantages over that of 'private trust'.

Tax advantages

Charities are largely exempt from income tax, corporation tax and capital gains tax. Inheritance tax is not chargeable on gifts to charities and transfers, conveyances and leases to charities are exempt from stamp duty.

Certainty of objects (see Chapter 2)

If there is a clear intention to give property for charitable purposes, the trust will not fail for uncertainty of objects.

The rule against perpetual trusts

This does not apply to charitable trusts which may continue forever.

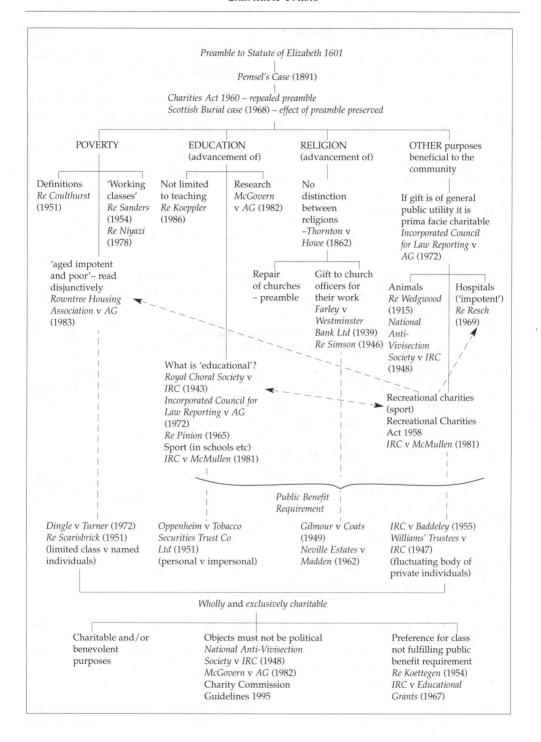

Preamble to Statute of Elizabeth 1601

Pemsel's Case (1891)

Charities Act 1960 – repealed preamble
Scottish Burial case (1968) – effect of preamble preserved

POVERTY

EDUCATION
(advancement of)

RELIGION
(advancement of)

OTHER purposes
beneficial to the
community

Definitions
Re Coulthurst
(1951)

'Working
classes'
Re Sanders
(1954)
Re Niyazi
(1978)

Not limited
to teaching
Re Koeppler
(1986)

Research
McGovern
v AG (1982)

No
distinction
between
religions
–*Thornton v
Howe* (1862)

If gift is of general
public utility it is
prima facie charitable
*Incorporated Council
for Law Reporting v
AG* (1972)

'aged impotent
and poor'– read
disjunctively
*Rowntree Housing
Association v AG*
(1983)

Repair
of churches
– preamble

Gift to church
officers for
their work
*Farley v
Westminster
Bank Ltd* (1939)
Re Simson (1946)

Animals
Re Wedgwood
(1915)
*National
Anti-
Vivisection
Society* v IRC
(1948)

Hospitals
('impotent')
Re Resch
(1969)

What is 'educational'?
Royal Choral Society v
IRC (1943)
*Incorporated Council for
Law Reporting* v AG
(1972)
Re Pinion (1965)
Sport (in schools etc)
IRC v *McMullen* (1981)

Recreational charities
(sport)
Recreational Charities
Act 1958
IRC v *McMullen* (1981)

*Public Benefit
Requirement*

Dingle v Turner (1972)
Re Scarisbrick (1951)
(limited class v named
individuals)

Oppenheim v *Tobacco
Securities Trust Co
Ltd* (1951)
(personal v impersonal)

Gilmour v *Coats*
(1949)
Neville Estates v
Madden (1962)

IRC v *Baddeley* (1955)
Williams' Trustees v
IRC (1947)
(fluctuating body of
private individuals)

Wholly and *exclusively charitable*

Charitable and/or
benevolent
purposes

Objects must not be political
*National Anti-Vivisection
Society* v IRC (1948)
McGovern v AG (1982)
Charity Commission
Guidelines 1995

Preference for class
not fulfilling public
benefit requirement
Re Koettegen (1954)
IRC v *Educational
Grants* (1967)

The rule against remoteness of vesting

The rule applies to charitable trusts except where a gift is made to one charity with a gift over to another on the occurrence of certain events: *Re Tyler* [1891] 3 Ch 252.

There is no statutory definition of what is charitable. In general, for a charitable trust to be valid it must fall within 'the spirit and intendment' of the preamble to the Statute of Elizabeth 1601 as classified by Lord Macnaghten in *Commissioners of Income Tax* v *Pemsel* [1891] AC 531. Strictly speaking, the preamble was repealed by the Charities Act 1960. However, its effect was specifically preserved by the court in *Scottish Burial Reform and Cremation Society Ltd* v *Glasgow Corporation* [1968] AC 138.

Trusts for the relief of poverty

a) Poverty does not mean destitution, rather 'going short': *Re Coulthurst* [1951] Ch 661.

b) 'Aged, impotent and poor' in the preamble should be read disjunctively so that a beneficiary need only fit one of these descriptions: *Rowntree Housing Association* v *Attorney-General* [1983] 1 All ER 288.

   (Note: if the beneficiary is aged or impotent rather than poor, then the trust will be valid under the fourth head and not under this head.)

c) It was held in *Re Sanders' Will Trusts* [1954] Ch 265 that the working classes do not constitute a section of the poor. However, in *Re Niyazi's Will Trusts* [1978] 1 WLR 910 a gift for the construction of a working men's hostel was held to be a valid charitable trust for the relief of poverty in view of all the circumstances.

Trusts for the advancement of education

a) Education is not restricted to a teacher-student in class situation: *Re Koeppler* [1985] 2 All ER 869. It includes the improvement of a useful branch of human knowledge and its public dissemination: *Incorporated Council of Law Reporting for England and Wales* v *Attorney-General* [1972] Ch 73, and research provided certain conditions are fulfilled: *McGovern* v *Attorney-General* [1982] Ch 321.

b) Many things are considered to be of educational value, from a search for the Bacon – Shakespeare manuscripts: *Re Hopkins' Will Trusts* [1965] Ch 669, to choral singing: *Royal Choral Society* v *IRC* [1943] 2 All ER 101.

   If the court does not feel able to decide whether something is of educational value, it will use expert evidence: *Re Pinion* [1965] Ch 85.

   A trust for sport will not of itself be educational, but if it is for sport in a school it will be a valid charitable trust under this head: *IRC* v *McMullen* [1981] AC 1.

c) Political purposes are not charitable but they may fall under the educational head. An attempt at this that failed is seen in *Southwood and Another* v *Attorney-General*

(1998) The Times 26 October. Here an organisation was for the advancement of the education of the public in the subject of militarism and disarmament. Upon investigation this was revealed to be a political body promoting disarmament.

Trusts for the advancement of religion

a) The court will not distinguish between religions unless a religion involves doctrines subversive of all morality – *Thornton* v *Howe* (1862) 31 Beav 14. Indeed the law 'assumes that any religion is at least likely to be better than none': *Neville Estates Ltd* v *Madden* [1962] Ch 832 per Cross J. Indeed in *Funnell* v *Stewart* [1996] 1 WLR 288 no particular religion was mentioned, rather the gift was for spititual work.

b) Gifts for the maintenance or repair of churches and churchyards are charitable by clear analogy to the preamble.

c) Whether a gift to a church officer as the holder of that office will be charitable, depends on the wording of the gift. *Farley* v *Westminster Bank* [1939] AC 430 – a gift to vicars and churchwardens for 'parochial work' was held not to be wholly and exclusively charitable as it could include work which is not, strictly speaking, for religious purposes.

Re Simson [1946] Ch 299 – a gift to a vicar 'to be used for his work in the parish' was held to be charitable.

Trusts for other purposes beneficial to the community

The trust must be for public purposes beneficial to the community or for the public welfare and it must be charitable within the 'spirit and intendment' of the preamble: *Attorney-General* v *National Provincial and Union Bank of England Ltd* [1924] AC 262. However, the emphasis was reversed in *Incorporated Council of Law Reporting for England and Wales* v *Attorney-General* [1972] Ch 73 where it was said that if a purpose is shown to be beneficial to the community or of general public utility, it is prima facie charitable and it is for those who oppose its charitable status to show that the object is not within the spirit and intendment of the preamble.

Trusts which have been held charitable under this 'fourth head' fall into three main categories.

Animals

Trusts in favour of animals generally or a class of animals (not specific animals – see Chapter 10) are charitable on the ground that they promote public morality by tending to discourage cruelty: *Re Wedgwood* [1915] 1 Ch 113.

However, not all such trusts will be charitable. In *Re Grove-Grady* [1929] 1 Ch 557, the court felt that the law had gone far enough in affording charitable status to such gifts and refused to hold a refuge for all animals to protect them again human molestation, charitable. And in *National Anti-Vivisection Society* v *IRC* [1948] AC 31 the plaintiff institution was held not to be charitable as it was not in the public interest and, more specifically, because it sought a change in the law.

Hospitals

Gifts to hospitals are charitable as for the relief of the impotent in the preamble even if a charge is made to patients, provided that it is not a profit-making body.

Recreational charities

A trust simply to promote sport is not charitable: *Re Nottage* [1895] 2 Ch 649. However, since the Recreational Charities Act 1958 recreational facilities can be charitable subject to the fulfilment of the conditions under the Act. *Guild (Executor Nominate of the Late James Young Russell) v IRC* [1992] 2 WLR 397 was the first House of Lords decision on the Act. One of the main issues decided was that in the case of a sports centre or other purpose in connection with sport, that there was no need to be providing for a deprived group.

The public benefit requirement

Even if a trust is prima facie charitable, it will not be a valid charitable trust unless it can also be shown to be for the public benefit. (This requirement does not apply to trusts for the relief of poverty.)

Trusts for the relief of poverty

The public benefit requirement does not apply: *Dingle* v *Turner* [1972] AC 601. However, a distinction must be drawn between a gift to a limited class and a gift to particular individuals. The former gift would be a valid charitable trust; the latter would not: *Re Scarisbrick's Will Trusts* [1951] Ch 622. In *Re Segelman* [1996] 2 WLR 173 a gift for the assistance of poor and needy members of the testator's family during the 21-year period from the testator's death was a valid and charitable gift, not being disqualified by the restricted nature of the class.

Other trusts

Judgments in some cases suggest that there is a single test to determine whether the public benefit requirement is satisfied, which applies to all three remaining heads. The decisions themselves, however, show that this is not the case.

a) Trusts for the advancement of religion

Following *Gilmour* v *Coats* [1949] AC 426 and *Neville Estates Ltd* v *Madden* [1962] Ch 832 a trust will satisfy the public benefit requirement if the members of the beneficiary organisation live in (rather than outside) the community. That is, the trust must be seen to be for the benefit of the community generally.

b) Trusts for the advancement of education; trusts for other purposes beneficial to the community

Two different tests exist.

i) *Oppenheim* v *Tobacco Securities Trust Co Ltd* [1951] AC 297 – the possible beneficiaries must not be numerically negligible and the quality which distinguishes them from other members of the public must not depend on their relationship to a particular individual. It must be an impersonal and not personal quality.

ii) *Williams' Trustees* v *IRC* [1947] AC 447 and *IRC* v *Baddeley* [1955] AC 572 – the possible beneficiaries must constitute a section of the public as contrasted with 'a fluctuating body of private individuals' or 'a class within a class'.

The trust must be wholly and exclusively charitable.

In other words, under the terms of the trust it must not be possible to apply the trust property for non-charitable purposes.

If the gift is to an organisation, the organisation and thus the gift will not be charitable if some of the purposes of the body are non-charitable (generally, political): *National Anti-Vivisection Society* v *IRC* [1948] AC 31; *McGovern* v *Attorney-General* [1982] Ch 321, and more than simply incidental to the body's main charitable purposes. Note also the relaxation of the rules as a result of the Charity Commission Guidelines 1995.

If the gift is for apparently charitable purposes, it will not be a valid charitable trust if the gift is worded in such a way that the trust property could be applied for non-charitable purposes. In particular, this may be the case where the gift includes a preference to benefit a limited class which fails to satisfy the public benefit requirement: *Re Koettgen's Will Trusts* [1954] Ch 252; *IRC* v *Educational Grants Association Ltd* [1967] Ch 993. The court will look at the reality of the situation.

The case of *Re Hetherington Dec'd* [1989] 2 WLR 1094 suggests, however, that if a gift could be carried out in a way which would satisfy the public benefit requirement but could also be carried out in a way which would not, the gift will be construed as a gift to be carried out only by the methods which satisfied the requirement and would thus be a valid charitable trust.

The need to be able to provide supervision

The case of *Gaudiya Mission* v *Bramachary* [1998] 2 WLR 175 concerned an Indian charity. The Court of Appeal decided that such a body could not be a charity for the purposes of the Charities Act 1993. This was because the court would be unable to provide supervision of such foreign institutions.

11.3 Key cases

- *Commisioners of Income Tax* v *Pemsel* [1891] AC 531
  Definition – Statute of Elizabeth 1601 – Lord Macnaghten classification

- *Dingle* v *Turner* [1972] AC 601
  Poverty – no public benefit requirement

- *Guild (Executor Nominate of the Late James Young Russell)* v *IRC* [1992] 2 WLR 397
  Recreational charity – no need for a deprived group

- *IRC* v *McMullen* [1981] AC 1
  Trust for sport – not educational – unless in a school

- *Re Simson* [1946] Ch 299
  Gift to a vicar – work in the parish – charitable – religion

- *Rowntree Housing Association* v *Attorney-General* [1983] 1 All ER 288
  Aged, impotent and poor – preamble – only one required

11.4 Questions and suggested solutions

QUESTION ONE

Consider the validity of the following dispositions to trustees made under the will of G:

a) '£500,000 to be applied for research to demonstrate the benefits to society of the retention of a National Health Service';

b) '£400,000 to be applied for the provision of recreational facilities for the Italian community of London';

c) '£300,000 to be applied for the promotion of the education of children of law graduates of London University'.

University of London LLB Examination
(for External Students) Law of Trusts June 1994 Q6

General Comment

This question has the advantage of being broken into broad-brush problem sections which both enable the candidate to answer the specific problem and to demonstrate more general knowledge about the subject. The area of valid charitable gifts is one in which the analysis is founded on degrees based on the facts. Therefore the answer must reflect a careful examination of the facts.

Skeleton Solution

a) National Health Service example.

b) Italian Community example.

c) Children of London University graduates.

Suggested Solution

These cases concern the creation of trusts where there may or may not be a charitable purpose. The advantages of a charitable trust are primarily tax-driven. Trusts for charitable purposes are not subject to the rule against perpetuities.

a) This disposition is faced with the problem whether the gift is for a valid charitable purpose.

The creation of a trust which is for the good of society will be for a charitable purpose, as will a provision which is for educational purposes.

Educational purpose trusts have been broadly interpreted, as in the case of *IRC* v *McMullen* [1981] AC 1 in the House of Lords where a trust for the promotion of association football was found to be educational because it contributed to the development of young people. The test, as in *Incorporated Council of Law Reporting for England and Wales* v *Attorney-General* [1972] Ch 73, is whether or not the trust performs a contribution to learning.

In this instance, the trust is not aimed specifically at learning; rather it is directed at encouraging others to share the settlor's own beliefs. As such, it is close to being a political-purpose trust. *National Anti-Vivisection Society* v *IRC* [1948] AC 31 was a case in which Lord Simonds found that the purpose of the society was political because it aimed to change the law and to change people's opinions about vivisection.

Lord Normand in *Bowman* v *Secular Society Ltd* [1917] AC 406 found that an organisation whose predominant aim was political could be a charity depending upon the degree to which its aim was to change the law or to perform charitable works in the community. However, *McGovern* v *Attorney-General* [1982] Ch 321 was a case in which, with reference to Amnesty International, the court demonstrated its reluctance to appraise whether the benefits of the trust would be for the public benefit if they are aimed at a change in the law or public opinion.

This trust is aimed at the retention of the National Health Service and therefore, on the balance of the authorities, it will be found to be a political purpose trust.

b) The issue in this disposition is whether or not this disposition will be a valid recreational charity or not. The closest parallel authority is the London Welsh case (*Williams' Trustees* v *IRC* [1947] AC 447) where the London Welsh Club for Welsh people living in London was found to be void as a charitable purpose because it was not for a broad enough section of the population.

However, the Recreational Charities Act 1958 expands this public benefit test to circumstances where facilities are provided to a section of the public with the intention of improving the quality of life for the people benefiting. Those benefiting must have a need of the facilities because of their social or economic circumstances and the facilities must be available to both men and women.

The case of *IRC* v *McMullen* [1981] AC 1 in the House of Lords found that this statute would only apply to people who were deprived in some way and whose conditions of life could be improved by the trust. As such, a London Scottish Centre (in that case) would not be a charity under the Act because it was not provided for a proportion of the community because they were deprived.

On these facts, the recreational facilities are not being provided for the Italian community because the Italian community is deprived and thereby in need of the facilities. Therefore, the trust will not acquire charitable status.

c) The issue here is whether or not the trust is for a valid educational purpose and thereby charitable. While the purpose of the trust is expressly for education there is an argument that the potential beneficiaries represent too narrow a part of the public to constitute a charitable purpose.

In *Oppenheim* v *Tobacco Securities Trust Co Ltd* [1951] AC 297, Lord Simonds found that a purpose could not be charitable where the beneficiaries had too close a personal nexus to the donor. 'Benefit', in his Lordship's words, must be to a 'section of the community'.

In *IRC* v *Educational Grants Association Ltd* [1967] Ch 993, it was found that a trust run for the benefit of the children of Metal Box employees, as to 80 per cent of the trust fund, was a de facto private trust. *Re Koettgen's Will Trusts* [1954] Ch 252 gives the Inland Revenue the power to investigate whether or not the trust is being run as a private or a public trust.

In the case of London University law students' children, it can be argued that law students form a part of the population. It would be open to anyone who could gain entry to a law degree at London University, which is a public institution, to acquire the benefit of this trust. Provided that, on the facts, it is not run as a private trust for a particular group of law students and their children, this would appear to be a valid charitable trust.

QUESTION TWO

a) 'It is difficult to see why trusts for political purposes should not be capable of being valid charitable trusts.'

Discuss.

b) Nick leaves £10,000 to provide the lecturers of the University of London with sporting facilities. Is this a valid charitable bequest? How, if at all, would your answer differ if the gift was intended to provide such facilities for the students of the University of London rather than the lecturers?

University of London LLB Examination
(for External Students) Law of Trusts June 1996 Q4

General Comment

Part (a) is an essay-type question, but more focussed than many. Part (b) concerns whether or not a gift is charitable.

Skeleton Solution

a) Discussion of the cases on whether or not trusts for political purposes are charitable – argument as to whether or not these decisions are sustainable.

b) Gift is not charitable, since it in no way involves the advancement of education; might be ancillary to that purpose – the alternative contingency is almost certainly charitable, either as being ancillary to the students' education or under the Recreational Charities Act 1958.

Suggested Solution

a) It is clearly established that trusts for political purposes are not charitable: eg *McGovern* v *Attorney-General* [1982] Ch 321 (where Slade J held that Amnesty International were too political to be charitable).

This approach embodies a number of strands of legal thought. Perhaps the most important is that a charity must be for public benefit and it is impossible to say whether that which is political is or is not for public benefit. Partly this reflects the desire of the English judiciary to keep their noses clean and to keep out of politics. It also reflects their desire and what they see as their duty to apply the laws which Parliament has passed and not to become involved in the desirability or otherwise of law reform.

In support of this approach it may cogently be argued that because of the substantial tax exemptions which charities enjoy, charitable status (and thus these tax exemptions) should only be enjoyed by what is clearly and generally agreed to be for public benefit. Politics is by its very nature far too controversial to fall within this category.

Against this the following points can be made. The judiciary themselves do from time to time in their judgments advocate law reform in that they express the view that a particular point should be looked at by the legislature. Also, they do sometimes allow that which is political through as being charitable. A clear example was *Re Koeppler* [1985] 2 All ER 869 (where money was left to 'the Warden and the Chairman of the Academic Advisory Council ... of the institution known as Wilton Park ... for the benefit at their discretion of the said institution as long as Wilton

Park remains a British contribution to the formulation of an informed international, public opinion and to the promotion of greater cooperation in Europe and the West in general ...') and this was held to be charitable. Equally, university departments of politics enjoy precisely the same charitable status as other university departments, despite the fact that their whole raison d'être is politics. The difficulty with this argument is that both they and Wilton Park study politics as an academic discipline rather than advocating reform or a particular political point of view.

It seems, therefore, that there are valid reasons for the present status quo.

b) A gift to promote the work of the lecturers of the University of London would unquestionably be a valid charitable bequest, as being for the advancement of education: *Attorney-General* v *Margaret and Regius Professors in Cambridge* (1682) 1 Vern 55. The question is whether providing sporting facilities for them is charitable.

The difficulty is that the provision of sporting facilities has no necessary nexus with their academic work or with the advancement of education. It in no way involves the propagation of learning, which is an essential element for a gift to be charitable as being for the advancement of education. It might be possible to argue that it is ancillary to their work as lecturers: *Re Coxen* [1948] Ch 747 (where the Court of Aldermen of the City of London were directed to manage a large trust fund for orthopaedic hospitals and given a maximum of £100 pa for a dinner – it was held that the whole gift was charitable). It is submitted, however, that this argument is unlikely to work here. Equally, it seems unlikely that the lecturers would be able to avail themselves of the Recreational Charities Act 1958, since they do not apparently belong to any class with a special need for these facilities.

Therefore it is submitted that this gift is unlikely to be held to be charitable.

In the alternative contingency, it is submitted that it would make a difference if the gift was for the students. Here the gift is very likely to be accepted as being ancillary to the education of the students: *Attorney-General* v *Ross and Others* [1985] 3 All ER 334 (where Scott J held that the students union at a London Polytechnic was charitable and that its non-charitable activities were ancillary to its main object). Alternatively, they might well be able to invoke the aid of the Recreational Charities Act 1958 and argue that by reason of their youth they need these facilities.

QUESTION THREE

Are the following purposes charitable:

a) providing scholarships to assist students to learn ballroom dancing while at university on the condition that the trustees may, in applying up to 75 per cent of the income of the trust, give preference to children of employees of ABC Ltd;

b) providing funds for the establishment of a modern national health service in Ruritrania, a country plagued by poverty and disease, where there are strong religious objections to medical procedures which involve any invasion of the body, including surgery and vaccination by syringe;

c) providing funds to persuade the Vatican to allow the ordination of women priests in the Roman Catholic church?

University of London LLB Examination
(for External Students) Law of Trusts June 1997 Q4

General Comment

This is a problem question and requires the candidate to determine whether certain dispositions are charitable.

Skeleton Solution

a) Gift is in itself probably charitable – but the expression of a preference probably vitiates its charitable status.

b) Gift is prima facie charitable – is it too political to be charitable?

c) Gift is probably too political to be charitable.

Suggested Solution

a) In order for a gift to be charitable, it must satisfy three conditions: (i) it must be for a purpose which the law regards as charitable (ie advancement of religion, relief of poverty, advancement of education, or other purposes beneficial to the community); (ii) it must be for public benefit; (iii) it must be wholly and exclusively charitable.

Universities are themselves charitable as being for the advancement of education: *Attorney-General* v *Margaret and Regius Professors in Cambridge* (1682) 1 Vern 55. Therefore providing scholarships for a university is ipso facto charitable. There seems no reason why providing scholarships to assist students to learn ballroom dancing while at university should not be charitable. Although this is presumably a recreational subject rather than one of the normal academic subjects, it could be argued that it was ancillary to the university's main purpose and thus still charitable: *Re Coxen* [1948] Ch 747 (Court of Aldermen of the City of London directed to manage a large trust fund for the benefit of orthopaedic hospitals and given a maximum of £100 pa for a dinner. Held charitable). Besides, it can probably be argued that promoting ballroom dancing is itself capable of being charitable: *Royal Choral Society* v *IRC* [1943] 2 All ER 101 (where the encouragement and advancement of choral singing in London was held charitable). It might also be charitable under the Recreational Charities Act 1958.

The difficulty is the expression of a preference for employees of ABC Ltd. A gift for the employees of a particular company is not charitable because it lacks the necessary element of public benefit: *Oppenheim* v *Tobacco Securities Trust Co Ltd* [1951] AC 297. There is authority for saying that a gift is still charitable even if it expresses a preference for relations or employees: *Re Koettgen's Will Trusts* [1954] Ch 252; *Caffoor Trustees* v *Commissioner of Income Tax, Colombo* [1961] AC 584. However, it is submitted that these cases are unlikely to be followed today.

That being so, it is submitted that this gift is not charitable.

b) The relief of poverty is itself most certainly charitable. Providing a voluntary hospital is also charitable: *Barclays Bank Ltd* v *Mercantile Bank Ltd, Re Smith* [1962] 1 WLR 763. So also is providing a hospital for paying patients. Therefore this gift is prima facie charitable.

The difficulty is the fact that in Ruritrania there are religious objections to what is being proposed. This raises the question as to whether or not the gift is too political to be charitable: *McGovern* v *Attorney-General* [1982] Ch 321 (where Slade J held that Amnesty International was too political to be charitable). Clearly the fact that Amnesty International is regarded as too political to be charitable indicates that the mere fact that something might prima facie be regarded as charitable is not sufficient to make it charitable in the eyes of English law. On the other hand what is being done here is, in this country at least, plainly charitable, whereas what Amnesty International was doing was distinctly political. A further complication is that it is only certain aspects of medicine (albeit important ones) which are regarded as objectionable. Clearly this might help, but on the other hand if the gift is held too political to be charitable, it might fall foul of the rule that a charitable gift must be wholly and exclusively charitable.

It is therefore difficult to say on which side of the dividing line this case falls. It is submitted that on balance it is not charitable, but it is difficult be be sure in the absence of a decision from a High Court judge.

c) The advancement of religion is itself unequivocally charitable. Again, however, the danger is that this gift is too political to be regarded as charitable. It is submitted that this gift is almost certainly not charitable, because (whatever one's personal views may be on the topic at issue) it has very little to do with the advancement of religion, and a lot to do with the promotion of a particular political point of view, whether ecclesiastico-political or otherwise. Indeed the mere fact that this is such a politically and theologically sensitive issue suggests that any judge would be most unwilling to regard such a gift as charitable.

QUESTION FOUR

a) What are the possible advantages and disadvantages of a statutory definition of the meaning of 'charity'?

b) Consider the validity of the following gifts:

 i) £10,000,000 to my trustees upon trust for the purpose of setting up an Olympic

Sporting Institute, for the better training of Great Britain's most promising young amateur athletes;

ii) £1,000 for the provision of condoms and other means of birth control to students in schools in London.

University of London LLB Examination
(for External Students) Law of Trusts June 1998 Q6

General Comment

This question raises some interesting points: why is there no statutory definition of charity or charitable purposes? This would need careful analysis under the pressures of an examination. Part (b) raises two problems which illustrate the nature of the flexibility of the charity concept: part (i) requires an analysis of the law relating to sport, and part (ii) raises a question not considered in existing case law, so that the candidate must argue by analogy.

Skeleton Solution

a) Definition in 1601 preamble – redefined by Lord MacNaghten – *Baddeley* – no limits; *Incorporated Council of Law Reporting* – limits; public benefit; exclusively charitable; no political activity – role of Charity Commissioners – dangers of statutory definition.

b) i) Trusts for sporting activities – *Re Nottage*; *City of Glasgow Police* – Recreational Charities Act 1958 – improving conditions of life – need – *Guild v IRC* – advancement of education – *McMullen*.

ii) Wide definition of education – *McMullen* – possibly illegal – *Re Shaw* – within spirit and intendment?

Suggested Solution

a) In fact, the definition of charitable activity is founded in statute – the preamble to the Statute of Charitable Uses 1601. Where earlier statutory provisions were repealed by s38(4) Charities Act 1960 (re-enacted in 1993), the preamble was preserved and given the status of precedent to be followed by the court.

The Statute of 1601 gives a list (but not a definition) of activities which were considered to be charitable, mainly because they relieved the public purse, and today, when considering whether an activity should be given charitable status, the court will consider, inter alia, whether that activity is within the 'spirit and intendment' of the 1601 preamble.

In *Commissioners of Income Tax v Pemsel* [1891] AC 531 Lord MacNaghten subdivided the preamble into four main categories: trusts for the relief of poverty; trusts for the advancement of education; trusts for the advancement of religion; and trusts for other purposes beneficial to the community. However, neither the 1601 Statute nor the Charities Act 1993 gives a detailed definition of 'charity' or 'charitable purposes'.

Viscount Simonds observed in *IRC* v *Baddeley* [1955] AC 572 that there is no limit to the ways in which a man will seek to benefit his fellows. Ultimately, the court decides which activities are charitable, although applications for charitable status are made initially to the Charity Commissioners.

The approach of the English courts appears to be to leave the definition of charity open in order to accommodate new activities, to which it is in the public interest to give charitable status (for example, accurate law reporting, as in the case of *Incorporated Council of Law Reporting for England and Wales* v *Attorney-General* [1972] Ch 73). At the same time, strict rules are applied that the activity must be for the public benefit, it must be exclusively charitable, and it must not be a political activity. This regime allows for flexibility, because the nature of the activity is not restricted, but the rules ensure that the activity is for the benefit of the public as a whole.

It was observed by Lord Wilberforce in *Scottish Burial Reform and Cremation Society Ltd* v *Glasgow Corporation* [1968] AC 138 that the law of charity is a moving subject and may well have evolved since Lord MacNaghten established his new classification in 1891.

There would undoubtedly be an advantage in providing a statutory definition which was drafted to give all the criteria in one text. This would have the benefit of certainty and clarity. The tests of what is 'exclusively charitable', of 'public benefit' and 'political' could then also be defined. A clear distinction could be made between activities which are acceptable as being ancillary to the charity's main objects, and those which are not because they involve proactive political campaigning. It should be noted, however, that much of this work has already been done by the Charity Commissioners, who produce very clear guidelines on what activities will be considered charitable.

The danger of a statutory definition would be its inflexibility, unless it were drawn very widely, which may then render it of no real assistance. In *IRC* v *McMullen* [1981] AC 1 it was pointed out that the concept of charity was not static, but changed to meet differing social values. For this reason, it is best to leave the legislation with no fixed definition, so that the concept can develop through the case law.

b) i) It was established in *Re Nottage* [1895] 2 Ch 649 that a trust to promote sporting activities per se could not be charitable. In that case, the testator gave money to provide a trophy for the winner of a yacht race. Similarly, in *IRC* v *City of Glasgow Police Athletic Association* [1953] AC 380 an association to promote sporting and general pastimes was refused charitable status, because its objects, in permitting merely recreational activities, were not exclusively charitable. Following this second decision, legislation which was both retrospective and prospective was introduced in order to save the many similar gifts which would have been refused charitable status on these grounds: Recreational Charities Act 1958.

An Olympic Sporting Institute would presumably have objects which were entirely sports-based. It would appear that the young people who are the intended beneficiaries could be drawn from all walks of life, and, since there is no personal nexus, the public benefit requirement would be satisfied. However, it does not serve the needs of a particular community, and so might be outside the scope of the Recreational Charities Act 1958 . To come within this legislation, there must be an element of 'social welfare'. There are two limbs to this requirement:

- the facilities must be provided with the object of improving the conditions of life of the intended beneficiaries; and

- those beneficiaries must have need of the facilities because of their youth, age, infirmity, poverty or social or economic circumstances.

In *Guild (Executor Nominate of the Late James Young Russell)* v *IRC* [1992] 2 WLR 397 the House of Lords established that the beneficiaries need not be deprived. However, the thrust of the Recreational Charities Act 1958 is to provide facilities for communities rather than for the whole country.

Could this be construed as a trust for the advancement of education? The provision of the facilities is to be made by setting up a Sporting Institute for young athletes. If this were run as part of, or in association with, a school or university, this trust would fall within Lord MacNaghten's second category.

In *IRC* v *McMullen* [1981] AC 1 it was established that the Football Association Youth Trust was charitable, but this was established to promote the playing of football in schools and universities. In *McMullen*, when defining 'for the advancement of education', Lord Hailsham took the Education Act 1944 as his starting point, but expressly recognised the value of extramural activities. He also noted that educational activities, to be charitable, need not be restricted to particular localities. He refused to restrict the application of charitable status to activities carried out in the classroom or the playground. It is likely, therefore, that the Institute would be given charitable status. It might have been different, however, if the provision were made for athletes of all ages rather than for young athletes.

ii) It was stated in *IRC* v *McMullen* that education contains spiritual, moral, mental and physical elements. This definition would probably be wide enough to encompass a sex education programme including the provision of condoms and other means of birth control.

If this provision were made to school students under the age of consent, however, it might be considered as immoral or illegal and thus, according to dicta of Harman J in *Re Shaw* [1957] 1 WLR 729 (that immoral purposes should be regarded as harmful) could not be a charitable activity.

An argument could be made that the activity was within the spirit and intendment of the Statute of Elizabeth 1601, in that birth control provision would lighten the demands on the public purse. A good arguable case could thus be put before the Charity Commissioners to allow this gift charitable status.

QUESTION FIVE

Are the following gifts charitable:

a) £1,000,000 to teach football to children from deprived inner-city areas;

b) £1,000,000 to campaign for state provision of free eye-sight tests for the poor;

c) £1,000,000 to educate the children of millionaires; and

d) £1,000,000 to endow a chair of political science in the University of London?

University of London LLB Examination
(for External Students) Law of Trusts June 1999 Q6

General Comment

The form of the question gives the structure to the essay – four sections of equal length. It is important to answer the specific question set for each part of the question, and to address the issues raised by the way in which the question is framed.

Skeleton Solution

a) Trusts for the advancement of education and the relief of poverty – Lord MacNaghten's categories – *IRC* v *McMullen* – Education Act 1944 – *Re Mariette* – no personal nexus; *Re Niyazi* – Recreational Charities Act 1958.

b) Political objects; *Attorney-General* v *Ross*; *McGovern* v *Attorney-General* – 1979 Government White Paper – *Bowman* v *Secular Society* – Charity Commissioners' guidelines – poor/impotent.

c) Trusts for the advancement of education – Goodman Committee – public benefit requirement – non profit-making.

d) Trusts for the advancement of education/political objects – *Re Koeppler*; *Southwood* v *Attorney-General*.

Suggested Solution

a) This gift could be charitable under more than one of Lord MacNaghten's heads of charity, as established in *Commissioners of Income Tax* v *Pemsel* [1891] AC 531.

A gift to teach football to children would be a trust for the advancement of education since 'education' is not limited to education in schools. In *IRC v McMullen* [1981] AC 1 the House of Lords looked to the Education Act 1944, which recognised that voluntary societies and those which provided extra-curricular activities make a contribution to state-provided education. Lord Hailsham rejected the concept that, in order to be charitable, educational activities must take place within the school or university system.

In *Re Mariette* [1915] 2 Ch 284 the court recognised the educational value of keeping children out of mischief by providing them with organised activities – in this case by providing squash courts. The fact that the provision is expressed to be for children would also assist in establishing that this gift was charitable.

The requirement that the activity must be for the public benefit is satisfied, since the beneficiaries are not connected by a family or an employment link and there is therefore no personal nexus: see *Oppenheim v Tobacco Securities Trust Co Ltd* [1951] AC 297.

Although the beneficiaries of a trust for the advancement of education do not have to be poor, this gift would also be charitable as the provision that the gift, if for 'children of deprived city areas', would be construed as such: see *Re Niyazi's Will Trusts* [1978] 1 WLR 910.

Even though the purpose of the gift is limited to the teaching of football to children, it would also fall within the scope of s1(2)(b)(i) Recreational Charities Act 1958, as provision of the facilities would be construed as being 'in the interests of social welfare': see *National Deposit Friendly Society v Skegness Urban District Council* [1958] 2 All ER 601.

b) While a gift for the provision of free eye-sight tests for the poor would be construed as charitable, either as a charity for the sick or for the relief of poverty, campaigning for state provision could be construed as political activity, which cannot be charitable, unless the activity is ancillary to the principal objects of a charity: see *Attorney-General v Ross and Others* [1985] 3 All ER 334. It would appear from the 1989 Government White Paper *Charities: A Framework for the Future* that such activity should be reactive rather than proactive. The reasons for this rule were given in *McGovern v Attorney-General* [1982] Ch 321:

i) the court cannot judge whether the proposed change in the law will be for the public benefit;

ii) cases must be decided on the basis that the law is right as it stands: to do otherwise would be contrary to the doctrine of the separation of powers;

iii) the court itself must be impartial politically.

On this basis, charitable status was refused to Amnesty International, and the judge, in giving judgment, went on to list the types of activity which would be refused charitable status, and included trusts to procure changes in the law in this country and trusts to bring about a reversal in Government policy. Similarly, in *Bowman* v *Secular Society* [1917] AC 406, a trust set up inter alia to campaign for the abolition of Sunday observance, to secularise education and disestablish the church was denied charitable status because its objects were to bring about changes in the law.

Initially, the Charity Commissioners would rule whether the organisation's objects were exclusively charitable. They publish guidelines on political activities by charities to the effect that the objects of a charity should not include a power to exert political pressure, except in a way which is ancillary to a charitable purpose.

In view of the size of the gift, however, it is unlikely that this activity would be construed as ancillary unless it were given to one of the large national charities, such as the Royal National Institution for the Blind. There is no indication of this, however, in the way in which the gift is expressed, and thus the gift cannot be charitable. As it stands, it is a gift for a purpose and therefore cannot be a valid express private trust, because there are no ascertainable beneficiaries.

c) Most, if not all, the public schools in England and Wales enjoy charitable status. Among their pupils are children of millionaires. *Re Mariette* [1915] 2 Ch 284 concerned the provision of squash courts for public school pupils.

The educational activity must be for the public benefit. This requirement is satisfied because, by providing for the education of these children, the donor is relieving the public purse from having to make such provision. This is a factor of such significance that, despite the recommendations of the Goodman Committee on Charity Law and Voluntary Organisations in 1976, there has never been legislation to revoke the charitable status of public schools. There is no requirement that the beneficiaries of an educational charity should be poor. There is no personal nexus between the beneficiaries, since 'millionaires' can come from all sectors of the population. The organisation which provides the education must be non-profit-making (*Re Girls' Public Day School Trust* [1951] Ch 400) so that, if the institutions charge fees, any surplus must be used for the purposes of the charity.

The gift places no age limit on the children who are to benefit, although children usually connotes youth: students at school and university. The Charity Commissioners would probably take this 'benignant' approach to the interpretation of the clause, especially as there seems to be no age limit on the activities under the head of trusts for the advancement of education.

d) A gift for the endowment of a chair in political sciences as part of a recognised university course would be construed as a valid charitable gift for the advancement of education. Education in politics is not considered to be political activity, since it involves a study of the political system, not an attempt to change it.

In *Re Koeppler* [1985] 2 All ER 869 a gift to Wilton Park, to fund educational conferences in order to promote cooperation between East and West, was recognised as charitable despite the political content of the conferences proposed.

McGovern v *Attorney-General* [1982] Ch 321 was distinguished on the grounds that in *Koeppler* the political nature of the discussions was incidental to the work undertaken by the charity. By contrast, the political activity was an essential part of the objects of Amnesty International.

Similarly, in *Attorney-General* v *Ross and Others* [1985] 3 All ER 334 it was held by Scott J that there can be a valid educational charity for the purpose of developing the political awareness of students and to enable them to form views on political issues.

In the case of *Southwood and Another* v *Attorney-General* (1998) The Times 26 October, charitable status was refused where the stated objects of the organisation were the advancement of education in the subject of militarism and disarmament. Rather than promoting peaceful means of dispute resolution, the activities challenged the policies of Western governments and were thus political activities. The aim of the political activity must be to inform rather than to influence the view of the students.

Chapter 12

The Cy-près Doctrine

12.1 Introduction

12.2 Key points

12.3 Key cases and statute

12.4 Questions and suggested solutions

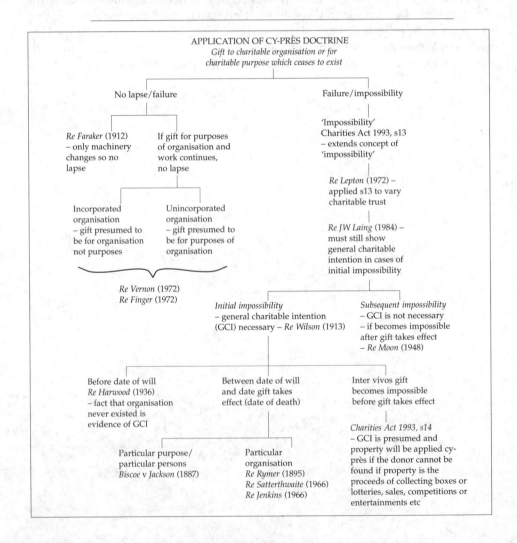

APPLICATION OF CY-PRÈS DOCTRINE
Gift to charitable organisation or for
charitable purpose which ceases to exist

No lapse/failure

Failure/impossibility

Re Faraker (1912)
– only machinery
changes so no
lapse

If gift for purposes
of organisation and
work continues,
no lapse

'Impossibility'
Charities Act 1993, s13
– extends concept of
'impossibility'

Re Lepton (1972) –
applied s13 to vary
charitable trust

Re JW Laing (1984) –
must still show
general charitable
intention in cases of
initial impossibility

Incorporated
organisation
– gift presumed to
be for organisation
not purposes

Unincorporated
organisation
– gift presumed to
be for purposes of
organisation

Re Vernon (1972)
Re Finger (1972)

Initial impossibility
– general charitable intention
(GCI) necessary – *Re Wilson* (1913)

Subsequent impossibility
– GCI is not necessary
– if becomes impossible
after gift takes effect
– *Re Moon* (1948)

Before date of will
Re Harwood (1936)
– fact that organisation
never existed is
evidence of GCI

Between date of will
and date gift takes
effect (date of death)

Inter vivos gift
becomes impossible
before gift takes effect

Charities Act 1993, s14
– GCI is presumed and
property will be applied cy-
près if the donor cannot be
found if property is the
proceeds of collecting boxes or
lotteries, sales, competitions or
entertainments etc

Particular purpose/
particular persons
Biscoe v Jackson (1887)

Particular
organisation
Re Rymer (1895)
Re Satterthwaite (1966)
Re Jenkins (1966)

12.1 Introduction

The issue is whether a court will use the cy-près doctrine to give effect to a charitable purpose in a trust which would otherwise be invalid. An understanding of charitable trusts (Chapter 11) is a prerequisite to studying the cy-près doctrine as the two topics are closely related. At first sight, the cases and statutory material concerning the topic appear to be relatively straightforward. Complexities do exist, however; notably in distinguishing whether a gift has been saved by an application of the cy-près doctrine or whether in fact the gift did not fail at all. This distinction, although many students find it difficult to draw, must be grasped before the cy-près doctrine as a whole can be mastered. Since s16 Charities Act 1993 the Charity Commissioners have a joint jurisdiction with the courts. Sections 74 and 75 contain specific provisions for the modification of small charities.

12.2 Key points

The cy-près doctrine comes into play when a gift is made to a charitable organisation which has ceased to exist or for a charitable purpose which cannot be carried out. The effect of an application of the doctrine is that the gift will be applied to another charitable organisation carrying out the same purposes or for a similar charitable purpose, rather than resulting to the donor via a resulting trust (or possibly to the Crown via bona vacantia – see Chapter 6).

If the gift is to a charitable organisation which appears no longer to exist, the gift may nevertheless be applied for charitable purposes not on the basis of a cy-près application, but rather because there has in fact been no failure of the gift at all. This is possible in two situations.

a) *Re Faraker* [1912] 2 Ch 488 – if the gift is to a charity which has been consolidated with other charities with similar purposes under a scheme. The gift did not fail because the charity was still in existence, only the machinery of it had changed.

   Re Faraker will not apply, though, if:

   i)   the charity is liable to termination under its constitution: *Re Stemson's Will Trusts* [1970] Ch 16;

   ii) the gift is made for an aspect of the the charity's work which cannot be carried out by the amalgamation: *Re Lucas* [1948] Ch 424.

b) If the gift can be construed as for the purposes of the organisation and the purposes are now being carried out by another body. The cases of *Re Vernon's Will Trusts* [1972] Ch 300n and *Re Finger's Will Trusts* [1972] Ch 286 drew a distinction for the purpose of such interpretation between incorporated organisations and unincorporated organisations.

   i)   A gift to an incorporated body is presumed to be for the body itself rather than for its purposes. Thus, if the body ceases to exist the gift fails. (It may still be applied cy-près if the conditions below are fulfilled.)

ii) A gift to an unincorporated body is presumed to be for the purposes of the body. Thus if the body ceases to exist but the purposes are carried on by another body the gift did not fail at all and would be applied for the new body.

If the gift has, however, failed (a case of 'impossibility') the possibility of cy-près application arises.

(Since s13 Charities Act 1960 (now s13 Charities Act 1993) the concept of 'impossibility' has been a very wide one enabling, in effect, the terms of gifts to be varied if they are impractical – as was done in *Re Lepton's Charity* [1972] 1 Ch 276. It has been underlined, however, that s13 expressly preserves the need for general charitable intention in cases of initial impossibility: *Re J W Laing* [1984] Ch 143.) *Oldham Borough Council v Attorney-General* [1993] Ch 210 and *Peggs and Others v Lamb and Others* [1994] 2 WLR 1 are two examples of the width of such powers. In *Varsani v Jesani* [1998] 3 All ER 273 it was made clear that the test to be used was whether the original purpose had ceased to provide a suitable and effective method of using the property, regard being had to the spirit of the gift.

The gift may be applied cy-près if the case is one of initial impossibility and general charitable intention is proved and if it is a case of subsequent impossibility in which case there is no need to prove a general charitable intention.

Initial impossibility

If a gift is initially impossible – becomes impossible before the gift takes effect – it can be applied cy-près if the donor can be shown to have had a general charitable intention.

a) If the gift becomes impossible before the date of the will.

In *Re Harwood* [1936] Ch 285 it was held that a gift to a body which had never existed showed a general charitable intention.

b) If the gift becomes impossible between the date of the will and the date the gift takes effect (date of death):

i) if the gift is for a particular purpose but can be construed as a gift to benefit a particular group of persons with only a desire for a particular mode which is impossible, the gift will be applied cy-près for those persons in other ways: *Biscoe v Jackson* (1887) 35 Ch D 460;

ii) if the gift is for a particular organisation then if the organisation is simply the machinery for carrying out a purpose which the gift is intended for, then the gift can be applied cy-près for that purpose via another body: *Re Rymer* [1895] 1 Ch 19. Whether the organisation was simply the machinery will be influenced by other gifts in the will from which a general charitable intention maybe inferred:

Re Satterthwaite's Will Trusts [1966] 1 WLR 277 and *Re Jenkins' Will Trusts* [1966] Ch 249.

c) If an inter vivos gift becomes impossible before the gift takes effect.

Charities Act 1993, s14 – if property is given for a specific charitable purpose, general charitable intention will nevertheless be presumed and the property will be applied cy-près if the donor cannot be found or if he executes a written disclaimer. It will be presumed that the donor cannot be found if the property is the proceeds of collecting boxes or lotteries, sales, competitions or entertainments, etc.

Subsequent impossibility

A gift is subsequently impossible if it becomes impossible after the gift takes effect: *Re Moon's Will Trusts* [1948] 1 All ER 300. The gift will be applied cy-près and there is no need to find a general charitable intention.

12.3 Key cases and statute

*   *Re Harwood* [1936] Ch 285
    General charitable intention – present – where body never existed

*   *Re Moon's Will Trusts* [1948] 1 All ER 300
    Subsequent impossibility – no need to find a general charitable intention

*   Charities Act 1993, s14 – general charitable intention – assumed – absent donor

12.4 Questions and suggested solutions

QUESTION ONE

In what circumstances, if any, may trust moneys be applied cy-près?

University of London LLB Examination
(for External Students) Law of Trusts June 1987 Q5(a)

General Comment

This is a very general question. In an answer the student is required to give a precis of the law relating to cy-près. This must necessarily be very concise due to the time constraints (this is only half of a question).

Skeleton Solution

Introduction – when cy-près applies; contrast with non-charitable trusts; requirement of general charitable intention – distinction between initial and supervening impossibility – initial impossibility: whether gift has in fact failed; requirement of general charitable intention – supervening impossibility – Charities Act 1993, ss13 and 14.

Suggested Solution

Trust monies may only be applied cy-près where the trust concerned is charitable in nature and it has failed. In private trusts failure will result in the property being returned on resulting trusts to the settlor in most cases. In charitable trusts the cy-près doctrine is designed to avoid money given for charitable trusts which fail being returned on resulting trusts if it can be said that there was a general charitable intention behind the gift. If such an intention can be found the money will be applied for the benefit of charitable objects which are similar to those of the original gift.

A gift to a charitable trust may fail because the trust has ceased to exist at the date the gift takes effect, for example, a gift under a will which comes into operation after the trust went out of existence, or because the trust ceased to exist after the gift took effect and it has not been exhausted by those trusts. The former is known as initial impossibility whilst the latter is known as supervening impossibility.

In cases of initial impossibility, it must be shown that the charitable trust ceased to exist before the gift took effect. Thus, there will be no room for the application of cy-près where the charity has been amalgamated with other charities and has lost its administrative machinery and name but not its identity as a trust.: *Re Faraker* [1912] 2 Ch 488. It must also be shown that there is a general charitable intention behind the gift and that the donor was not intending it as a specific gift for a specific purpose: *Re Rymer* [1895] 1 Ch 19. There are often problems in determining if there is a general charitable intention and to this end the court has devised a number of rules which are designed so that the gift can be applied cy-près. In *Re Vernon's Will Trusts* [1972] Ch 300n Buckley J held that a gift to an unincorporated charity without more was prima facie to be construed as a gift for its purposes so that if the charity ceased to exist but its work was still being carried on a cy-près application could be made. This principle does not apply to incorporated charities as these are considered as taking any gifts to them beneficially. In *Re Satterthwaite's Will Trusts* [1966] 1 WLR 277 it was held that a general charitable intention might be drawn from a long list of gifts which had a common charitable theme but included a gift which was unidentifiable as a gift to a known charity, that gift could be applied cy-près: *Re Harwood* [1936] Ch 285.

Supervening impossibility does not require that a general charitable intention be shown to exist behind the gift because once money is effectively dedicated to charitable purposes it is always held for charitable purposes. All that is necessary in supervening impossibility is that it is a gift which took effect and since then the charity has ceased to exist. Thus, in *Re Slevin* [1891] 2 Ch 236 a gift was made by Will to an orphanage. Shortly after the will took effect the orphanage closed but the gift was nevertheless applied cy-près.

There are also some statutory provisions on initial impossibility. Under s13 Charities Act 1993 the court may order that a cy-près application be made in certain cases even though there is no impossibility in applying the gift. This may be done where, for example, the original purposes have been carried out as far as may be or where they are no longer a practical or useful way of applying the money. Under s14 Charities Act 1993 cy-près is applied to monies from unidentified sources as part of a collection for a charitable purpose which cannot be carried out. The object of this provision is to overcome the difficulties of returning the money to the donors.

QUESTION TWO

a) On what basis does the law determine whether a proposed trust, which appears to provide for a novel purpose, ie, one not found to be charitable or uncharitable by a previous judicial decision, is charitable? Are any reforms of the law indicated?

b) Siegfried died, leaving in his will '£50,000 to the Stepney Grammar School for scholarships to deserving boys' and '£50,000 for the work of Stepney Food for the Homeless'. Stepney Grammar School, though it previously had only male pupils, is now mixed, and the current board of governors have advised the trustees that they would not administer a scholarship scheme for boys only. Stepney Food for the Homeless was a corporate charitable body which has since been wound up; its work, however, was continued and is now carried on by East London Food for the Homeless. Advise the trustees.

University of London LLB Examination
(for External Students) Law of Trusts June 2000 Q5

General Comment

For part (a) the manner in which the law grows by analogy in the light of prevailing circumstances needs to be appreciated. Clearly such an approach causes uncertainty – hence the need to consider the possibilities of reform. Whilst suggestions can be made, none of them are a panacea for all ills. The important thing to realise in part (b) is that what is required is some quite specific material in relation to the cy-près doctrine, rather than general material on charities.

Skeleton Solution

a) Growth by analogy – the living preamble – the *MacNaghten* classification – proposals for reform.

b) Cy-près rather than charities generally – initial and subsequent failure – general charitable intention – *Re Lysaght* – the position of incorporated bodies.

Suggested Solution

a) There is no statutory definition of what is charitable. In order to be charitable a matter should fall within the remit of the preamble to the Statute of Elizabeth 1601. Whilst this was repealed, its principles were reaffirmed by the House of Lords in *Scottish Burial Reform and Cremation Society Ltd v Glasgow Corporation* [1968] AC 138. This includes matters such as the relief of aged, impotent and poor people. The courts have adopted a 'growth by analogy approach' from the preamble. The different kinds of charitable purposes were categorised into four by Lord MacNaghten in the case of *Commissioners of Income Tax* v *Pemsel* [1891] AC 531: trusts for the relief of poverty, trusts for the advancement of education, trusts for the advancement of religion and trusts for other purposes beneficial to the community. Russell LJ in *Incorporated Council of Law Reporting for England and Wales* v *Attorney-General* [1972] Ch 73 argued that with respect to the fourth category, the court should make a determination of what is beneficial to the community from first principles, though this novel approach has not been followed and is in conflict with *Williams' Trustees* v *IRC* [1947] AC 447. Whilst we thus have a living preamble as a guide to novel cases, the aim of the courts is very much to develop in the light of social needs rather than being ruled by the antiquated language of that preamble. In their decisions the courts are clearly guided by the earlier case law and the particular circumstances of the gift and of the time.

With growth by analogy there is continuing uncertainty and it has been suggested that a statutory definition would be the answer. It is argued that the lack of such a definition results in apparently arbitrary decisions as to whether an organisation is charitable, and makes it difficult, if not impossible, to be certain what does constitute a charity. No one, however, has yet been able to produce a definition of charity that has met with general approval, and even if such a definition were to be put forward there would still be borderline cases. As the law stands there is a real, if limited, possibility of adapting the law to changing social circumstances, which might be diminished by a statutory definition. The matter was reconsidered in the White Paper *Charities: A Framework For The Future* (1989), where three possible ways of defining charity were discussed:

i)   by listing the purposes which are deemed to be charitable;

ii) by enacting a definition of charity based on Lord Macnaghten's classification;

iii) by defining 'charitable purposes' as 'purposes beneficial to the community'.

The view taken in the White Paper was that, so far as the first way is concerned, even if a list could be agreed, it might be inflexible and quickly outdated by changing public opinion; as to the second way, the incorporation of Lord Macnaghten's classification into statute would throw the law into confusion and uncertainty by depriving the courts of recourse to previous decisions, but if the existing case law were in some way to be preserved little would be achieved; and the third way would have the merit of simplicity, but would greatly expand the ambit of charity in ways which might be far from desirable, would be notably subjective and likely to give rise to a great deal of litigation. The conclusion drawn was that there are few advantages in attempting a wholesale redefinition of charitable status, and many real dangers would arise from doing so.

b) Both dispositions in the will are clearly charitable but they fail or experience difficulties at the outset; what needs to be considered is the cy-près doctrine. This allows the court to save trusts for charitable purposes that would otherwise fail. The system works in relation to charitable bodies that have ceased to exist, as in the case of Stepney Food for the Homeless, and also where the charitable purpose may not be possible to carry out – as in the case of the Stepney Grammar School gift. What would happen is that another charitable body that had similar aims would receive the money for the same or similar purposes. Otherwise the money would go back to the estate following resulting trust principles. In the case of initial failure, such as a failure between the date of the will and the testator's death, the gift can be applied cy-près if there is a general charitable intention. With subsequent failure, where the difficulty arises after the will, there is no need to find a general charitable intention.

The Stepney Grammar School gift requires consideration of the case *Re Lysaght* [1996] Ch 191. Here funds were left to the Royal College of Surgeons to fund medical scholarships. Restrictions were imposed: the student were to be males, the sons of qualified British-born medical men and not of the Jewish or Roman Catholic faiths. The gift was not acceptable in those terms and the court thought that there was a general charitable intention, the outcome being that the gift took effect without the religious qualifications. The School in the question should seek to make use of this in order to allow the use of the money for females as well as males. The gift to Stepney Food for the Homeless may, according to *Re Vernon's Will Trusts* [1972] Ch 300n, be a poor candidate for the use of the cy-près doctrine because it was made to a defunct corporate body. Dicta in the above case states that a gift to a corporate body that performs charitable purposes is a gift to the body beneficially, which will lapse if that body ceases to exist before the testator dies. The only alternative would be where it could be shown that the institution in question was to take the property on trust for charitable purposes.

Part Two
The Nature of Trusteeship

Chapter 13

Appointment, Retirement and Removal of Trustees

13.1 Introduction

13.2 Key points

13.3 Key case and statutes

13.4 Questions and suggested solutions

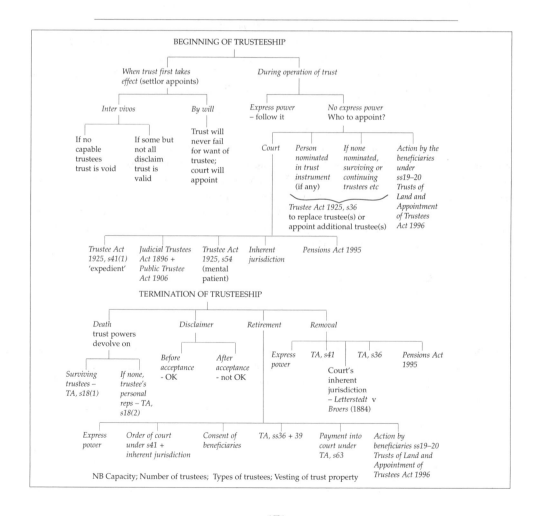

13.1 Introduction

This chapter covers introductory points which relate to trusteeship, knowledge of which is vital before the more intricate aspects of trustees' powers and duties can be considered. Neither these introductory points nor the law concerning the appointment of trustees and the termination of trusteeship, present any difficult concepts. Instead, the topics are technical and require the student to familiarise himself fully with the relevant statutory provisions. Note the changes made by the Charities Act 1993, the Pensions Act 1995 and the Trusts of Land and Appointment of Trustees Act 1996.

13.2 Key points

Introductory

Types of trustees

In addition to individuals (with capacity), various other types of trustees may be appointed and may act as trustee. These include, primarily, firms of solicitors; trust corporations (often banks and insurance companies); judicial trustees (appointed by the court under the Judicial Trustees Act 1896); the Public Trustee (who may be appointed by whoever is entitled to appoint under the Public Trustee Act 1906).

Capacity

Any person who has capacity to hold property has capacity to be a trustee. An infant, therefore, cannot validly be appointed a trustee of any property (Law of Property Act (LPA) 1925, s20). However, if the situation arises, he can hold personal property on resulting or constructive trust. He cannot do so in the case of realty as he cannot validly hold the legal estate in land. Section 32 Charities Act 1993 made provision for the disqualification of certain categories of person, such as brankrupts, from the holding of the position of trustee in relation to charities.

Number of trustees

The only limitations are statutory.

a) Maximum number

   If the trust involves realty, the number of trustees shall not exceed, nor be increased beyond, four: Trustee Act (TA) 1925, s34(2). Section 34(3), however, identifies exceptions to this rule including trusts involving land held for charitable, ecclesiastical or public purposes.

b) Minimum number

   i) A sole trustee of land (not being a trust corporation) cannot act effectively as he cannot give a valid receipt for the proceeds of sale or other capital money under the LPA 1925 and the Settled Land Act (SLA) 1925 as relevant.

ii) If more than one trustee was originally appointed, then a sole surviving trustee cannot retire from the trust and appoint a sole trustee (not being a trust corporation).

Appointment of trustees

Initial appointment by the settlor

a) Inter vivos trust

The settlor will appoint the first trustee(s). If for some reason the appointment is invalid, the trust will fail. If, however, the appointment is valid, but the trustee(s) disclaim the trust, the trust is valid and the court will appoint new trustees provided that it is not, 'of the essence … that the trustees selected by the settlor and no-one else shall act as the trustees of it': *Re Lysaght* [1966] Ch 191 per Buckley J.

b) Trust created by will

The trust will never fail for want of a trustee even if none were appointed; if necessary, the court will appoint.

Subsequent appointments

If there exists an express power concerning appointment of new trustees, then this will determine who can appoint and in what circumstances. If no such provision exists, or if such provision addresses only the question of who can appoint, then resort must be had to statutory provisions and to the court's inherent jurisdiction.

a) If the trust instrument states who is to exercise any power of appointment, and all such persons exist.

If this is the case, such person(s) will have a power of appointment under TA, s36 (see (b) below).

b) If no person(s) exist under (a) above but if there exist surviving or continuing trustee(s) or personal representatives of the last surviving or continuing trustee. (A trustee who is retiring as a result of the appointment below falls within this category. If all the trustees predecease the testator, the personal representatives of the last to die do not fall within this category.)

If this is the case, such person(s) will have the power of appointment under s36.

Under TA, s36, the power of appointment can be exercised by the relevant persons in eight situations.

i) Where a trustee is dead (including a trustee who dies before the testator – s36(8)).

ii) Where a trustee remains outside the United Kingdom for more than 12 months (uninterrupted period: *Re Walker* [1901] 1 Ch 601).

iii) Where a trustee wants to retire from a part of or from all of the trusts.

iv) Where a trustee refuses to act (including a disclaimer).

v) Where a trustee is unfit to act (including a trustee who is bankrupt).

vi) Where a trustee is incapable of acting (not including bankruptcy).

vii) Where a trustee is an infant.

viii) Where a trustee has been removed under a power contained in the trust instrument. (This does not confer a power to remove a trustee.)

An appointment under s36 must be in writing but cannot be made by will.

Under s36(1) more than one trustee can be appointed to replace only one trustee, thus increasing the number of trustees. Trustees may also be appointed under s36(6) if no vacancy exists by the same persons and in the same way provided that no more than three trustees are already acting. The effect of an appointment under s36 is that the new trustee(s) are in the same position as if they had been appointed by the trust instrument: s36(7).

c) The court

The court can appoint new trustee(s) under the following provisions.

i) TA, s41(1): whenever it is expedient to appoint and inexpedient, too difficult or impracticable to do so without the assistance of the court. The provision can be used to appoint new trustee(s) in substitution for or in addition to existing trustee(s), if any.

ii) Its inherent jurisdiction. In view of the width of s41, this is rarely used unless a dispute exists and the trustee is to be removed against his will.

iii) TA, s54: where a mental patient is a trustee.

iv) Judicial Trustees Act 1896 and Public Trustee Act 1906.

The effect of an appointment is the same as that under s36 above.

In exercising its power of appointment, the court will follow certain principles laid down in *Re Tempest* (1866) LR 1 Ch App 485 – it will have regard to the wishes of the settlor; it will not appoint someone who is likely to prefer certain of the beneficiaries over others; it will consider whether the appointment will promote the execution of the trust, and in *Re Parsons* [1940] Ch 973, it will not appoint someone if there is a conflict between his duty and his interest.

The court will not use its powers to interfere with an appointment by a person in (a) or (b) above.

The Pensions Act 1995 provided the court with additional powers to appointment in relation to pension funds.

d) The beneficiaries

In theory, the trustees have a duty to consult the beneficiaries before appointing a new trustee. However, if they do not do so, the court will not interfere with the appointment. Sections 19 and 20 Trusts of Land and Appointment of Trustees Act 1996 have provided for some powers of appointment and removal of trustees by beneficiaries. This applies in relation to trusts of land. Section 11 adds a duty to consult with the beneficiaries on the part of the trustees.

Vesting of the trust property

In general, a conveyance or transfer by the old trustee(s) is necessary. If, however, the appointment is by deed, s40(1) TA provides that the trust property will automatically vest in the new trustee unless the property is of a type listed under s40(4) which identifies exceptions to the rule (mortgages, leases and shares). If the court appoints or if for some reason there are problems concerning vesting, the court has wide powers to make vesting orders under the TA.

Termination of trusteeship

This may occur in four ways.

Death

The trust estate and the trust powers (under s18(1) and s18(2) TA) devolve on the surviving trustee(s) or if none, on the personal representatives of the last surviving trustee.

Disclaimer

A trustee can disclaim at any time before acceptance of the office, but not after: *Re Shannon* [1942] Ch 311. Partial disclaimer is impossible: *Re Lister* [1926] Ch 149. Acceptance may be express or implied, and whether it will be implied will depend on the circumstances. It is now clearly established that any suggestion that one of several trustees cannot disclaim is incorrect: *Broomhead (JW) (Vic) Pty Ltd v J W Broomhead Pty Ltd* [1985] VR 891.

Retirement

This is possible in six ways.

a) Express power in trust instrument.

b) Under TA:

   i) s36 – a trustee can retire on appointment of a replacement;

   ii) s39 – a trustee can retire, in any event, if the trustees who will continue (not being less than two in number or a trust corporation) by deed consent to his retirement.

c) Under an order of the court.

The court can make such an order under s41 on the appointment of a new trustee, or under its inherent jurisdiction in an action to administer the trust.

d) By consent of the beneficiaries.

This is an application of the rule that it is a defence to an action for breach of trust that the beneficiaries (being sui juris) all consented to it.

e) By the beneficiaries in some cases, under the Trusts of Land and Appointment of Trustees Act 1996.

f) Payment into court.

This amounts to retirement to an extent although he remains a trustee for certain purposes.

Removal

This is possible in five ways.

a) Express power.

b) Under TA, s36 – if trustee falls within one of the eight situations.

c) Under TA, s41 – the court can do so when appointing a new trustee but will not do so if there is a dispute.

d) Under the court's inherent jurisdiction.

e) For pension funds, by the court, under the Pensions Act 1995.

This was done in *Letterstedt* v *Broers* (1884) 9 App Cas 371 and in *Clarke* v *Heathfield (No 2)* [1985] ICR 606.

13.3 Key case and statutes

* *Letterstedt* v *Broers* (1884) 9 App Cas 371
  Removal under the inherent jurisdiction of the court

* Trustee Act 1925

  * ss18, 36 and 41 – some methods to remove, replace or appoint trustees

  * s36 – power to replace or appoint

  * ss36, 39 and 63 – some methods of retirement

* Pensions Act 1995 – additional powers to appoint and remove

13.4 Questions and suggested solutions

QUESTION ONE

In what circumstances and by whom may a trustee of a personalty settlement be removed from his trusteeship?

University of LLB Examination
(for External Students) Law of Trusts June 1987 Q6(a)

General Comment

This is a very general question requiring a structured and concise answer in view of the time constraints.

Skeleton Solution

Introduction; when and by whom an appointment can be made under s36 – when the court will appoint under s41 and under its inherent jurisdiction.

Suggested Solution

A new trustee of personalty may be removed under the provisions of s36 or s41 Trustee Act (TA) 1925 or under the court's inherent jurisdiction. Section 36 is primarily concerned with the appointment of new trustees outside court but this can only be done where at the same time an existing trustee is departing from the trusts. The circumstances in which this section may be used are set out therein and they include a number of circumstances which are tantamount to removal. These are where the trustee has remained outside the United Kingdom for a continuous period of 12 months, where he refuses to act in the trusts, where he is incapable of acting or unfit to act, is an infant or is being removed under an express power in the trust instrument. Removal of a trustee under s36 can only be on the grounds specified in the section and the power to remove thereunder is vested in any person appointed to carry out appointments and removals under the trust instrument or the surviving or continuing trustees of the trust for the time being. Continuing trustees means those who will still be in the trusts after the removal has been made: see *Travis v Illingworth* (1865) 2 Drew & SM 344. In all circumstances s36 will require a new trustee to be appointed in place of the trustee being removed.

Under s41 TA 1925 the court has power to appoint a new trustee or trustees where it is 'inexpedient, difficult or impracticable' to do so without its assistance. This provision is primarily concerned with appointment but it also extends to cases of removal of trustees. This might occur where a trustee is, for example, incapable of acting in the trust and refuses to retire, the use of s36 could lead to problems and the court's assistance can be sought in such circumstances to remove and replace him: see *Re Woodgate* (1857) 5 WR 448. The court also has power to remove a trustee under its inherent jurisdiction. This will be used in instances where s41 is inapplicable as where the beneficiaries do not want the trustees to continue acting in the trusts as they have lost confidence in them. The court will consider whether the best interests of the beneficiaries are served by a removal here and, if necessary, effect one: see *Letterstedt* v *Broers* (1884) 9 App Cas 371.

QUESTION TWO

a) Is it necessary or useful for a new trustee to be appointed by deed rather than by writing under hand?

b) Tug and Tow are trustees of a personalty settlement. Tug has been continuously abroad for the past 14 months. Advise Tow whether it is necessary or advisable for a new trustee to be appointed in place of Tug and if so in what manner this can be done.

c) Can a trustee who retires ever be made liable for breaches of trust which take place after his retirement and if so, in what circumstances?

University of London LLB Examination
(for External Students) Law of Trusts June 1984 Q8

General Comment

An essay question divided into three related areas, this question simply requires the student to state the relevant rules. Part (c) requires consideration of liability for breach of trust after retirement (Chapter 20) and usefully illustrates how this topic may be introduced into a question primarily on appointment and retirement of trustees.

Skeleton Solution

a) Automatic vesting provisions under TA, s40(1) – appointment by deed, although not necessary, is advisable unless the trust property is of a type listed in s40(4).

b) Section 36 ground – trustee who has been outside the United Kingdom for a period greater than 12 months can be removed from office – another can be appointed in his place.

c) Exceptions to the general rule that a trustee will not remain liable after retirement (see Chapter 20).

Suggested Solution

a) Under s36(1) Trustee Act (TA) 1925 the appointment of a new trustee need only be in writing, a deed is not necessary. However, if only writing is used then it will only amount to a bare appointment and further steps will have to be taken to vest the trust property in the new trustee. This is implicit in s36(7) which deals with the effect of a s36 appointment providing that he has the same powers, authorities and discretions as the original trustees 'as well as before as after all the trust property

— 178 —

becomes ... vested in him'. To avoid the necessity of executing conveyances of property, etc to vest the trust property in the existing trustees and the new trustees an appointment of the trustees by deed is preferable. Under s40(1)(a) if a deed appointing a trustee contains a declaration that the trust property is to vest in him then it will vest in him on appointment together with the existing trustees without the need for any conveyance or assignments. Even if the deed of appointment contains no such declaration, then unless there is an express provision to the contrary, it will operate as if it did contain such a declaration: see s40(1)(b). However, these provisions are subject to s40(4) which requires an express conveyance where land belonging to the trust is mortgaged or is leasehold and the lease contains a covenant not to assign or let without licence or consent and where the company comprises stocks and shares. In these cases the automatic vesting by deed could have the effect of breaching covenants and other restrictions concerning the transfer of the property.

b) Under s36(1) Trustee Act (TA) 1925 a new trustee may be appointed in place of, inter alia, a trustee who has remained out of the United Kingdom for more than 12 months. As Tug has been continuously abroad it might be possible to remove him under this provision. But '12 months' here means an uninterrupted period of 12 months so in *Re Walker* [1901] 1 Ch 601 the power did not apply where the trustee had been in London for one week in the relevant period. If this provision is to be used it must be clear that Tug has at no time returned to the United Kingdom in the last 12 months. This seems to be the case as the word 'continuously' is used. However, if events prove this not to be so then there would be no other ground on which he could be safely removed under s36(1), it may then be necessary to ask the court to substitute a new trustee in his place under s41(1) TA 1925 on the ground that it is 'inexpedient, difficult or impracticable' to make an appointment out of court. This assumes that there are no special powers in the trust instrument to remove a trustee in these circumstances.

It may well be more expedient for Tow not to bother trying to have Tug removed as a trustee at all. As this trust is one of personalty there is no limit (practical considerations aside) on the maximum number of trustees. Contrast trusts of land where the maximum number of trustees is four: see s34 TA 1925. It may be inconvenient for Tug to remain as trustee if his signature on documents will be required and it will not be possible to obtain this easily. It is dangerous for Tug to remain as trustee if he is not already involved in the trust, as if Tow commits a breach of trust Tug may well be liable for failing to keep an adequate check on Tow's actions.

If Tow decides on Tug's removal as a trustee then the person given the power to nominate new trustees under the trust will have to undertake the task of removal and replacement. If there is no such person nominated Tow will have to exercise this power. He must remember that a mere removal of a trustee without more cannot be carried out under s36(1), a replacement must be made at the same time. Thus, he must chose a suitable person to act with him in the trusts. Further, he might well consider if he cannot carry on in the trusts by himself alone but this really depends on the circumstances of the trust.

c) A trustee will remain liable for his own breaches of trust even after his retirement: see *Dixon* v *Dixon* (1879) 9 Ch D 587, but he will not be liable for breaches which take place after his retirement, as a general rule. There are, however, some circumstances where he may well be held liable for breaches after his retirement. This might arise where he retired knowing that his co-trustees would commit a breach of trust after his retirement or simply retired in order to facilitate a breach of trust: see *Head* v *Gould* [1898] 2 Ch 250. Thus, if a trustee objected to a proposed course of action by his fellow trustees which amounted to a breach of trust he cannot escape the consequences of the breach by asking them to release him from the trust. He has a duty in such circumstances to seek an injunction to prevent the breach or if necessary, to seek their removal: see *Re Strahan* (1856) 8 De GM & G 291.

However, the mere fact that a breach of trust ensues shortly after a trustee retires is not enough, in itself, to hold him liable for that breach. In *Head* v *Gould* Kekewich J said it would not suffice to show that the breach was rendered easy by reason of his retirement. It had to be shown that the breach which took place was contemplated by the trustees before his retirement. Further, if the trustee intended a breach of trust after his retirement, proof of this alone will not suffice to render him liable unless that particular breach actually took place. Should a trustee be sued for breach of trust in these circumstances then the usual defences such as in ss61 and 62 TA 1925 and the limitation periods will be available to him.

Chapter 14

Trustees' Fiduciary Duties

14.1 Introduction

14.2 Key points

14.3 Key cases and statute

14.4 Questions and suggested solutions

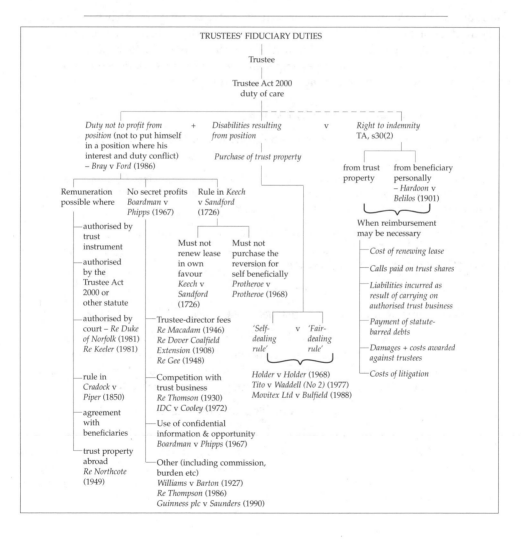

TRUSTEES' FIDUCIARY DUTIES

Trustee

Trustee Act 2000
duty of care

Duty not to profit from + *Disabilities resulting* v *Right to indemnity*
position (not to put himself *from position* TA, s30(2)
in a position where his
interest and duty conflict) *Purchase of trust property*
– *Bray* v *Ford* (1986)

from trust   from beneficiary
property   personally
– *Hardoon* v
Belilos (1901)

Remuneration   No secret profits   Rule in *Keech*
possible where   *Boardman* v   v *Sandford*
              Phipps (1967)   (1726)

When reimbursement
may be necessary

—authorised by
trust
instrument   Must not   Must not   — *Cost of renewing lease*
              renew lease   purchase the
—authorised   in own   reversion for   — *Calls paid on trust shares*
by the   favour   self beneficially
Trustee Act   *Keech* v   *Protheroe* v   — *Liabilities incurred as*
2000 or   *Sandford*   *Protheroe* (1968)   *result of carrying on*
other statute   (1726)   *authorised trust business*

—authorised by   —Trustee-director fees   — *Payment of statute-*
court – *Re Duke*   *Re Macadam* (1946)   'Self-   v   'Fair-   *barred debts*
of Norfolk (1981)   *Re Dover Coalfield*   dealing   dealing
Re Keeler (1981)   *Extension* (1908)   rule'   rule'   — *Damages + costs awarded*
              Re Gee (1948)   *against trustees*

—rule in   —Competition with   *Holder* v *Holder* (1968)   — *Costs of litigation*
Cradock v   trust business   *Tito* v *Waddell* (No 2) (1977)
Piper (1850)   *Re Thomson* (1930)   *Movitex Ltd* v *Bulfield* (1988)
              IDC v *Cooley* (1972)

—agreement
with   —Use of confidential
beneficiaries   information & opportunity
              Boardman v *Phipps* (1967)
—trust property
abroad   —Other (including commission,
Re Northcote   burden etc)
(1949)   *Williams* v *Barton* (1927)
              Re Thompson (1986)
              Guinness plc v *Saunders* (1990)

14.1 Introduction

The student often finds that this topic is one of the more interesting aspects of the law concerning trusteeship. The law is based on both common-law principles and statutory provision and certain aspects of the rules have been and continue to be the subject of debate, and are criticised for being too harsh on the trustee. The topic presents no real conceptual difficulties except perhaps when distinguishing between the 'self-dealing' and 'fair-dealing' rules concerning the situation where a trustee purchases trust property. The reverse aspect of the duties not to profit is that if a trustee does so he will be a constructive trustee of such profits (see Chapter 8).

14.2 Key points

The Trustee Act 2000, in s1, provides for a duty of care on the part of trustees in relation to their functions under this Act. The functions include investment and delegation. The duty operates in addition to other duties that they have. The level of care and skill that will be required will relate to any special knowledge or experience that a trustee has or purports to have, for example in relation to his profession.

Duty not to profit from position as trustee

This duty was expressly underlined by the court in *Bray* v *Ford* [1896] AC 44 by Lord Herschell:

> 'It is an inflexible rule of a Court of Equity that a person in a fiduciary position … is not, unless otherwise expressly provided, entitled to make a profit; he is not allowed to put himself in a position where his interest and duty conflict.'

This general duty can be broken down into three main 'sub-duties'.

Remuneration is possible in the following instances

a) He is authorised to do so by the trust instrument.

Any such clause will be strictly construed: *Re Chapple* (1884) 27 Ch D 584.

The Trustee Act 2000, in s29, provides for situations in which trustee renumeration has not been mentioned in the trust instrument. It permits reasonable renumeration so long as the trustees agree to this in writing. Such authorisation is not required for trust corporations. These systems do not apply to charitable trusts.

b) He is authorised to do so by a court order under its inherent jurisdiction.

In deciding whether to exercise its jurisdiction, the court must balance two aspects of the beneficiaries' interests. Clearly, it is in the beneficiaries' interest that trust expenses should be kept to a minimum. However, it is also in their interest that the trust should be well administered and this may require remuneration to be paid to the trustee(s): *Re Duke of Norfolk's Settlement Trusts* [1981] 3 All ER 220. It is clear from *Re Keeler's Settlement Trusts* [1981] 1 All ER 888 that the court can use its jurisdiction to authorise both future remuneration and the retention of past remuneration.

c) He is authorised to do so by other statutes.

The Judicial Trustees Act 1896 provides for a judicial trustee; and the Public Trustee Act 1906 allows the Public Trustee to charge fixed fees.

d) All the beneficiaries (who are all sui juris) authorise him to do so.

e) Trust property is situated abroad and the law of that country allows trustees to receive remuneration: *Re Northcote's Will Trusts* [1949] 1 All ER 442.

f) The rule in *Cradock* v *Piper* (1850) 1 Mac & G 664 applies.

The rule is limited to allowing a solicitor/trustee to charge his usual professional costs for work done for himself and his co-trustees in a court matter provided that his activities have not increased the expense. The rule does not apply to non-court work. In that situation, the solicitor/trustee can employ any of his partners provided that it would be proper to employ a solicitor and that the solicitor/trustee receives no benefit.

Duty not to receive secret profits

a) Trustee/director fees.

If the trustee becomes director of a company in which the trust has a substantial shareholding, he will, in general, be liable to account as constructive trustee for any salary received (provided that the trust instrument does not authorise him to retain it): *Re Macadam* [1946] Ch 73. The rule will not apply if the trustee/director became director before he became trustee: *Re Dover Coalfield Extension Ltd* [1908] 1 Ch 65, or if the trustee became director by using his own personal shareholding. This is because the trustee must have received the fee as a result of his position as trustee.

b) Competition with the trust business.

A trustee will be liable to account as constructive trustee for profits made by him from a business which competes with a business of the trust: *Industrial Development Consultants Ltd* v *Cooley* [1972] 1 WLR 443, provided that the businesses are in direct competition: *Re Thomson* [1930] 1 Ch 203.

c) Use of confidential information and opportunity derived from position as trustee.

The idea that confidential information constitutes trust property was introduced by *Boardman* v *Phipps* [1967] 2 AC 46 and has been criticised.

d) Other situations.

A trustee will be liable to account as constructive trustee for commission received by virtue of his office as in *Williams* v *Barton* [1927] 2 Ch 9. It appears from *Guinness plc* v *Saunders* [1990] 2 AC 663 and from *Re Thompson's Settlement* [1988] Ch 99 that if a trustee concurs in a transaction in which he has an interest which he fails to disclose, he will be liable for any profits thereby received.

The rule in Keech v Sandford

The rule is that if part of trust property comprises a lease, the trustee must not renew the lease for his own benefit even if the lessor has refused to renew it for the benefit of the trust. In *Protheroe* v *Protheroe* [1968] 1 WLR 519 the rule was applied to the purchase of the reversion; it was held that, in the same way, the trustee could not purchase the reversion for his own benefit.

Disabilities resulting from the trustee's position

The main disability is to be found in the general rule that a trustee cannot purchase trust property. The rule, however, is not an absolute one. A distinction has been drawn between the situation where a trustee purchases trust property from himself – the 'self-dealing rule' – and where he in fact purchases trust property from the beneficiaries – the 'fair-dealing rule': *Tito* v *Waddell (No 2)* [1977] Ch 106. If a trustee buys a beneficial interest in the trust from one of the beneficiaries, the onus is on the trustee to show that he did not exercise any undue influence; but if he can discharge this onus, the transaction is valid. If a trustee buys trust property, the transaction can always be set aside at the option of the beneficiaries even if the trustee paid the true market price. The trustee can seek the sanction of the court and in an exceptional case, as in *Holder* v *Holder* [1968] Ch 353, the court may ratify the transaction retrospectively. It was said in *Movitex Ltd* v *Bulfield* [1988] BCLC 104, that a trustee who does not satisfy the requirements of the 'fair-dealing' rule is guilty of a breach of his duty to the beneficiaries to act fairly but is not, strictly speaking, guilty of breach of trust.

Right to indemnity

Section 31(1) Trustee Act 2000 provides that a trustee can reimburse himself out of the trust for all expenses incurred in the execution of the trust (provided that they are properly incurred).

The trustee also has, in certain circumstances, a right of indemnity from the beneficiaries personally, as shown in *Hardoon* v *Belilos* [1901] AC 118.

14.3 Key cases and statute

* *Boardman* v *Phipps* [1967] 2 AC 46
  Confidential information – trust property – criticised

* *Re Duke of Norfolk's Settlement Trusts* [1981] 3 All ER 320
  Court authorisation – trustee renumeration

- *Re Macadam* [1946] Ch 73
  Trustee – duty – no secret profits

- Trustee Act 2000

  - s1 – duty of care; trustees; functions under this Act

  - s29 – provides for situations in which trustees remuneration will be possible

14.4 Questions and suggested solutions

QUESTION ONE

In what circumstances may a trustee be remunerated for his services to the trust?

University of London LLB Examination
(for External Students) Law of Trusts June 1991 Q6(a)

General Comment

This is a straightforward question on the law of trustee remuneration.

Skeleton Solution

Bray v *Ford* – trustee remuneration – the six exceptions.

Suggested Solution

It is a fundamental principle of the law of trusts that a trustee must not place himself in a position where his interest and duty conflict – Lord Hershell in *Bray* v *Ford* [1896] AC 44. One aspect of this principle was that a trustee was in general under a duty to act without remuneration. However, this did not mean that there was anything unlawful in a trustee being paid for his work: rather, it is that such remuneration will not be paid unless the trustee can point to some rule of law or trust provision that authorises such payment for work done. In general, a trustee may be remunerated for his services in the following situations.

a) Where there is an express remuneration clause in the trust instrument. Although such a clause will receive a strict interpretation (*Re Gee* [1948] Ch 284), such clauses are today common especially where it is the intention that professional trustees (eg a bank) be appointed.

b) The Trustee Act 2000, in s29, provides for situations in which trustee renumeration has not been mentioned in the trust instrument. It permits reasonable renumeration so long as the trustees agree to this in writing. Such authorisation is not required for trust corporations. These systems do not apply to charitable trusts.

c) A trustee may receive remuneration under a contract for services made with a beneficiary. However, the trustee must provide some new consideration for his remuneration as promising to fulfil the trust duties is not enough: he is already obliged to do this.

d) There are a number of ad hoc statutory provisions which provide that payment may be made to special kinds of trustee; eg s42 Trustee Act 1925 in respect of corporate trustees and the Judicial Trustees Act 1896.

e) A trustee is entitled to keep any remuneration received by virtue of his administering trust assets situated abroad, if such is received without his volition: *Re Northcote's Will Trusts* [1949] 1 All ER 442.

f) Under the rule in *Cradock* v *Piper* (1850) 1 Mac & G 664 a solicitor trustee is entitled to receive the normal profit-costs for his work done as solicitor to the trust on behalf of himself and his co-trustees in legal proceedings, provided that the costs are not more than would have been incurred by the trust if the solicitor had been acting only for his co-trustees and not himself.

g) A trustee may be awarded remuneration under the inherent jurisdiction of the court to ensure the smooth and efficient administration of the trust – *Re Duke of Norfolk's Settlement Trusts* [1981] 3 WLR 455. Remuneration will be ordered if it would be for the benefit of the administration of the trust and can include varying the remuneration actually authorised. The court must consider all factors, but especially the need to protect beneficiaries from unscrupulous trustees.

In all other cases, a trustee will be called to account as constructive trustee for any payment received by virtue of his position as trustee. He can, however, be reimbursed for expenses: s31(2) Trustee Act 2000 and *Hardoon* v *Belilos* [1901] AC 118.

QUESTION TWO

'The defendant in *Williams* v *Barton* is held to be a constructive trustee of a commission which he has earned in good faith yet the defendant in *Lister* v *Stubbs* is held not to be a constructive trustee of an illicitly obtained bribe … This inconsistency in the imposition of constructive trusts cannot be justified [and] it is therefore suggested that, despite the eminence of the members of the Court of Appeal who decided *Lister* v *Stubbs*, a constructive trust should have been imposed in that case.' (Oakley, *Constructive Trusts* (1987).)

Discuss.

University of London LLB Examination
(for External Students) Law of Trusts June 1994 Q8

General Comment

This question requires a precise knowledge of the two cases referred to and therefore should only be attempted by a candidate who is confident of the base of knowledge of those cases. This area is also theoretically complex and, therefore, must be approached logically and concisely.

Skeleton Solution

Distinguish between constructive trust and liability to account – *Lister & Co v Stubbs* analysed – *Williams* v *Barton* analysed – seeking a solution in the 'secret profits' cases.

Suggested Solution

There is a distinction between a constructive trust and a mere accountability to pay in concept. Under constructive trust principles, the strict code of rules relates to the responsibilities of trustees. Mere accountability to pay is the relationship between debtor and creditor.

The real difference is that under a constructive or express trust, a trustee is not permitted to make any profits from his position as a trustee: *Boardman* v *Phipps* [1967] 2 AC 46. If there is no trust found on the facts, then the individual will only be a creditor and therefore is able to make profits provided that the debt is repaid.

Mere accountability claims are subject to a six-year limitation period, after which the claim cannot made (Limitation Act 1980). Constructive trust claims have no such time limitation.

In *Lister & Co v Stubbs* (1890) 45 Ch D 1, Stubbs had an obligation to pay and account to Lister & Co. Lindley LJ found that it would be wrong for Stubbs to have to account to Lister & Co for any profits made. As a creditor, Stubbs is only required to repay the debt. As a trustee, he would have been required to account for any profits made. The difference is in the quality of the obligation owed.

It is possible for an individual to make a secret profit where the individual is only a creditor, provided that the debt is repaid. The nature of a fiduciary obligation is that no secret profits can be made by the trustee using the property that is subject to the trust. In *Williams* v *Barton* [1927] 2 Ch 9 there was an express trust relationship in which the trustee was also an agent in the Stock Exchange. The trustee made extra commission for his stockbroking firm at the instruction of the other trustees. The beneficiaries sued him to repossess these monies on the basis that there was a conflict of interests between the agent acting as a trustee and a stockbroker investing the trusts assets. It was held that the prohibition on trustees making profit from the trust is not confined simply to situations where those profits are made wrongly from trust property but also where the profits arise in the situation where the person making the profit also happens to be a trustee.

This was not a case which sought to exclude the ability of the trustees to contract with persons for remuneration for acting either as trustees or as agents of the trust.

Therefore, much of any explanation of the difference between *Lister & Co v Stubbs* and *Williams* v *Barton* must centre on the feelings of the court or the individual's status in dealing with the trust as a commercial third party. Deciding whether someone is a trustee or ought to be made a constructive trustee will depend on the court's sense of the ethical obligations which ought to be imposed on the individual, as much as any fine theoretical distinction. What is clear is that a trustee can never profit from the trust in a way that is not laid out in the trust deed.

The approach of the courts in secret profits-type cases is illustrated by the decision in *Boardman* v *Phipps* [1967] 2 AC 46. In that case, the House of Lords looked hard for a way in which the trustee, who had made secret profits while making the beneficiaries a very large amount of money which they would otherwise not have made, could still be rewarded for the work he had done. The House of Lords was here dealing with a situation in which there was an express trust and therefore the issue of constructive trusts did not arise. This illustrates the way in which the courts will look at the equity of the situation not only in terms of strict theoretical interests but also as to the rights which ought to be accorded to the parties on all the facts.

There is also the case of *Attorney-General's Reference (No 1 of 1985)* [1986] QB 491 where a secret profit was made by a public-house tenant who made money selling beer not bought from the brewery which owned his public house, but using the brewery's equipment to serve it. It was argued that the tenant must be a constructive trustee required to account for the secret profits to the brewery. However, this case was found to concern a debtor-creditor relationship and not a constructive trust. In that case, it was found undesirable for the criminal law to look to issues of constructive trusts law. As a result, it was found that appropriate criminal penalties should apply and that secret profits made should be repaid on a debtor-creditor relationship.

The requirement of a trustee to make good any profit is in line with the general rule that a trustee must not benefit from the trust to the detriment of the beneficiaries. With such an absolute rule, there are likely to be hard cases, such as *Williams* v *Barton* [1927] 2 Ch 9, where there appears to be justification for the trustee making some profit (as with *Boardman* v *Phipps*). There is also the point that, in the case of investment trusts, the beneficiaries are not always in the class of 'widows and orphans', that is people who require protection. However, in these instances the trustees can protect their ability to make profits in the trust agreement. The more important cases are the family-type trusts in which the professional trustees (lawyers and bankers) will be required to look after the financial interests of the beneficiaries under the trusts. As such they should only be entitled to make profits from their agreed professional fees.

The difference in the case of a debtor-creditor relationship is that there is no reason to impose a greater obligation on the creditor than the repayment of the debt. Therefore, the issue is whether, on any particular set of facts, the individual is possessed of a level of responsibility which enhances the quality of his or her obligations to the level of responsibility which equity will normally recognise and enforce.

QUESTION THREE

'A trustee should not profit from his position.'

Discuss how accurately this represents the law relating to either breach of fiduciary duty or remuneration of trustees.

University of London LLB Examination
(for External Students) Law of Trusts June 1996 Q5

General Comment

This question invites a discussion of the law and cases on the conflict of interest rule in relation to either breach of trustees' fiduciary duty or trustees' remuneration.

Skeleton Solution

Breach of fiduciary duty (either option)

Quotation does accurately represent the law, though there are certain limits to its application – *Keech* v *Sandford* – exceptions to the principle need to be appreciated.

Remuneration of trustees (or option)

Quotation provides some guidance but under modern conditions there are a number of very important exceptions – if the profit actually derives from the trusteeship (but only then) the trustee is accountable – consider the range of exceptions to the general rule.

Suggested Solution

Breach of fiduciary duty (either option)

It is a fundamental rule of equity that a trustee must not profit from his position: see, eg, *Vyse* v *Foster* (1874) LR HL 318. This is part of a wider rule that a trustee must not allow his duty and his interest to conflict: eg *Bray* v *Ford* [1896] AC 44; *Broughton* v *Broughton* (1855) 5 De GM & G 160. The rule does not depend on fraud or mala fides, but on the mere fact that a profit was made: *Regal (Hastings) Ltd* v *Gulliver* [1942] 1 All ER 378. In the American case of *Wormley* v *Wormley* (1823) 21 US 421 Johnson J said 'There are canons of the court of equity which have their foundation, not in the actual commission of fraud, but in that hallowed orison "lead us not into temptation" '. The rule is thus very much a recognition of the frailty of human nature. It is also there primarily to protect the beneficiaries.

The leading case on this point is *Keech* v *Sandford* (1726) Sel Cas t King 61, where the trustee of a lease of Romford Market applied for renewal, which was refused. The trustee then procured renewal for himself. Lord King LC said:

'I very well see, if a trustee, on the refusal to renew, might have a new lease to himself, few trust-estates would be renewed to cestuis que use; though I do not say there is a fraud in this case, yet he should rather have let it run out, than to have had the lease to himself.'

This illustrates the above points very clearly.

This case is difficult to reconcile with the later case of *Re Biss* [1903] 2 Ch 40, where a yearly tenant of a shop died intestate. The widow took out letters of administration and with her two adult children carried on the business. The landlord refused to renew the lease. Later one of the children obtained a renewal. The Court of Appeal held that the child would be allowed to keep the lease, because the landlord's refusal of a renewal to the widow had extinguished any hope of renewal to the estate. It seems that the rule in this case is that if the lessee can prove that he in no way abused his position or intercepted an advantage coming to the estate and is not guilty of any breach of faith, then he will be allowed to keep the lease. However, this is difficult to prove. It might be possible to regard *Re Biss* as an exception to the rule in *Keech* v *Sandford* (1726) Sel Cas t King 61, but there, too, the renewal had been refused.

On any view and in both cases the rule is applied that a trustee must not make a profit from his trusteeship. The difficulty in these cases is how it applies where the trustee obtains a benefit which has already been denied to the estate.

The rule is also applied in other situations. For example in *Williams* v *Barton* [1927] 2 Ch 9 a stockbroker trustee had his firm employed to value the trust securities and it was held that he was accountable. Equally, where trustees appoint themselves company directors using voting rights which are part of the trust property they are accountable for their directors fees: *Re Macadam* [1946] Ch 73. There are, however, a number of exceptions to this rule. One is if the shares which qualified the trustee for the directorship were trust property without more: *Re Dover Coalfield Extension Ltd* [1908] 1 Ch 65. Another is if the trustee would have been appointed even if the trust shares had been used to vote against the appointment: *Re Gee* [1948] Ch 284. A further exception is if for some other reason the remuneration came to him without his volition: *Re Northcote's Will Trusts* [1949] 1 All ER 442. There is finally an exception if the trust instrument authorises the trustee to retain this type of remuneration: *Re Llewellin's Will Trusts* [1949] Ch 225. Most modern trusts contain such a clause. Apart perhaps from the last exception, the rationale running through both this basic rule and all its exceptions is that if the profit actually derives from the trusteeship (but only then) the trustee is accountable.

It is therefore submitted that the quotation does accurately represent the law in respect of the fiduciary duties of trustees, though it perhaps needs some reinterpretation in the light of modern conditions.

Remuneration of trustees (or option)

It is a fundamental rule of equity that a trustee must not profit from his position: see, eg, *Vyse* v *Foster* (1874) LR HL 318. This is part of a wider rule that a trustee must not allow his duty and his interest to conflict: eg *Bray* v *Ford* [1896] AC 44; *Broughton* v *Broughton* (1855) 5 De GM & G 160. The rule does not depend on fraud or mala fides, but on the mere fact that a profit was made: *Regal (Hastings) Ltd* v *Gulliver* [1942] 1 All ER 378. In the American case of *Wormley* v *Wormley* (1823) 21 US 421 Johnson J said 'There are canons of the Court of equity which have their foundation, not in the actual commission of fraud, but in that hallowed orison "lead us not into temptation" '. The rule is thus very much a recognition of the frailty of human nature.

The leading case on this point is *Keech* v *Sandford* (1726) Sel Cas t King 61, where the trustee of a lease of Romford Market applied for renewal, which was refused. The trustee then procured renewal for himself. Lord King LC said:

> 'I very well see, if a trustee, on the refusal to renew, might have a new lease to himself, few trust-estates would be renewed to cestuis que use; though I do not say there is a fraud in this case, yet he should rather have let it run out, than to have had the lease to himself.'

This illustrates the above points very clearly.

When this rule is applied to trustees' remuneration, it manifests itself in the fact that a trustee must act gratuitously: eg *Robinson* v *Pett* (1734) 3 P Wms 132. Even where the trustees carry on a business which is required by the trust instrument, they are not normally allowed to be paid: eg *Brocksopp* v *Barnes* (1820) 5 Madd 90. Equally, a solicitor-trustee is not generally entitled to charge for professional work done: eg *Re Barber* (1886) 34 Ch D 77.

There are, however, exceptions to this rule. First, a trustee may be remunerated where the beneficiaries (being sui juris) agree: eg *Ayliffe* v *Murray* (1740) 2 Atk 58. Second, s29 Trustee Act 2000 provides for those situations in which trustee renumeration has not been mentioned in the trust instrument. The Act permits reasonable renumeration so long as the trustees agree to this in writing. Such authorisation is not required for trust corporations. These systems do not apply to charitable trusts. Third, they may be remunerated where there is a court order authorising the remuneration: eg *Re Keeler's Settlement Trusts* [1981] 1 All ER 888; *Re Duke of Norfolk's Settlement Trusts* [1981] 3 WLR 455. Fourth, the Public Trustee is given a statutory power to charge the fees fixed by the Treasury: s9 Public Trustee Act 1906. Fifth, the rule in *Cradock* v *Piper* (1850) 1 Mac & G 664 allows a solicitor-trustee to charge profit costs for acting as the solicitor to the trust in legal proceedings on behalf of himself and his co-trustees jointly. Finally, a trustee may be remunerated where there is authority in the trust instrument.

In practice nowadays it is very common for a trust instrument to allow professional trustees (such as solicitors and accountants) to be remunerated. Therefore in fact there are in practice a large number of exceptions to the rule that a trustee must not profit from his position. However, these are in many ways apparent exceptions, because the fundamental principle still holds good, that there must be no conflict of interest. Professional trustees under modern conditions are generally of great benefit to their trust because of the special expertise which they bring to the trust. They normally 'earn their keep' and the beneficiaries (who are after all the whole raison d'être of the trust) gain more from having professional trustees than they lose in paying their remuneration.

It is therefore submitted that the quotation does accurately represent the law in respect of the remuneration of trustees, though it perhaps needs some reinterpretation in the light of modern conditions.

QUESTION FOUR

'While it is of utmost importance that trustees should be strictly liable for breach of the "no-conflict" rule, the imposition of a constructive trust on the profits arising from any breach is justified only rarely.'

Discuss.

University of London LLB Examination
(for External Students) Law of Trusts June 1997 Q1

General Comment

This is an essay question. It requires a discussion of the relevant case law together with an argument based on it and on the quotation in the question. A good answer requires some original thought as well.

Skeleton Solution

Firstly, is the rule that a trustee's duty and interest must not conflict correct – issues raised include the frailty of human nature – not being led into temptation – is *Keech* v *Sandford* correct?

Secondly, should a constructive trust be imposed on the fruits of any breach of this rule as a matter of course or only rarely – issues raised include the effect which the honesty or otherwise of the trustee should have on the destination of the profit – whether a trustee should be remunerated for work actually done in good faith.

Suggested Solution

This quotation in essence supports the strict application of the rule against allowing a trustee's duty and a trustee's interest to conflict, while objecting to the imposition of a constructive trust on the profits which any trustee makes from a breach of that rule, except in very rare cases.

The quotation therefore falls into two parts and, likewise, needs to be examined in two parts.

It is submitted that it is essential that there be a strict rule of equity against allowing the interests and the duties of a trustee to conflict. The reason for this is simply the frailty of human nature. Human nature is such that it is impossible to expect ordinary people not to be led into temptation. If they are allowed to make a personal profit for themselves with impunity, while in a position of trust, there is automatically a very real danger that the interests of those whose interests they are supposed to be looking after

PRO TANTO
TO THAT EXTENT

(na) will suffer. Plainly that must not be allowed to
hap v (or in this case equity) to prevent that happening.

Thi siderable judicial support. In the American case of
Wo 21 Johnson J said 'There are canons of the Court of
Equity which have their foundation, not in the actual commission of fraud, but in that
hallowed orison "lead us not into temptation" '. This quotation makes it clear that
human nature is by its essence frail and for that reason the beneficiaries need
protection. Actual fraud does not have to be established.

The leading and perhaps fundamental English authority on this topic is the famous and
venerable case of *Keech v Sandford* (1726) Sel Cas t King 61. Here the trustee of a lease
of Romford Market applied for renewal. This was refused. The trustee then obtained
renewal for himself. Lord King LC:

> 'I very well see, if a trustee, on the refusal to renew, might have a new lease to himself,
> few trust-estates would be renewed to cestuis que use; though I do not say there is a fraud
> in this case, yet he should rather have let it run out, than to have had the lease to himself.'

The learnèd judge thus makes it clear again that the rationale behind the rule is to
protect the trust property from a trustee who is not necessary dishonest or fraudulent
but merely a normal human being.

It is submitted that this rule is necessary for the protection of beneficiaries. This is
particularly so since fraud is (and rightly so) difficult and onerous to prove.

The second limb of the quotation poses more difficult problems. The rationale behind
this part of the rule is clear. If one were to allow a trustee who had made a profit by a
breach of trust to retain that profit, then there would be no effective sanction to prevent
any trustee from committing any breach of trust. In many cases this must surely be
correct and pro tanto the quotation cannot therefore be supported. Therefore the
imposition of a constructive trust on the profits arising from a breach of trust can be
justified and justified very strongly. This must be particularly so where the trustees
have acted fraudulently or dishonestly. Indeed it is submitted that where the trustee
has acted dishonestly or fraudulently, there can be no justification for not imposing a
constructive trust on the profits. Are there any exceptions to this general proposition?

It is submitted that there are exceptions. Plainly all of these concern a situation where
the trustee has acted honestly. It might be possible to argue that there should be a
general exception for trustees who act honestly, but then this is the present position in
that the court is given a discretion to release a trustee who has acted honestly under s61
Trustee Act 1925.

That said, perhaps the main exception concerns the remuneration of trustees. There is
certainly an argument for saying that the present rule (namely no remuneration
without the sanction of the trust instrument, the court or all the beneficiaries being sui
juris) is too strict. Indeed the idea has already been mooted and it is being actively
considered that this rule should be modified, particularly in the case of professional

trustees, who are not usually willing to act gratis. The same is true of the rule that a trustee who uses trust shares to procure a directorship for himself is accountable for the profits: *Re Macadam* [1946] Ch 73. The counter arguments to this are firstly that these rules can be (and under modern drafting practice usually are) modified by the trust instrument, secondly that equity must provide default provisions and thirdly that the present state of the law represents realistic default provisions, which settlors are free to modify if they so choose.

Here, too, there is arguably a need for an escape route in cases of honesty. However, here too again there is such a provision already in place. In *Boardman* v *Phipps* [1967] 2 AC 46 the trustees had acquired all the remaining shares in a company in which the trust had a holding. They made use of information they had received in their capacity as trustees. The House of Lords held that the trustees were accountable for the profit which they personally had made. However, as they had acted honestly but mistakenly and in a manner which was highly beneficial to the trust, they would be generously rewarded for the work they had done. This is an important exception, because it ensures that honest trustees are remunerated for the benefits which they have conferred on the trust fund.

It is important to remember when discussing this topic that modern conditions (where professional trustees who insist on remuneration can be of immense benefit to trust funds) are very different from the conditions which prevailed in the days when the present rules of equity were laid down and trustees usually acted gratis as a matter of course. The Trustee Act 2000 also makes some provision for renumeration.

In conclusion, there are arguments on both sides as to whether the second limb of the quotation is or is not justified. It is submitted that in a number of cases the imposition of a constructive trust is not justified, but that there are more cases where it is justified than the quotation suggests.

QUESTION FIVE

Jude is the Chief Planning Officer for Wessex District Council. For years he has accepted money from various property developers to ensure that they received planning permission for their projects, which he has paid into a bank account at his local branch of Wesland Bank used exclusively for this purpose. Jude purchases a large house with money from the account, which he staffs with a large body of servants. On the strength of the account balance, Jude is able to get 'platinum' credit cards from three companies, each with a credit limit of £15,000.

Jude approaches his bank manager to open an account for one Tess Durbyfield, though he cannot produce proof of her identity or existence. Jude tells the manager that Tess is a Ruritranian refugee who is evading the authorities, that she is ill and cannot come into the bank, but that she needs a bank account to receive electronic fund transfers from abroad from relatives. The bank manager initially objects, but relents when Jude presents him with a case of Ruritranian sparkling wine as a token of Tess's appreciation. Jude then forges documentation to convince the Council finance office that he has hired the non-existent Tess as his personal assistant, and the Council transfers her wages monthly into the Tess Durbyfield account at the bank. Jude dissipates the funds in the account, withdrawing money using 'Tess's' cash machine card.

As Chief Planning Officer of Wessex, Jude procures information from the Chief Planning Officer in neighbouring Avonshire District about a large development there about to receive planning permission. Jude invests heavily in shares in the development company, and makes a profit of £100,000. He uses £10,000 of the money to pay off a loan with which he purchased his car, and dissipates the rest.

Both Jude's account and the Tess Durbyfield account are now empty, the credit limit of £15,000 has been reached on each of the three credit cards, and Jude owes £20,000 wages to his servants. His only significant assets are his car, worth £15,000, and the house, which is worth £500,000.

Discuss.

University of London LLB Examination
(for External Students) Law of Trusts June 1998 Q5

General Comment

This is a straightforward problem question about breach of fiduciary duty, tracing and accessory liability. Note that *Attorney-General of Hong Kong* v *Reid and Others* [1994] 1 AC 324 does not overrule *Lister & Co* v *Stubbs* (1890) 45 Ch D 1, the former case being a Privy Council case and thus only persuasive authority.

Skeleton Solution

Significance of proprietary claim – breach of fiduciary duty: *Attorney-General* v *Reid*; *Lister & Co* v *Stubbs* – credit cards – Tess Durbyfield account – liability of bank – *Baden Delvaux* categories – *Brinks Ltd* – backwards tracing into car – *Bishopsgate* v *Homan* – conclusion.

Suggested Solution

If the Council can establish that it has a proprietary claim under a constructive trust, the sums acquired from Jude's breach of fiduciary duty will be paid back in preference to any claim of Jude's unsecured creditors.

The abuse of his position as Chief Planning Officer is analogous to the breaches of Reid, Crown Counsel in Hong Kong, who abused his position by accepting bribes from criminals (*Attorney-General of Hong Kong* v *Reid and Others* [1994] 1 AC 324). The Attorney-General for Hong Kong, representing the Crown, sought to recover the property represented by the bribe on the ground that Reid was a fiduciary. Reid used the sums received to purchase property in New Zealand, which increased in value considerably. The Privy Council drew an analogy with a fiduciary who took a secret profit, and imposed a constructive trust on Reid, who had to account for the sums received. The Privy Council permitted the Hong Kong Government to trace into the New Zealand properties, and held that Reid must account for his profit, which was held on constructive trust for his principal (the Hong Kong Government). The opinion has been criticised, because it is argued from the principle 'equity looks on as done that which ought to be done', leading to the conclusion that the bribes were a debt owed to the principal. The imposition of the constructive trust also raised questions.

Nevertheless, although this is a Privy Council case and thus must be considered merely persuasive authority, it is likely that a future court would follow this rather than the English decision in *Lister & Co v Stubbs* (1890) 45 Ch D 1, where the Court of Appeal refused to declare a constructive trust of bribes, which would have enabled the principal to trace into the sums received by the defendant. The defendant had to repay the money received to his principal, but did not have to account for profits. Further, the principal was unable to trace into the property which now represented the bribes, whereas the Hong Government were permitted to trace into the three New Zealand properties purchased by Reid, including two purchased in the names of others.

The acquisition of the credit cards is a benefit deriving from his fiduciary position, but it carries no benefits in these circumstances for which Jude would be obliged to make full account.

With regard to the bank account opened in the name of Tess Durbyfield, the court may be prepared to find that the bank was put on notice that the account was in fact operated by Jude, because their enquiries were not answered satisfactorily. The gift of wine to the bank manager might be construed as a bribe, leaving us with the possibility of a constructive trust based on accessory liability. However, it was established in *Baden Delvaux v Société Générale* [1993] 1 WLR 509 that for a constructive trust to be established on the grounds of accessory liability, the constructive trustee must have either had actual knowledge, or have wilfully shut their eyes to the obvious, or have wilfully and recklessly failed to make such enquiries as an honest and reasonable man would make. The bank manager did make enquiries, and it is difficult to say with hindsight whether the answers received should have put him on enquiry. Would Tess's purported evasion of the authorities put the bank on notice of an entirely different fraudulent/illegal purpose? *Brinks Ltd v Abu-Saleh and Others (No 3)* [1996] CLC 133, established that the requisite knowledge must be of the fraud which was in fact being perpetrated. On the facts, it is doubtful whether the bank manager knew of the fraudulent receipt of wages into the account. The bank is therefore unlikely to be made a constructive trustee.

However, the wages paid into the account remain an unmixed fund representing Jude's second fraud on the Council, and tracing at common law should therefore be possible; unfortunately, in any event, there are no funds left in the bank account.

Jude's investment in the Avonshire development occured as a result of a use of information received by virtue of his fiduciary position as Chief Planning Officer, rendering him liable to account to his employer as a constructive trustee: see *Boardman v Phipps* [1967] 2 AC 46. His use of £10,000 to pay off the car loan could be 'backwards' traced into the car. Here, Jude had already acquired title to the car before he made the profit on the development. He mixed £10,000 of the constructive trust funds with his own repayments to pay off the loan. It was suggested in *Bishopsgate Investment Management Ltd (In Liquidation)* v *Homan and Others* [1994] 3 WLR 1270 that it was 'at least arguable' that there should be an equitable charge over the asset. If the court accepted this argument, the Council could regain £10,000 of the proceeds of sale of the car. Since the car itself is worth more than the sum originally paid (though its overall value is likely to have depreciated in the meantime), the court might divide the value of the car between the Council and the unsecured creditors in proportion to the car's original value and the £10,000 paid out of the bank account: see *Re Hallett's Estate* (1880) 13 Ch D 696. However, in *Re Tilley's Will Trusts* [1967] 2 All ER 303, it was suggested that the trust fund would receive back the full amount of the initial contribution.

Thus, following *Attorney-General of Hong Kong v Reid and Others* [1994] 1 AC 324, the Council could trace into the house which Jude acquired with the bribes, tracing at common law through his unmixed bank account. They will receive the full value of the property, or the property itself, because they have a proprietary claim. The Council would have no liability in respect of the credit cards, even though the credit was obtained because the bribes in the fund made Jude appear creditworthy.

There is nothing in the Tess Durbyfield account into which the Council can trace, but they can trace through at common law (as another unmixed fund) into the value of the car to the extent of the £10,000 paid to pay off the car loan.

The personal claims against Jude as a constructive trustee will be worthless unless Jude has other assets in his personal capacity which are not disclosed here, in which case the Council will rank as an unsecured creditor along with the credit card companies and Jude's employees.

Chapter 15

Powers of Investment

15.1   Introduction

15.2   Key points

15.3   Key statute

15.4   Question and suggested solution

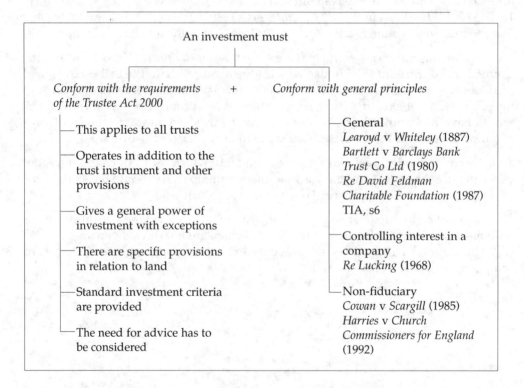

An investment must

Conform with the requirements   +   Conform with general principles
of the Trustee Act 2000

— This applies to all trusts

— Operates in addition to the
trust instrument and other
provisions

— Gives a general power of
investment with exceptions

— There are specific provisions
in relation to land

— Standard investment criteria
are provided

— The need for advice has to
be considered

— General
Learoyd v Whiteley (1887)
*Bartlett v Barclays Bank
Trust Co Ltd* (1980)
*Re David Feldman
Charitable Foundation* (1987)
TIA, s6

— Controlling interest in a
company
Re Lucking (1968)

— Non-fiduciary
Cowan v Scargill (1985)
*Harries v Church
Commissioners for England*
(1992)

15.1 Introduction

What a trustee's powers of investment are depends in part on the trust instrument, and the nature of the trust property. The law in this area has been greatly altered by the general power of investment introduced by the Trustee Act 2000.

15.2 Key points

General principles

Whilst these principles still provide a background, full regard must be given to the Trustee Act 2000. It was said in *Learoyd* v *Whiteley* (1887) 12 App Cas 727 that the trustee when investing trust property must not only act as a business man of ordinary prudence, but must also avoid all investments of a hazardous nature. In *Bartlett* v *Barclays Bank Trust Co Ltd* [1980] Ch 515, a distinction was drawn between a prudent degree of risk and hazard; the former would be acceptable. In accordance with trustees' fiduciary duties (see Chapter 14), a trustee will not be allowed to invest in anything in which he has a personal interest: *Re Feldman (David) Charitable Foundation* [1987] 58 OR (2d) 626.

Non-fiduciary considerations

The best interests of the beneficiaries are generally their financial interests. Thus, non-financial considerations must not be taken into account when deciding what to invest in, except in the exceptional situation when all the actual or potential beneficiaries are adults with very strict moral views on particular matters: *Cowan* v *Scargill* [1985] 3 WLR 501; see also *Harries and Others* v *Church Commissioners for England and Another* [1992] 1 WLR 1241 on the issue of ethical investments.

When the trust property includes a controlling interest in a company

The application of the general principles above to this particular situation was considered in *Re Lucking's Will Trusts* [1968] 1 WLR 866. It was said that the trustee should not simply consider the information he receives as shareholder, but should be, in some way, represented on the board. The extent of such representation will depend on the circumstances; he may be required to act as managing director or he may only need to ensure that he has a nominee on the board who can report back to him. This was interpreted more liberally in *Bartlett* v *Barclays Bank Trust Co Ltd* [1980] Ch 515 in which it was said that the trustee need not always be represented on the board if the circumstances did not require this; other methods of control over the company's affairs may be sufficient.

General power of investment

A general power of investment is provided by s3 Trustee Act (TA) 2000. Subject to some limitations, a trustee may make any kind of investment that he could make if he were absolutely entitled to the assets of the trust.

Investments in land

The general power of investment does not permit a trustee to make investments in land other than in loans secured on land. There are, however, powers to acquire land provided by s8 TA 2000. These include situations where this is for the purpose of an investment. A person invests in a loan secured on land if he has rights under any contract under which one person provides another with credit, and the obligation of the borrower to repay is secured on land.

Standard investment criteria

Section 4 TA 2000 provides for trustees to have regard to standard investment criteria, in the exercise of any power of investment. A trustee must from time to time review the investments of the trust and consider whether, having regard to the standard investment criteria, they should be varied. The standard investment criteria, in relation to a trust, are:

a) the suitability to the trust of investments of the same kind as any particular investment proposed to be made or retained and of that particular investment as an investment of that kind, and

b) the need for diversification of investments of the trust, in so far as is appropriate to the circumstances of the trust.

The need to take advice

Section 5 TA 2000 requires that advice on investments be obtained, except in circumstances where the trustee reasonably concludes that in all the circumstances it is unnecessary or inappropriate to do so. Thus normally before exercising any power of investment, a trustee must obtain and consider proper advice about the way in which, having regard to the standard investment criteria, the power should be exercised. Also, when reviewing the investments of the trust, a trustee must obtain and consider proper advice about whether, having regard to the standard investment criteria, the investments should be varied. Proper advice is the advice of a person who is reasonably believed by the trustee to be qualified to give it by his ability in, and practical experience of, financial and other matters relating to the proposed investment.

Application to all trusts

The general power of investment is in addition to powers conferred on trustees otherwise than by the TA 2000, but subject to any restriction or exclusion imposed by the trust instrument or by any enactment or any provision of subordinate legislation. These provisions apply to all trusts whether created before or after the Act's commencement in 2001.

In addition to following the general principles, a trustee must limit his investments to those authorised either by the trust instrument or by statutes, particularly the Trustee Act 2000.

In relation to these powers the trustee will, nevertheless, be subject to certain limitations. Although in *Re Harari's Settlement Trusts* [1949] 1 All ER 430 it was held that such a power would not be interpreted restrictively, the case of *Re Power's Will Trusts* [1947] Ch 572 (distinguishing *Re Wragg* [1919] 2 Ch 58) established that the word 'invest' implied a yield of income and, thus, non-income-producing property would not be permissible as an investment.

15.3 Key statute

* Trustee Act 2000

    * s3 – general power of investment

    * s4 – standard investment criteria; suitability; need for diversification

    * s5 – need for advice; when making or reviewing investments; unless unnecessary or inappropriate

    * s8 – this section provides a means to acquire land for purposes, including investment

15.4 Question and suggested solution

QUESTION ONE

Edgar and Frank are the trustees of a Trust Fund which is valued at £500,000. The trust funds are held on trust for Herbert for life, with remainder to his children in equal shares.

Edgar tells Frank that as Herbert is a confirmed teetotaller, does not smoke and is a pacifist, none of the trust funds should be invested in any company which is engaged in the alcohol or tobacco trade or the manufacture of armaments.

Advise Frank.

University of London LLB Examination
(for External Students) Law of Trusts June 1985 Q8(b)

General Comment

This question addresses the problem of whether trustees' personal views on particular investments can properly be taken into consideration, and requires an application of what was said in *Cowan* v *Scargill* [1985] 3 WLR 501 to the facts.

Skeleton Solution

Introduction identifying the issue; statement of general rule in *Cowan* v *Scargill* – exception to the rule and whether it can apply to the facts in question – conclusion.

Suggested Solution

The main issue in this problem is whether Edgar and Frank, as trustees, can refrain from exercising their investment powers so as to ensure that the trust funds are not invested in a company which either they or the beneficiaries object to on moral or social grounds. This problem was considered in *Cowan* v *Scargill* [1985] 3 WLR 501 where five trustees of a National Coal Board pension fund refused to assent to investments in, inter alia, any industry which competed with the coal industry in the provision of energy. Megarry V-C pointed out that trustees when making investments had a duty to put the interest of their beneficiaries first and the interests of the beneficiaries were normally their best financial interests. Thus, if a trustee failed to make an investment on moral or social grounds which was in the best financial interests of the beneficiaries his conduct would be open to criticism. Further, a trustee had to put his own personal views aside when making trustee investments. Edgar and Frank cannot allow their personal views to determine whether or not investments should be made in companies engaged in the alcohol or tobacco trades or the manufacture of armaments.

However, it may be that the beneficiaries would or do object to investments under the trust being made in certain types of industry. In *Cowan* v *Scargill* Megarry V-C pointed out that if the only actual or potential beneficiaries are all adults and they consider that, for example, investment in alcohol or tobacco trades is objectionable, then it could be concluded that such was not for their 'benefit'. 'Benefit' is construed widely and could include arrangements which worked to the financial disadvantage of a beneficiary where better financial returns could only be obtained from sources that the beneficiary considered evil. It is unlikely that this dicta could be applied here since the trust is for the benefit of Herbert and his children. The trustees could not consider Herbert's views alone when considering the matter of investment so that if his children had no particular objection to investment in alcohol or tobacco companies or armaments manufacture their duty would be to look to financial benefits. If Herbert's children are infants the position would be no different because the dicta in *Cowan* v *Scargill* on this point were limited to trusts where all the beneficiaries are adults. It therefore seems that Edgar and Frank should consider their duty as being to obtain the best financial return on the trust fund even if this means investing in industries which Herbert regards as objectionable. However, if they can find investments which are as good as those Herbert might object to they could purchase these because it would be difficult to hold such investments to criticism.

Chapter 16

Powers of Advancement and Maintenance

16.1   **Introduction**

16.2   **Key points**

16.3   **Key case and statute**

16.4   **Questions and suggested solutions**

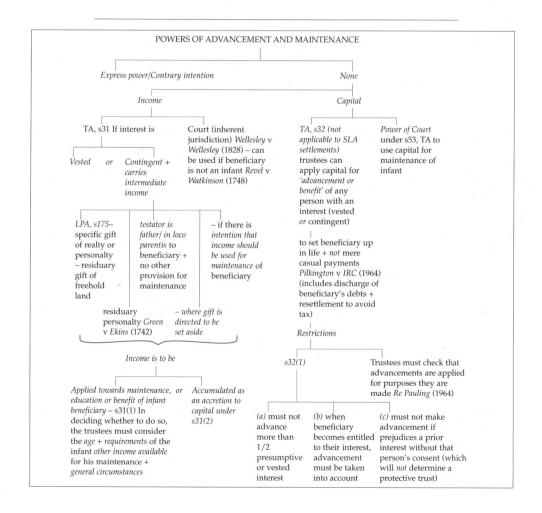

POWERS OF ADVANCEMENT AND MAINTENANCE

Express power/Contrary intention — *None*

Income — *Capital*

TA, s31 If interest is

Vested or *Contingent + carries intermediate income*

Court (inherent jurisdiction) *Wellesley* v *Wellesley* (1828) – can be used if beneficiary is not an infant *Revel* v *Watkinson* (1748)

TA, s32 (not applicable to SLA settlements) trustees can apply capital for *'advancement or benefit'* of any person with an interest (vested *or* contingent)

Power of Court under s53, TA to use capital for maintenance of infant

LPA, s175– specific gift of realty or personalty – residuary gift of freehold land

testator is father/ in loco parentis to beneficiary + no other provision for maintenance

– if there is intention that income should be used for maintenance of beneficiary

to set beneficiary up in life + *not* mere casual payments *Pilkington* v *IRC* (1964) (includes discharge of beneficiary's debts + resettlement to avoid tax)

residuary personalty *Green* v *Ekins* (1742)

– where gift is directed to be set aside

Income is to be

Applied towards maintenance, or education or benefit of infant beneficiary – s31(1) In deciding whether to do so, the trustees must consider the *age + requirements* of the infant *other income available* for his maintenance + *general circumstances*

Accumulated as an accretion to capital under s31(2)

Restrictions

s32(1)

(a) must not advance more than 1/2 presumptive or vested interest

(b) when beneficiary becomes entitled to their interest, advancement must be taken into account

(c) must not make advancement if prejudices a prior interest without that person's consent (which will *not* determine a protective trust)

Trustees must check that advancements are applied for purposes they are made *Re Pauling* (1964)

16.1 Introduction

The law on this topic is derived primarily from two sections of the Trustee Act (TA) 1925 which must be learnt. The aspect which students tend to have most difficulty with is the distinction between vested and contingent interests and the question of whether the latter carry intermediate income. The answer can be found by reference to a combination of common sense, statutory provisions and individual decisions and must be fully understood before s31 can be applied.

16.2 Key points

The Trustee Act 1925, ss31 and 32, give trustees wide powers to use income and capital for the maintenance of infant beneficiaries and for the advancement or benefit of all beneficiaries, provided that the trust instrument shows no contrary intention.

Income

In the absence of any express power, income under a trust can be used for the benefit of a beneficiary who is not in receipt of such income under TA 1925, s31 or under the court's inherent jurisdiction.

TA 1925, s31

The trustees can use the income for the 'maintenance, education or benefit' of an infant beneficiary under a trust whose interest carries 'intermediate income'. To the extent that it is not so used, the income must be accumulated and added to the capital under s31(2). If the infant dies before reaching the age of 18 or marrying, his estate will not be entitled to these accumulations even if his interest is vested: *Re Delamere's Settlement Trusts* [1984] 1 All ER 588. At the age of 18 or upon earlier marriage, the income (but not the accumulated income) will be paid to the beneficiary. The beneficiary becomes entitled to the accumulations when he becomes entitled to the capital.

a) 'Maintenance, education or benefit'

When deciding whether to use the income for such purposes, the trustees must consider the age and requirements of the infant, whether other income is available for his maintenance and the general circumstances of the case. If the discretion is exercised in good faith the court will not interfere: *Bryant* v *Hickley* [1894] 1 Ch 324.

b) 'Intermediate income'

A vested gift (eg 'To X') will always carry intermediate income. A contingent gift, however (eg 'To X on attaining 21') will not. It will carry intermediate income, and thus s31 will apply, in the following circumstances.

i) Under the Law of Property Act 1925, s175, a specific gift of realty or personalty or a residuary gift of freehold land will carry intermediate income.

ii) A gift of residuary personalty carries intermediate income: *Green* v *Ekins* (1742) 2 ALK 743.

iii) If the settlor is the father of or stands in loco parentis to the infant beneficiary and the contingency is attaining the age of 18 or earlier marriage, the gift will carry intermediate income.

iv) Where the gift is directed in the instrument to be set aside.

v) If the instrument shows an intention that the income should be used for the maintenance of an infant beneficiary: *Re Selby-Walker* [1949] 2 All ER 178.

Court's inherent jurisdiction

The court's inherent jurisdiction to allow income to be used for an infant's maintenance was underlined in *Wellesley* v *Wellesley* (1828) 2 Bli NS 124, and it was stated in *Revel* v *Watkinson* (1748) 1 Ves Sen 93 that the jurisdiction could also be used to grant maintenance when the beneficiary is not an infant.

Capital

In the absence of any express power, trust capital can be used for the benefit of a beneficiary who is not yet entitled to such capital under TA 1925, ss32 and 53.

TA 1925, s32

The trustees can apply the capital for the 'advancement or benefit of any person with an interest in it (vested or contingent). Section 32 does not apply to Settled Land Act 1925 settlements.

a) 'Advancement or benefit'

This means setting up the beneficiary in life: *Pilkington* v *IRC* [1964] AC 612, and includes the discharge of the beneficiary's debts and a resettlement of capital to avoid tax (although note the rules against perpetuities).

b) Restrictions of the power of advancement

   i) The trustees must ensure that the advancements are applied for the purposes for which they are made: *Re Pauling's Settlement Trusts (No 1)* [1964] Ch 303.

   ii) Section 32(1)(a): the trustees must not advance more than half of the beneficiary's presumptive or vested share or interest.

   iii) Section 32(1)(b): when the beneficiary becomes absolutely entitled to their interest the advancement must be taken into account.

   iv) Section 32(1)(c): an advancement must not be made if it prejudices a prior interest unless the person with such an interest gives consent to the advancement. If the life tenant under a protective trust gives consent, the protective trust will not be determined under s33 TA 1925.

TA 1925, s53

The court has power to order the use of capital for an infant's maintenance.

16.3 Key case and statute

- *Pilkington v IRC* [1964] AC 612
  Advancement or benefit – setting up the minor for life

- Trustee Act 1925

  - s31 – infant beneficiary; maintenance, education or benefit

  - s32 – apply the capital; advancement or benefit

  - s53 – power of the court; use of capital; benefit of a minor

16.4 Questions and suggested solutions

QUESTION ONE

Under the trusts of a settlement, a personalty fund worth £150,000 is held by the trustees upon trust for such of the settlor's grandchildren, Tom, Dick and Harriet, as attain the age of 25 in equal shares absolutely. Tom is now 25, Dick is 18 and Harriet is 13. Advise the trustees:

a) whether they may now distribute one-third of the capital of the trust fund to Tom;

b) whether they should distribute any, and if so what, trust income and to whom;

c) whether they may advance the sum of £25,000 out of capital to enable Dick to train for a commercial pilot's licence;

d) whether they may pay out of trust moneys the school fees of Harriet who is about to go to a boarding school.

University of London LLB Examination
(for External Students) Law of Trusts June 1987 Q3

General Comment

The main issues in this question are the provisions contained in ss31 and 32 of Trustee Act (TA) 1925, although a consideration of the rule in *Saunders v Vautier* (1841) is also necessary in the first part (see Chapter 18).

Skeleton Solution

a) Application of the rule in *Saunders v Vautier* to Tom and of the class-closing rules.

b) Consideration of the trust income as applied in accordance with TA 1925, s31 distinguishing present income and past accumulated income and in each case, taking each beneficiary in turn.

c) Whether the trustees can advance £25,000 to Dick depends on whether an application of TA 1925, s32 is possible.

d) The school fees may be able to be paid under either s31 or s32 and both must be considered.

Suggested Solution

a) The trustees may distribute one third of the capital to Tom, if he demands it, as he has now fulfilled the contingency of attaining 25 as imposed by the trust. Under the rule in *Saunders* v *Vautier* (1841) 4 Beav 115 a beneficiary of full age who has an absolute, vested and indefeasible interest in property may at any time, notwithstanding any direction to accumulate, demand his share. Tom's interest became indefeasible in one-third of the fund when he attained 25 but not before then because it was liable to be defeated if he died before 25: see *Berry* v *Green* [1938] AC 575. He may receive further capital in the future if other beneficiaries do not attain 25 as the gift is 'to such grandchildren as attain 25' in equal shares.

The distribution to Tom cannot be prevented by the fact that the other beneficiaries have not attained 25 as the gift is not contingent on all of them attaining that age. It will not be prevented by the nature of the property in the trust as this will have to be sold, if necessary, in order to pay him his share. Thus, for example, if the trust had control of a company which it would lose because Tom demanded his share, this could be used to stop him demanding that share: see *Re Weiner* [1956] 2 All ER 482 and *Lloyd's Bank plc* v *Duker* [1987] 3 All ER 193. The possibility of further grandchildren being born will not prevent distribution of one-third to Tom as the class of beneficiaries closed at the latest on Tom attaining 25.

b) The trust income has to be considered in two parts, the accumulated income from past years, if any, and income arising in the current financial year. The former is held by the trustees as an accretion to the capital of the property from which it arose and as one fund with this capital for all purposes: see s31(2)(iii) TA 1925. Thus, when Tom attained 25 he should have been given the accumulated income on his share together with the capital, if he exercised the rule in *Saunders* v *Vautier*. The accumulations on the shares of Dick and Harriet may not, as a general rule, be paid to them until they fulfil the contingency under s31(2). However, this general rule is subject to one exception in that the trustees may use the accumulated income for the maintenance of infant beneficiaries under s31 and this would allow them to maintain Harriet but not, of course, Dick as he is now 18.

Income arising in the current financial year should be paid over to Tom, should he wish the trust to continue in respect of his share, and to Dick, as it arises. When a beneficiary attains 18 then under s31(1)(ii) TA 1925 all the income on his share must be paid to him as it arises. The income on Harriet's share will have to be accumulated under s31 as she is unable to give a valid receipt therefore. The trustees may, however, use the whole or such part of it, as they in their absolute discretion think fit, for Harriet's maintenance, education or benefit under s31(1) TA 1925.

c) An advance of £25,000 to Dick to enable him to train for a commercial pilot's licence is possible under s32 TA 1925 provided the settlor has not excluded the power of advancement thereunder. The sum of £25,000 is however, the maximum advance that can be made to Dick as s32(1)(a) only permits total advancements of up to one-half of a beneficiary's presumptive share. If Dick has already received advancements from the trust for other purposes then these will have to be taken into account in deciding the maximum advance that can be made. When distribution of the fund eventually takes place the amount that is advanced to Dick will have to be brought into account as part of his share under s32(1)(b) TA 1925. In determining whether to advance the trustees will have a complete discretion but they are obliged to ensure that the purpose for which the advance is required is prudent and that the money is applied to it: see *Re Pauling's Settlement Trusts (No 1)* [1964] Ch 303.

d) Harriet's school fees may be paid by the trustees exercising their powers either under ss31 or 32 TA 1925. As Harriet is still an infant the power of maintenance is available in her case and this allows the trustees to apply the income on her share for, inter alia, her education. The trustees could use both current and accumulated income for this purpose. Alternatively the trustees could use the power of advancement under s32 and apply the capital of Harriet's share to pay her school fees. This would be necessary if the total income was insufficient to do so, which would appear to be unlikely in this case.

The limitations under s32 in making advancements would apply and once the trustees had advanced more than one-half of her presumptive share they would have to seek the approval of the court to make further advancements. It would appear more prudent to use s31 in this case in view of the size of Harriet's share.

QUESTION TWO

By her will, Celia, after appointing Tug and Tow to be her executors and trustees, left her residuary estate to them upon trust to divide it into two equal parts and to hold such parts upon the following trusts:

a) as to one part, upon trust to pay the income thereof to her husband, Henry, for life upon protective trusts and subject thereto upon trust for such of her children as should attain the age of 25;

b) as to the other part, upon trust in equal shares for such of her children as should be living when her youngest child attains the age of 18.

Celia died last year leaving Henry and three children surviving, Tom, Dick, and Harriet, aged three, 14 and 21.

Advise Tug and Tow:

a) whether they may have recourse to the trust income of either fund to pay school fees for Dick;

b) whether they may apply trust capital from either fund to enable Harriet to purchase a fast food franchise (a business in which she has five years' experience);

c) pending the attainment by Tom of the age of 18, what they should do with the income of fund (b);

d) in the event of Henry's bankruptcy, what they should do with the income of fund (a).

University of London LLB Examination
(for External Students) Law of Trusts June 1991 Q4

General Comment

Questions on a trustee's power of maintenance or advancement are often difficult and always involve complicated factual situations. They repay careful reading and should be attempted only if you have a clear understanding of the difference between the powers and a sure grasp of the concept of 'intermediate income'.

Skeleton Solution

Maintenance: s31 Trustee Act 1925 – protective trusts – prior interests – advancement: s32 Trustee Act 1925 – meaning of 'benefit'.

Suggested Solution

This problem concerns the trustees' powers of maintenance and advancement. The power of maintenance is the power to apply income of a trust fund for the maintenance, education or benefit of an infant beneficiary – the trustees being unable to give the infant his or her share of the income because the infant cannot give a valid receipt. The power of advancement is the power to give a beneficiary part of the capital sum under a trust which he or she would receive (but is not yet entitled to) should he or she fulfil the terms of the trust, eg, reach a specified age. In this case, as there is neither an express power of maintenance or advancement, the trustees' powers arise under ss31 and 32 Trustee Act (TA) 1925. These powers have not been expressly excluded.

a) *Dick's school fees*

The issue here is whether the trustees may exercise the statutory power of maintenance in Dick's favour by using part of the income from either part of the trust to pay his school fees. Clearly, there is a prima facie chance that the power may be exercisable as Dick is under 18 and he is one of the beneficiaries of both trusts. Again, there is no doubt that the proposed purpose is within s31 TA 1925 as this specifically authorises income to be paid for an infant beneficiary's 'maintenance, education or benefit'. However, the major problem is whether the income arising from Dick's share is actually available for his use. In other words, whether Dick is entitled to the income; sometimes expressed as 'whether the gift or trust carries the intermediate income'.

The income from part (a) of the trust is not available to Dick as there is a prior interest – the income is to be paid to Henry under the protective trust. There can be no maintenance from this part.

The income from part (b) may well be available for Dick's maintenance. There is not a deferred gift, but rather a gift contingent on a future event. The gift is therefore either or both (we are not told) a contingent residuary gift of realty and/or personalty. A contingent gift of residuary personalty carries all income earned from the testator's death until the beneficiary actually becomes entitled: *Re Adams* [1893] 1 Ch 329. Further, under s175 Law of Property Act 1925, contingent residuary gifts of freehold land (leasehold being personalty for these purposes) will carry the intermediate income. Thus there can be maintenance from this part.

b) The issue here is whether the trustees may exercise their power of advancement in Harriet's favour. This depends on whether s32 Trustee Act 1925 is applicable. Advancement is the payment of capital sums to a beneficiary before the time comes when he or she is actually entitled to the fund, although under s32 only half the capital sum due to Harriet can be paid by way of advancement. An immediate problem is whether the proposed use of the capital is for the 'advancement or benefit' of Harriet within s32, for if it is not, the power cannot be exercised. Following *Pilkington* v *IRC* [1964] AC 612, where a wide definition was given to 'advancement and benefit', it seems likely that the proposed use is within the section, especially since this is intended to be Harriet's career and is not speculative due to her previous experience. The question therefore arises whether the other conditions of s32 are fulfilled. Section 32 enables trustees to advance capital held on trust for any beneficiary (infant or adult), with any interest in the property (contingent, deferred or vested). Thus, the trustee may advance up to one half of the capital from part (b) of the fund to Harriet, even though she may never actually receive an interest (eg because she dies before the youngest child is 18). However, where there are prior interests – as with Henry's life interest under part (a) of the fund – the trustees may only advance capital if the person with the prior interest is of full age and gives his written consent s32(1)(c).

c) Pending the attainment of 18 by Tom, the youngest child, (at which date the trust property can be distributed) s31(2) Trustee Act 1925 directs that the residue of income from each beneficiary's share not applied for their maintenance while they are a minor should be accumulated by investment during the minority. This becomes available for their future maintenance.

d) The creation of the trust in part (a) of the fund is designed clearly to fall within s33 Trustee Act 1925. Under this section, if income is directed to be held on 'protective trusts' for the benefit of any person for their life (as here), then the income is held on the trusts set out in the section. This is simply a shorthand way of establishing an effective protective trust. In the event of a bankruptcy – which would terminate the life interest – the income is to be held on trust for the maintenance, support or benefit of all or any of the following: (i) the former life tenant (called the 'principal beneficiary' – Henry) and his spouse and issue or (ii) if the principal beneficiary has no spouse or issue, the principal beneficiary and the persons who would be entitled to the capital if the principal beneficiary were dead. All of Henry, Tom, Dick and Harriet are within (ii) and Henry and possibly the children if they are his issue are within (i).

Chapter 17

Delegation by Trustees

17.1   **Introduction**

17.2   **Key points**

17.3   **Key statutes**

17.4   **Question and suggested solution**

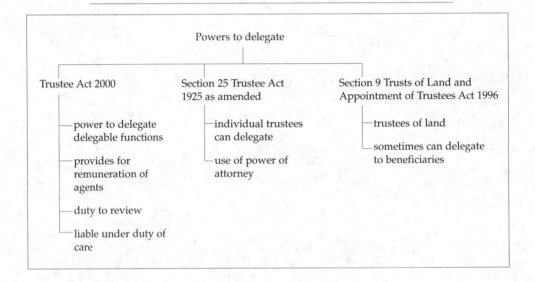

Powers to delegate

Trustee Act 2000

— power to delegate delegable functions

— provides for remuneration of agents

— duty to review

— liable under duty of care

Section 25 Trustee Act 1925 as amended

— individual trustees can delegate

— use of power of attorney

Section 9 Trusts of Land and Appointment of Trustees Act 1996

— trustees of land

— sometimes can delegate to beneficiaries

17.1 Introduction

This area has been completely transformed by the provisions in the Trustee Act 2000.

17.2 Key points

The general rule was that trustees were under a duty not to delegate the trust. The main exception to this, prior to 1925, was that delegation was possible in cases of legal and moral necessity: *Speight* v *Gaunt* (1883) 22 Ch D 727, which was interpreted in *Fry* v *Tapson* (1884) 28 Ch D 268 as meaning that agents could be employed whenever a prudent man of business would do so. The Trustee Act 1925 introduced far more extensive powers of delegation, and the Trustee Act 2000 has extended the possibilities of delegation.

a) The Trustee Act (TA) 2000 makes the following provisions for delegation by trustees. The Act also provides for the use of nominees and custodians as well as agents. The powers conferred by these provisions are in addition to powers conferred on trustees otherwise than by this Act, but subject to any restriction or exclusion imposed by the trust instrument or by any enactment or any provision of subordinate legislation. These provisions apply to all trusts, whether created before or after the commencement of the TA 2000 in 2001.

i) Section 11

Subject to exceptions, this section allows trustees to appoint an agent to exercise any or all of their delegable functions. For trusts other than a charitable trust, the trustees' delegable functions consist of any function other than: any function relating to whether or in what way any assets of the trust should be distributed; any power to decide whether any fees or other payment due to be made out of the trust funds should be made out of income or capital; any power to appoint a person to be a trustee of the trust; or any power conferred by any other enactment or the trust instrument which permits the trustees to delegate any of their functions or to appoint a person to act as a nominee or custodian.

ii) Section 12

This section states that the trustees can appoint each other as agents, but beneficiaries may not be used. The trustees may not authorise two (or more) persons to exercise the same function unless they are to exercise the function jointly.

iii) Section 14

This allows for remuneration of agents and also for the provision of terms of appointment. Certain terms can only be made use of where it is reasonably necessary to do so. The terms are: those permitting the agent to appoint a substitute; restricting the liability of the agent or his substitute to the trustees or any beneficiary; and permitting the agent to act in circumstances capable of giving rise to a conflict of interest.

iv) Section 15

Restrictions are imposed on the delegation of asset management functions.

v) Section 22

This section provides for the requirement of a review where agents, nominees and custodians are being used by trustees. Intervention must be resorted to when any review suggests that this is appropriate.

vi) Section 23

This states that a trustee is not liable for any act or default of the agent, nominee or custodian unless he has failed to comply with the duty of care applicable to him.

vii) Section 24

Where trustees exceed their powers this does not invalidate the authorisation or appointment.

b) Section 25 Trustee Act 1925: as amended by s5 Trustee Delegation Act 1999, by power of attorney an individual trustee can delegate.

The trustee remains personally liable for all defaults of or loss occasioned by his agent.

c) Section 9 Trusts of Land and Appointment of Trustees Act 1996 allows trustees of land to delegate to beneficiaries in certain circumstances.

17.3 Key statutes

- Trustee Act 2000 (generally) – power to delegate; delegatable functions

- Trustee Act as 1925, s25 (as amended) – power of attorney; allows individual trustees to delegate

- Trusts of Land and Appointment of Trustees Act 1996, s9 – delegation to beneficiaries; trusts of land

17.4 Question and suggested solution

QUESTION ONE

a) Explain the circumstances in which delegation by trustees is possible under the Trustee Act 2000.

b) To what extent are trustees liable for the actions of those to whom they delegate power under the Trustee Act 2000?

c) Explain the arrangements that trustees are able to make with regard to the terms of appointment when they delegate under the Trustee Act 2000.

d) Outline the statutory provisions, in addition to the Trustee Act 2000, that authorise delegation by trustees.

Written by the Author

General Comment

When the Trustee Act 2000 and the Trustee Delegation Act 1999 were introduced, this produced a situation in which rather straightforward accounts of the legislation were likely to be the main requirements in examination questions.

Skeleton Solution

a) The TA 2000 makes the following provisions: applies to all trusts – delegable functions – restrictions on the delegation of asset management functions – can appoint each other as agents but beneficiaries may not be used.

b) The main points on terms are: renumeration of agents – certain terms of appointment can only be made use of where it is reasonably necessary – substitutes, restricting the liability of the agent or his substitute to the trustees or any beneficiary – permitting the agent to act in circumstances capable of giving rise to a conflict of interest.

c) The main points to make are: duty of care – review – intervention.

d) The following statutes must be noted: s25 TA 1925, as amended by the TDA 1999 – Enduring Power of Attorney Act 1985 – 6 TDA 1999 – s9 Trusts of Land and Appointment of Trustees Act 1996 – s1 TDA 1999.

Suggested Solution

a) The Trustee Act (TA) 2000 makes the following provisions for delegation by trustees. The Act also provides for the use of nominees and custodians, as well as agents.

The powers conferred by these provisions are in addition to powers conferred on trustees otherwise than by this Act, but subject to any restriction or exclusion imposed by the trust instrument or by any enactment or any provision of subordinate legislation. These provisions apply to all trusts, whether created before or after the commencement of the TA 2000 in 2001. Section 11 TA 2000 states that subject to exceptions, the section allows trustees to appoint an agent to exercise any or all of their delegable functions. For trusts other than charitable trusts, the trustees' delegable functions consist of any function other than: any function relating to whether, or in what way, any assets of the trust should be distributed; any power to decide whether any fees or other payment due to be made out of the trust funds should be made out of income or capital; any power to appoint a person to be a trustee of the trust; or any power conferred by any other enactment or the trust instrument which permits the trustees to delegate any of their functions or to appoint a person to act as a nominee or custodian. By s15 TA 2000 restrictions are imposed on the delegation of asset management functions. Section 12 TA 2000 provides that the trustees can appoint each other as agents but beneficiaries may not be used. The trustees may not authorise two (or more) persons to exercise the same function unless they are to exercise the function jointly.

b) Section 14 TA 2000 allows for the remuneration of agents and also for the provision of terms of appointment. Certain terms can only be made use of where it is reasonably necessary to do so. The terms are: those permitting the agent to appoint a substitute; restricting the liability of the agent or his substitute to the trustees, or any beneficiary; and permitting the agent to act in circumstances capable of giving rise to a conflict of interest.

c) The main point to be made concerns s23 TA 2000. This states that a trustee is not liable for any act or default of the agent, nominee or custodian unless he has failed to comply with the duty of care applicable to him. Section 22 TA 2000 provides for the requirements of a review where agents, nominees and custodians are being used by trustees. Intervention must be resorted to when any review suggests that this is appropriate. Section 24 TA 2000 states that where trustees exceed their powers, this does not invalidate the authorisation or appointment.

d) The following are the more important of the possibilities. Section 25 of the TA 1925, as amended by the Trustee Delegation Act (TDA) 1999, allows delegation by individual trustees. This involves the use of a power of attorney. This is in relation to not just ministerial acts but also discretion in relation to, for example, investment decisions. Whether payment is possible under this provision is debatable. The appointment is for a maximum of a year. Written notice of the details of the power must be given within seven days to the other trustees. Failure to give notice does not affect the grant of the power. The Enduring Power of Attorney Act 1985 allows powers of attorney to be created which will survive any subsequent mental incapacity of the donor. Section 2(8) of the Enduring Power of Attorney Act 1985 provides that a power of attorney granted under s25 TA 1925 could not be an enduring power. The TDA 1999, in s6, repealed this in relation to powers created after the commencement of that Act. Thus an enduring power of attorney can be used to delegate functions under s25 TA 1925. As a result of s9 Trusts of Land and Appointment of Trustees Act 1996, delegation to beneficiaries by trustees, for any period, is possible for trusts of land. They have to use a power of attorney. The beneficiaries have to be of full age and beneficially entitled to an interest in possession in land. In deciding whether to delegate any of their functions, and, where the delegation is not irrevocable, in carrying out their obligations in relation to keeping the delegation under review, the duty of care under s1 TA 2000 applies. The power of attorney can be an enduring power of attorney. Finally, assistance is provided for co-ownership in relation to land by s1 TDA 1999. This section provides for extra powers and a way round restrictions that would otherwise exist.

Chapter 18

Miscellaneous Powers and Duties of Trustees

18.1   Introduction

18.2   Key points

18.3   Key case and statutes

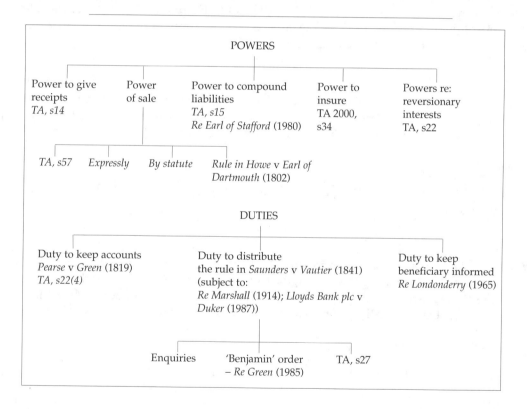

18.1   Introduction

This chapter groups together those powers and duties of trustees which the student must be aware of, but which do not justify chapters of their own, nor fit neatly into chapters concerning other topics. Questions involving these miscellaneous duties can be found in several other chapters in the second half of this book.

18.2 Key points

Powers

In addition to the powers which have already been considered in previous chapters, trustees have several more minor powers as follows.

Power of sale

Specific powers of sale can be found in various statutory provisions including the Settled Land Act 1925, the Law of Property Act 1925, the Trustee Act 1925 (s16), the Trustee Act 2000 (s4) and the Trusts of Land and Appointment of Trustees Act 1996 (s6). In addition, the trust instrument may itself empower the trustees to sell trust property and where the property in question is residuary personalty, a power may arise under the rule in *Howe* v *Dartmouth (Earl of)* (1802) 7 Ves 137. If a power of sale is not available in one of these ways, the trustees can, as a last resort, apply to the court for an order for sale under the Trustee Act (TA) 1925, s57.

Power to give receipts

Under TA 1925, s14 trustees are empowered to give receipts even if the trust instrument shows a contrary intention. If the receipt is for proceeds of sale of land, at least two trustees or a trust corporation are required to give a good receipt.

Power to insure

The TA 1925, s19 gives trustees power to insure trust property against such risks as they think fit.

Power to compound liabilities

The trustees have power to compound liabilities in respect of external disputes under TA 1925, s15. In exercising this power, the trustees must take into account the interests of the beneficiaries: *Re Stafford (Earl of)* [1980] Ch 28. They can act as they think expedient subject to the duty of care under s1 Trustee Act 2000.

Powers concerning reversionary interests

These are dealt with under TA 1925, s22.

Duties

Duty to distribute

Trustees are under a duty to distribute the trust property to those who are rightfully entitled to it. Under the rule in *Saunders* v *Vautier* (1841) 4 Beav 115, if all the beneficiaries are of full age and have between them an absolute vested interest in the trust property, they can call on the trustees to hand it over to them, and individual beneficiaries who satisfy the requirements can also do so to the extent of their share: *Berry v Green* [1938] AC 575. It was shown in the case of *Re Smith, Public Trustee v Aspinall* [1928] Ch 915 that the rule applies equally to discretionary trusts. Indeed, the only limitation on the rule is found in the nature of the trust property. Although in *Re Marshall* [1914] 1 Ch 192 it was underlined that the beneficiary has a right to have his share handed over to him, in *Lloyds Bank plc v Duker* [1987] 3 All ER 193, a beneficiary was not allowed to take his share of the trust property (a majority shareholding in a private company) in specie as to do so would unduly prejudice the other beneficiaries.

In order to distribute according to their duty, trustees should make enquiries, fulfil the requirements of TA 1925, s27 and, if a known beneficiary cannot be found, obtain a 'Benjamin' order from the court as was done in *Re Green's Will Trusts* [1985] 3 All ER 455.

Duty to keep accounts

This duty is imposed on trustees with a related duty to produce the accounts to the beneficiaries when asked to do so: *Pearse v Green* (1819) 1 Jac & W 135. The TA 1925, s22(4) allows the trustees to have the accounts audited should the circumstances require this.

Duty to keep the beneficiaries informed

It was held in *Re Londonderry's Settlement* [1965] Ch 918 that beneficiaries were entitled to inspect all trust documents containing information which they were entitled to know, although beneficiaries under a discretionary trust were not so entitled as far as confidential information concerning the exercise of the discretion was concerned.

18.3 Key case and statutes

* *Saunders v Vautier* (1841) 4 Beav 115
  Beneficiaries of full age and full entitlement – in agreement – can call for distribution

* Trustee Act 1925

  * s14 – power to give receipts

  * s22 – power re reversionary interests

  * s57 – power of sale

* Trustee Act 2000, s34 – power to insure

Chapter 19
Variation of Trusts

19.1   **Introduction**

19.2   **Key points**

19.3   **Key statutes**

19.4   **Questions and suggested solutions**

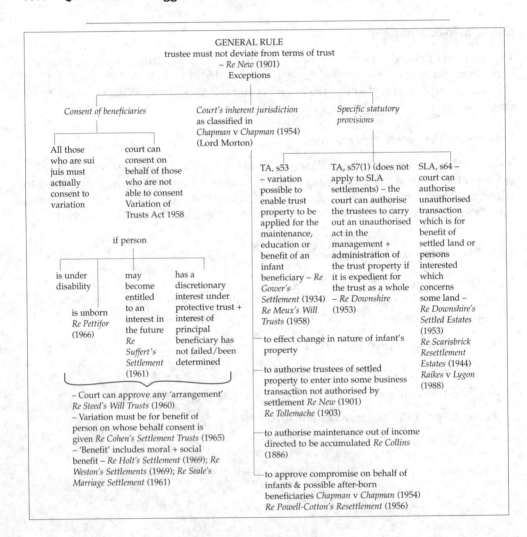

GENERAL RULE
trustee must not deviate from terms of trust
– *Re New* (1901)
Exceptions

Consent of beneficiaries

Court's inherent jurisdiction
as classified in
Chapman v *Chapman* (1954)
(Lord Morton)

Specific statutory provisions

All those who are sui juris must actually consent to variation

court can consent on behalf of those who are not able to consent Variation of Trusts Act 1958

if person

is under disability

is unborn
Re Pettifor (1966)

may become entitled to an interest in the future
Re Suffert's Settlement (1961)

has a discretionary interest under protective trust + interest of principal beneficiary has not failed/been determined

– Court can approve any 'arrangement' *Re Steed's Will Trusts* (1960)
– Variation must be for benefit of person on whose behalf consent is given *Re Cohen's Settlement Trusts* (1965)
– 'Benefit' includes moral + social benefit – *Re Holt's Settlement* (1969); *Re Weston's Settlements* (1969); *Re Seale's Marriage Settlement* (1961)

TA, s53 – variation possible to enable trust property to be applied for the maintenance, education or benefit of an infant beneficiary – *Re Gower's Settlement* (1934) *Re Meux's Will Trusts* (1958)

— to effect change in nature of infant's property

— to authorise trustees of settled property to enter into some business transaction not authorised by settlement *Re New* (1901) *Re Tollemache* (1903)

— to authorise maintenance out of income directed to be accumulated *Re Collins* (1886)

— to approve compromise on behalf of infants & possible after-born beneficiaries *Chapman* v *Chapman* (1954) *Re Powell-Cotton's Resettlement* (1956)

TA, s57(1) (does not apply to SLA settlements) – the court can authorise the trustees to carry out an unauthorised act in the management + administration of the trust property if it is expedient for the trust as a whole – *Re Downshire* (1953)

SLA, s64 – court can authorise unauthorised transaction which is for benefit of settled land or persons interested which concerns some land – *Re Downshire's Settled Estates* (1953) *Re Scarisbrick Resettlement Estates* (1944) *Raikes* v *Lygon* (1988)

19.1 Introduction

This topic is commonly considered by students to be a difficult one. Much of the difficulty stems from a misconception of the application of the most important statutory provision in this area – the Variation of Trusts Act 1958 – which, rather than giving the court a general power to authorise variations, is simply an aspect of the well established rule that variation is possible if all the beneficiaries consent. Once this idea is grasped, neither the Act itself, nor the other aspects of the topic should raise any serious problems.

19.2 Key points

The general rule is that variation of trusts is not possible due to the duty that trustees must not deviate from the terms of a trust: *Re New* [1901] 2 Ch 534. This rule is, however, subject to a number of important exceptions.

Statutory provisions

a) Trustee Act 1925, s53

Under this provision, the court can authorise variations which enable the transfer of trust property so that the capital or the income can be used for the maintenance, education or benefit of an infant beneficiary.

It was held in *Re Gower's Settlement* [1934] Ch 365 that the court could authorise a mortgage of trust property under s53, and in *Re Meux's Will Trusts* [1958] Ch 154 the sale of the whole of the beneficial interest was authorised where the proceeds were to be resettled on new trusts. It would not be so authorised if no resettlement was intended.

b) Trustee Act 1925, s57(1)

This section, which is not applicable to Settled Land Act (SLA) 1925 settlements, enables the court to authorise an otherwise unauthorised act involved in the management and administration of the trust, if it is expedient for the trust as a whole. It is clear that this provision in no way enables the alteration of beneficial interests: *Re Downshire* [1953] 2 WLR 94. An application under s57 could be made to authorise an investment outside the powers of the trustees.

c) Settled Land Act 1925, s64

This provision (which applies both to SLA 1925 settlements and to land held on trust for sale) allows the court to authorise any transaction affecting land which benefits either the settled land or the persons interested in it. Unlike the previous statutory provision in (b) above this section does allow the alteration of beneficial interest: *Re Downshire* [1953] 2 WLR 94.

In *Re Scarisbrick Resettlement Estates* [1944] Ch 229, trustees were authorised to sell capital to enable the continued and necessary occupation of the land, and in *Raikes* v *Lygon* [1988] 1 WLR 281, the use of some settled property to maintain other settled property was allowed despite the difference in potential beneficiaries under the two settlements.

d) The effect of the Trusts of Land and Appointment of Trustees Act 1996 is that trustees of land will have the powers of an absolute owner: s6. Under the Act change also takes place in relation to (c) above. Whilst no new strict settlements can be created, old ones can be continued. The trust for sale will cease to exist and land will for the future be held on a trust of land.

The court's inherent jurisdiction

The court will authorise variations of trusts under its inherent jurisdiction in limited circumstances, as classified by Lord Morton in *Chapman* v *Chapman* [1954] AC 429.

a) The court can authorise changes in the nature of an infant's property.

This head was relevant in the light of pre-1926 law and is no longer of importance.

b) The court can authorise transactions which are unauthorised by the settlement.

This head was previously underlined in *Re New* [1901] 2 Ch 534 in which it was said that authority would be given when such a transaction is desirable for the benefit of the estate and of all the beneficiaries. This flexible approach as applied in *Re New* was considered in *Re Tollemache* [1903] 1 Ch 955 in which *Re New* was described as the 'high-water mark' of the court's inherent jurisdiction to vary trusts. This head does not enable the court to authorise the alteration of beneficial interests.

c) The court can authorise maintenance out of income which was directed to be accumulated.

This was done in *Re Collins* (1886) 32 Ch D 229.

d) The court can approve a compromise on behalf of infants and of possible after-born beneficiaries.

This is possible only where dispute existed as to beneficial interests: *Chapman* v *Chapman* [1954] AC 429 and *Re Powell-Cotton's Resettlement* [1956] 1 All ER 60 and such a variation would clearly involve the alteration of beneficial interests.

Consent of the beneficiaries

It is generally accepted that consent of all beneficiaries (provided they are sui juris) is a defence to any breach of trust, including a breach of the duty not to deviate from the terms of the trust. A problem arises when the beneficiaries are not, for some reason, in a position to consent. In this situation, the court may be able to consent on those beneficiaries' behalf under the Variation of Trusts Act 1958. (Those beneficiaries who are in a position to consent must still do so.)

Under the Variation of Trusts Act 1958, s1, the court can approve any 'arrangement' varying the trust on behalf of, and provided that it is for the 'benefit' of, any of the following persons.

a) Persons under a disability – in particular, infants (s1(1)(a)).

b) Persons who may become entitled to an interest in the future (s1(1)(b)).

   If a person already has an interest, albeit contingent, s1(1)(b) will not apply: *Re Suffert's Settlement* [1961] Ch 1, and the beneficiary in question must themself actually consent.

c) Persons unborn (s1(1)(c)).

   If there is no possibility of a person ever being born – for example, if the class of beneficiaries is children of a woman who is beyond child-bearing age as in *Re Pettifor's Will Trusts* [1966] Ch 257 – an application under s1(1)(c) is inappropriate and unnecessary.

d) Persons with a discretionary interest under a protective trust which has not been determined (s1(1)(d)). In this case the variation need not be for the benefit of the person concerned. It is this that will prevail rather than the view of the settlor. This was seen in *Goulding* v *James* [1997] 2 All ER 239.

The word 'arrangement' was intended to be a wide and flexible one, and thus a proposal will qualify as an 'arrangement' unless it studies at the root of the settlor's intention – *Re Steed's Will Trusts* [1960] Ch 407.

The proposed variation must be for the benefit of the person on whose behalf the court's approval is sought: *Re Cohen's Settlement Trusts* [1965] 3 All ER 139.

The term 'benefit' includes moral and social benefit: *Re Holt's Settlement* [1969] 1 Ch 100. Whether tax advantages will qualify as a 'benefit' depends on whether they are the primary reason for the proposed variation. If they are, they will not so qualify and the variation will not be allowed: *Re Weston's Settlements* [1969] 1 Ch 223; if the advantages are simply incidental to the primary purpose of the trust, the variation will be allowed: *Re Seale's Marriage Settlement* [1961] Ch 574.

19.3 Key statutes

- Settled Land Act 1925, s64 – court order; variation; includes beneficial interests

- Trustee Act 1925

  - s53 – court order; variation; infant beneficiary

  - s57 – where expedient; unauthorised acts allowed

- Trusts of Land and Appointment of Trustees Act 1996, s6 – trustees of land; powers of absolute owner

- Variation of Trusts Act 1958, s1 – system of court consent to variation; disability; future interest; protective trust

19.4 Questions and suggested solutions

QUESTION ONE

Is there, and if so, should there be a difference between the formality requirements of the following:

a) a declaration of a bare sub-trust and other sub-trusts;

b) a disclaimer at the outset of a beneficial interest under a trust and a surrender of an existing beneficial interest under a trust;

c) a direction to trustees to transfer the legal title in trust property to X, and a direction to trustees to transfer the legal title in trust property to Y on trust for X;

d) a declaration of a trust of land and a declaration of a trust of personalty?

University of London LLB Examination
(for External Students) Law of Trusts June 1997 Q7

General Comment

This is a problem question concerning the need (or otherwise) for writing on certain dispositions.

Skeleton Solution

a) Declarations of bare sub-trusts need to be and should be in writing – where the sub-trust is not a bare trust of personalty, however, writing is arguably not needed.

b) A subsequent surrender of a beneficial interest certainly needs to be in writing – an initial disclaimer does not need to be in writing.

c) The actual transfer of the legal title has to be by the appropriate formality – how the direction is done only matters if it could be used to transfer the equitable interest, in which case it needs to be in writing.

d) A declaration of trust of land does need to be in writing – a declaration of trust of personalty does not.

Suggested Solution

a) In practice most trusts are created by a deed. Among other advantages, this means that any requirement for writing is automatically satisfied.

The requirement for writing is laid down by s53 Law of Property Act 1925. Subsection (1)(a) requires writing for the creation or disposal of any interest in land. Subsection (1)(b) requires any declaration of trust relating to land to be evidenced in writing. Subsection (1)(c) requires the transfer of any subsisting equitable interest or trust to be in writing.

The rationale behind these rules is to prevent fraud. That being so, the courts have been careful not to allow the absence of writing to be used as an engine for fraud: eg *Bannister* v *Bannister* [1948] 2 All ER 133.

A declaration of a bare sub-trust must in almost every case (if not every case) constitute the disposition of an equitable interest, so that it will have to be in writing under s53(1)(c). If, for example, T holds on trust for A who declares that he holds on bare trust for B, then arguably writing is needed because A drops out of the picture leaving T holding on bare trust for B, so that A is disposing of his equitable interest to B within s53(1)(c): *Grainge* v *Wilberforce* (1889) 5 TLR 436; *Re Lashmar* [1891] 1 Ch 258. If, however, the sub-trust is a true sub-trust and leaves A with duties as a sub-trustee (eg for B for life with remainder to C), then there is arguably no disposition of an equitable interest and thus no need for writing if the trust concerns personalty: *Onslow* v *Wallis* (1849) 1 Mac & G 506. If land is involved the creation of the sub-trust will, however, need to be evidenced in writing under s53(1)(b).

There can thus be a difference between a declaration of a bare sub-trust and and other type of sub-trust. It is submitted, however, that there is no logical reason why there should be any difference.

b) It is submitted that an initial disclaimer by a beneficiary does not need to be in writing, because it is not a disposition of an equitable interest within s53(1)(c) – rather it is simply declining to accept a beneficial interest. It 'operates by way of avoidance and not by way of disposition': *Re Paradise Motor Co Ltd* [1968] 1 WLR 1125.

A subsequent surrender of a beneficiary interest must clearly be in writing, since it is unquestionably a disposition of an equitable interest. It has been argued that a surrender takes effect by way of extinguishment of the pre-existing equitable interest and therefore is not a disposition. It is submitted, though, that the surrender in fact disposes of the interest to the person to whom it is surrendered.

Thus there probably is a difference between an initial disclaimer and a subsequent surrender. It is submitted that again there is no logical reason why there should be any such difference.

c) A direction by the beneficial owner of property to the trustees to hold that trust property on trust for someone else does have to be in writing: *Grey* v *IRC* [1960] AC 1. However, a transfer of the legal ownership (which carries the beneficial interest with it) as distinct from a transfer of the beneficial interest by itself, which is made by the trustee at the instigation of the beneficiary, does not have to be in writing: *Vandervell* v *IRC* [1967] 2 AC 291.

Here in both cases we are concerned with the transfer of the legal title in property. The transfer of the legal title itself would have to be done by the method appropriate to the nature of the property (eg transfer of shares and transfer or conveyance of land). Unless and until this is done the direction will have no effect on the legal title. Nor will it (of itself) give rise to any right on the part of the recipient to enforce the transfer of the legal title, because there is no specifically enforceable contract for transfer. Nor will the direction alone affect the equitable interest because of s53(1)(c). Once the transfer of the legal title had been put into effect, it is submitted that the direction would probably be otiose. Presumably what is envisaged here is a *Saunders* v *Vautier* (1841) 4 Beav 115 situation. If so, the transfer of the legal title to X would carry the beneficial ownership with it under *Vandervell* v *IRC* [1967] 2 AC 291. The transfer to Y on trust for X is more complicated. Arguably the transfer of the legal title carries with it the beneficial ownership within *Vandervell* v *IRC*, and *Grey* v *IRC* [1960] AC 1 is distinguishable. Thus the trust of personalty could be created without writing, though if the trust were of realty writng would be needed under s53(1)(b). However, depending on the status quo before the direction, it might be arguable that there is a transfer of the equitable interest which requires writing within s53(1)(c). If the trust for X commenced after the transfer the legal title to Y, then the transfer of the equitable interest would certainly need to be in writing to satisfy s53(1)(c): *Grey* v *IRC*.

Thus there is some doubt as to whether or not there is any difference between the formality requirements. It is submitted that if there is, this is anomalous and could profitably be removed.

d) A declaration of trust of land does have to be in writing: s53(1)(b). A declaration of trust of personalty, on the other hand, does not: *Benbow* v *Townsend* (1833) 1 My & K 596.

Here, therefore, there is a clear difference in the formalities required. It is certainly possible to argue that this distinction is outdated under modern conditions, but it is submitted that on balance the distinction is justified since, even under modern conditions, land is a more complex commodity and dealings in land need to be approached in a more serious fashion than those of mere personalty.

QUESTION TWO

'On the whole, settlors are better advised to give their trustees power to vary the beneficial interests in a trust than to leave the matter to the vagaries of *Saunders* v *Vautier* and Variation of Trusts Act applications.'

Discuss.

University of London LLB Examination
(for External Students) Law of Trusts June 1995 Q3

General Comment

This is a general essay question which provides scope for the candidate to discuss the range of trust powers in the light of *Saunders* v *Vautier* (1841) 4 Beav 115 and the Variation of Trusts Act 1958. Clearly, there is a requirement for knowledge of these two general aspects of trusts' law, but there is also room for a careful, common-sense discussion of the drafting of trust documents.

Skeleton Solution

Consider the scope of *Saunders* v *Vautier* powers – consider the use of the 1958 Act – apply each to examples in the case law – conclusion.

Suggested Solution

There is a need for settlors to focus on flexible powers for trustees, provided that the powers given to the trustees are justiciable, rather than to leave it to the courts, or the beneficiaries themselves, to control the application of trust property.

The matter depends upon the settlor's purpose and confidence in the trustees. The *Saunders* v *Vautier* (1841) 4 Beav 115 principle provides that the full set of vested beneficiaries under a settlement, acting together, can call for the trust property to be delivered to them, and can then distribute the property or deal with it as they agree to act. In the case of *Re Bowes* (1896) 1 Ch 507, for example, the application of trust property for the maintenance and planting of trees was held to be an unimportant purpose compared to the needs of the beneficiaries to that property.

In those circumstances there was a need for the settlor's intention to be overridden. This approach is deeply interventionist on the part of the courts, but perhaps it does achieve a more useful result for the beneficiaries. Therefore, there may be circumstances in which circumventing the wishes of the settlor is a useful power for the trustees and beneficiaries.

The purpose behind the Variation of Trusts Act 1958 is aimed primarily at legally unqualified or unadvised settlors who make settlements which are either unlawful, unfortunate or commercially inefficient. For example, a change in tax law may mean that a lay settlor who is not properly advised might create a settlement which attracts a higher rate of tax than another form of settlement which might achieve substantially similar results. The advantage of the Variation of Trusts Act 1958 is that it gives power to the trustees to alter the terms of the trust to benefit the beneficiaries.

The Variation of Trusts Act 1958 enables the court to approve a variation of the trust on behalf of a person having a direct or indirect interest in the trust, or on behalf of a person who may become interested in the subject matter of the trust. The importance of this statute is that, in the wake of the decision in *Re Holt's Settlement* [1969] 1 Ch 100 and the judgment of Megarry J, the 1958 Act ousts s53(1)(c) Law of Property Act 1925 and the risk of making a disposition of an equitable interest otherwise than by writing, because the court is empowered to alter the terms of the trust without the need for s53(1)(c) formalities.

The issue is, therefore, twofold. On one hand, it is possible that trustees might alter trusts in terms which would not be sanctioned by a court if they were presented to it. Therefore, if a trust provided broad powers for trustees to alter the terms of the trust, it is possible that some beneficiaries will be preferred rather than others, or that the trustees may fail to present the best possible solution where they act without proper advice. Where the Variation of Trusts Act 1958 or the *Saunders* v *Vautier* (1841) 4 Beav 115 mechanisms are used, the court has the ability to oversee the use of the power by the trustees.

On the other hand, requiring the trustees to go to court to have the terms of the trust altered does require an amount of trust funds being spent in seeking legal advice and representation to have the alteration carried out. In many cases there will be no complicated legal points involved, no tax ramifications caused by the alteration, and no beneficiaries seeking to object to the variation. In such cases, the expense would be difficult to justify.

Therefore, the answer to the question posed will depend upon the circumstances in which the trust is created. The settlor should be encouraged to promote certainty in the drafting of the trusts, and to reduce the stress and expense that would be required by litigation to give full effect to the settlement. Therefore, giving the trustees fiduciary powers to alter the trusts (rather than personal powers) does reduce cost while maximising flexibility. It remains open to the beneficiaries who are discontented with the variation to commence litigation to challenge the exercise of the fiduciary power.

QUESTION THREE

a) In what circumstances, if any, may the administration of an English trust be transferred abroad (in the sense of the trust fund being invested in overseas investments and the trustees being non-UK residents)?

b) Under the terms of a settlement, investments worth £500,000 are held upon trust to hold the income on protective trusts for Mary during her life and subject thereto for such of her children as attain the age of 21 in equal shares.

Mary is a widow aged 50 and has three children aged 18, 20 and 23. Mary and her children are all agreed that they would like to terminate the trust and divide the investments amongst themselves in agreed shares.

Consider whether this may be done (i) without an application to the court, and (ii) by making such an application.

University of London LLB Examination
(for External Students) Law of Trusts June 1991 Q8

General Comment

This is quite a technical question, on the edge of the syllabus and probably would not be attempted by many students. It is quite straightforward in itself and does involve some of the more familiar Variation of Trusts Act 1958 problems.

Skeleton Solution

a) Variation of Trusts Act 1958 – adult beneficiaries – infant beneficiaries.

b) Meaning of 'benefit' – tax saving – *Re Weston*.

Suggested Solution

a) There are various reasons why the trustees of an English trust may wish the investment funds of the trust to be transferred abroad and the management of the trust be placed in the hands of foreign trustees. The most obvious is, of course, that the beneficiaries intend to live in the foreign jurisdiction or, at least, intend to have some real and genuine link with that jurisdiction. It is clear, however, that another important reason why such a move might wish to be made is for the purpose of minimising the tax liability of the trust. This is particularly evident in cases where it is desired to move the investment and administration of the trust to 'off-shore' tax havens, such as the Channel Isles or the Isle of Man.

It is of course perfectly possible for the trust instrument to contain a power authorising the trustees both to invest overseas and, if appropriate, transfer the administration of the trust to foreign trustees. The exercise of such a power may, or may not, be made dependent on the consent of the beneficiaries. Similarly, the appointment of a foreign trustee may be made without any need to have recourse to the court if all the beneficiaries are of full age, sui juris and consent to the changes – as in *Re Whitehead's Will Trusts* [1971] 1 WLR 833.

However, in the normal case, it is clear that a trust can only be 'exported' if the terms of the trust can be varied so as to meet the requirements of the foreign law and to authorise the appointment of foreign trustees. All adult beneficiaries who are sui juris can, of course, consent for themselves to such a variation and if they are the only beneficiaries no problem arises. This is, however, unlikely for the trust is likely to include infant beneficiaries or even persons not yet born who will become such beneficiaries – eg future children of the settlor. Such persons cannot consent to a variation as they have no legal capacity and so application must be made to the court under the Variation of Trusts Act 1958 for approval on their behalf.

Under this Act, the court has the power to approve variations on behalf of four classes of persons – persons unborn (eg future children), infants, any person who has a discretionary interest under a protective trust, and any person who would be a member of a class of beneficiaries at a future date, where the class is ascertainable only at a future time. However, in order to be able to approve a variation on behalf of these persons (except a person with an interest under a discretionary trust), the court must be satisfied that the proposed variation is for their 'benefit'. This is the most difficult hurdle to overcome when asking for the approval of a variation which transfers the trust property and the administration of the trust abroad.

The most potent and obvious type of benefit is financial benefit and if the tax saving resultant on such a move is substantial then the court would find it difficult to deny that there is 'benefit' within the Act. Similarly, if the beneficiaries are emigrating permanently to a foreign jurisdiction then there may well be an additional intangible benefit in exporting the trust, as in *Re Seale's Marriage Settlement* [1961] Ch 574 and *Re Windeatt's Will Trusts* [1969] 2 All ER 324. Problems do arise, however, if the link with the foreign jurisdiction is tenuous because it is clear that the court must consider moral and social benefit as well as that which is financial. The leading authority here is *Re Weston's Settlements* [1969] 1 Ch 223 where the Court of Appeal refused consent on behalf of infant beneficiaries to a resettlement of the trusts in Jersey – the object being legitimate tax avoidance. According to the court, 'there are many things in life more worthwhile than money. One of these is to be brought up in this our England, which is still "the envy of less happier lands". I do not believe that it is for the benefit of children to be uprooted from England and transported to another country simply to avoid tax.' There is here, of course, a certain reluctance to approve variations whose sole purpose is tax avoidance ('the avoidance of tax may be lawful, but it is not yet a virtue'), but there is the greater point that the court's responsibility goes beyond fiscal considerations and approval must not be given where such would imperil the 'true welfare' of the children, born or unborn. It is, in essence, that the court must balance fiscal considerations with rather more intangible 'benefits'. Of course, the decision becomes easier if the beneficiaries can demonstrate a genuine link with the new jurisdiction. Finally, we must note that the court has power to order a variation of trust – it does not have power to consent to a complete re-settlement on completely new trusts which change the whole 'substratum' of the original scheme: *Re Ball's Settlement* [1968] 2 All ER 438. This would, of course, depend on the terms of the proposed variation.

b) i) Under this protective trust, Mary is the life tenant and her children are entitled in remainder. All the children are adult, but not all have obtained vested interests. However, under a protective trust it is difficult for the beneficiaries to effect a variation without recourse to the court. First, the rule in *Saunders* v *Vautier* (1841) 4 Beav 115 is inapplicable because not all of the beneficiaries are of full age, sui juris and together absolutely entitled. This is because under a protective trust governed by s33 Trustee Act 1925 (as this appears to be), when or if the life tenant's interest ends (eg due to an act of bankruptcy), the income is to be paid to the life tenant, his or her spouse and any issue or the persons absolutely entitled (the three children). The problem is that a potential and future spouse of Mary would have an interest under the trust – as would any future children – a possibility despite Mary's age. Thus, there are persons with contingent and future interests who would need to consent, but cannot.

ii) Application to the court to vary may be made in a number of ways, although only the last of these is relevant in the circumstances of this case. A court has inherent power to vary the terms of the trust in cases of absolute necessity to preserve the value of trust property eg *Re New* [1901] 2 Ch 534. This is not relevant here. Likewise, the extended jurisdiction to make variations in the administration of the trust which are 'expedient' under s57(1) Trustee Act 1925 does not assist in this case. Section 57 authorises changes in terms relating to administration of the trust, not changes in beneficial interests. The clearest ground for approaching the court is to gain approval for a variation under the Variation of Trusts Act 1958. As seen above, the court may approve a variation on behalf of incompetent persons and persons who had a discretionary interest under a protective trust. In this case, the court could approve the application on behalf of the unborn children (provided it was satisfied that it was for their benefit) and on behalf of any person who would acquire an interest under the discretionary trusts which would arise if the protective trusts should determine (such as a future spouse) and to this class of persons the requirement of benefit does not apply.

QUESTION FOUR

What principles does the court apply when an application to vary a trust is made?

University of London LLB Examination
(for External Students) Law of Trusts June 2000 Q7

General Comment

Quite a straightforward question for which knowledge of both principles and the various statutory possibilities of variation needs to be demonstrated.

Skeleton Solution

Trust instrument – inherent jurisdiction of the court – Trustee Act 1925 – Settled Land Act 1925 – Trusts of Land and Appointment of Trustees Act 1996 – Variation of Trusts Act 1958.

Suggested Solution

The House of Lords in *Chapman v Chapman* [1954] AC 429 stated that the basic rule is that the trustees must act in accordance with the trust instrument. This idea has meant that the role of the court is limited in terms of its inherent jurisdiction, there being only a limited set of circumstances in which variation is possible. There are, however, a number of statutory provisions that provide the means to vary a trust.

The court will authorise variations of trusts under its inherent jurisdiction in limited circumstances, as classified by Lord Morton in *Chapman v Chapman*. The court can authorise changes in the nature of an infant's property – a matter of largely historical importance now. The court can authorise transactions which are unauthorised by the settlement. In *Re New* [1901] 2 Ch 534 it was said that authority for variation would be given when such a transaction is desirable for the benefit of the estate and of all the beneficiaries. This does not enable the court to authorise the alteration of beneficial interests. The court can authorise maintenance out of income which was directed to be accumulated, as in the case of *Re Collins* (1886) 32 Ch D 229. Finally, the court can approve a compromise on behalf of infants and of possible after-born beneficiaries. This is possible only where dispute exists as to beneficial interests, as in both *Chapman* v *Chapman* [1954] AC 429 and *Re Powell-Cotton's Resettlement* [1956] 1 All ER 60.

Under s57 Trustee Act 1925 the court can confer the power on trustees to effect any transaction which is expedient in the management or administration of the trust but which the trustees have no power to do under the trust instrument. The aim of this provision is to ensure that the trust is managed as advantageously as possible in the interests of the beneficiaries, and it has therefore been used to authorise the sale of chattels, land and a reversionary interest. However, s57 does not give the court power to alter beneficial interests under a trust. It should also be noted that this section is not applicable to Settled Land Act (SLA) 1925 settlements. Under the Trustee Act 1925, s53, the court can authorise variations which enable the transfer of trust property, so that the capital or the income can be used for the maintenance, education or benefit of an infant beneficiary. It was held in *Re Gower's Settlement* [1934] Ch 365 that the court could authorise a mortgage of trust property under s53, and in *Re Meux's Will Trusts* [1958] Ch 154 the sale of the whole of the beneficial interest was authorised, where the proceeds were to be resettled on new trusts. It would not be so authorised if no resettlement was intended.

By s64(1) Settled Land Act 1925 the court can authorise any transaction for the benefit of settled land or land held on trust for sale or for the beneficiaries thereunder, if such a transaction could have been effected by an absolute owner. The courts have taken a wide view of the notion of a transaction. It appears to allow variation of beneficial interests as well as permitting trustees to exercise powers that they do not have under the trust instrument. In *Re Scarisbrick Resettlement Estates* [1944] Ch 229, trustees were authorised to sell capital to enable the continued and necessary occupation of the land, and in *Raikes* v *Lygon* [1988] 1 WLR 281, the use of some settled property to maintain other settled property was allowed, despite the difference in potential beneficiaries under the two settlements. The effect of the Trusts of Land and Appointment of Trustees Act 1996 is that trustees of land have the powers of an absolute owner: s6. Under the Act change also takes place in relation to the s64 power above. Whilst no new strict settlements can be created, old ones can be continued. The trust for sale will cease to exist and land will, for the future, be held on a trust of land.

The Variation of Trusts Act 1958 also provides a power of variation. It is generally accepted that the consent of all beneficiaries (provided they are sui juris) is a defence to any breach of trust, including a breach of the duty not to deviate from the terms of the trust. A problem arises when the beneficiaries are not, for some reason, in a position to consent. In this situation, the court may be able to consent on those beneficiaries' behalf under the Variation of Trusts Act 1958. Those beneficiaries who are in a position to consent must still do so. The Variation of Trusts Act 1958 gives the court extensive powers to approve variation of trusts. Under s1(1) of the Act the court can approve an arrangement on behalf of infants and others incapable of consenting, persons who are more than one contingency away from attaining an interest in the trust, persons unborn and persons with an interest under a protective trust where the interest of the principal beneficiary has not failed or determined. Under the 1958 Act the court will only approve an arrangement on behalf of the first three groups if it is for their benefit. Benefit for these purposes includes financial benefit and moral and cultural benefit. The court also has power to vary trusts under divorce legislation, and to vary trusts after the breakdown of marriage. In the case of *Goulding* v *James* [1997] 2 All ER 239 the Court of Appeal provided a review of the principles to be applied in this area. Whilst the first instance judge refused to approve a suggested variation of trust, as it was so far removed from what was originally intended, the Court of Appeal took a different view. Mummery LJ gave the lead judgement. He said that the discretion of the court whether or not to approve a proposed arrangement is fettered only by the proviso to s1, which prohibits the court from approving an arrangement which is not for the benefit of the classes noted above. The court will look at the arrangement as a whole, in all the circumstances. The court's concern involves, inter alia, a practical and business-like consideration of the arrangement, including the total amounts of the advantages which the various parties obtain, and their bargaining strength. In many cases, the intentions and wishes of the testator or settlor carry little, if any, weight on the issue of approval on behalf of those who have not the capacity to give consent themselves, and on the facts of the case approval should be given. It does not matter that the object of the proposed variation is to improve the position of the beneficiaries from the point of view of taxation or death duties, and this is in fact the most frequent motive behind applications under the Act. The court will not, however, sanction an arrangement involving approval of an appointment which was a fraud on a power.

Chapter 20

Remedies for Breach of Trust

20.1   Introduction

20.2   Key points

20.3   Key cases and statute

20.4   Questions and suggested solutions

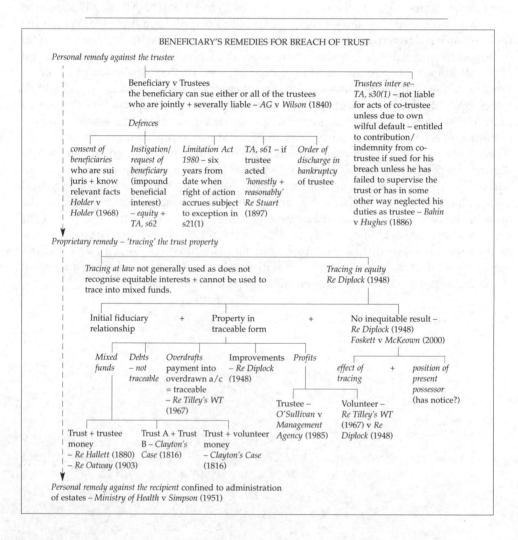

BENEFICIARY'S REMEDIES FOR BREACH OF TRUST

Personal remedy against the trustee

Beneficiary v Trustees
the beneficiary can sue either or all of the trustees
who are jointly + severally liable – *AG* v *Wilson* (1840)

Defences

| consent of beneficiaries who are sui juris + know relevant facts *Holder* v *Holder* (1968) | Instigation/ request of beneficiary (impound beneficial interest) – equity + TA, s62 | Limitation Act 1980 – six years from date when right of action accrues subject to exception in s21(1) | TA, s61 – if trustee acted 'honestly + reasonably' Re Stuart (1897) | Order of discharge in bankruptcy of trustee |

Trustees inter se–
TA, s30(1) – not liable
for acts of co-trustee
unless due to own
wilful default – entitled
to contribution/
indemnity from co-
trustee if sued for his
breach unless he has
failed to supervise the
trust or has in some
other way neglected his
duties as trustee – *Bahin*
v *Hughes* (1886)

Proprietary remedy – 'tracing' the trust property

Tracing at law not generally used as does not
recognise equitable interests + cannot be used to
trace into mixed funds.

Tracing in equity
Re Diplock (1948)

Initial fiduciary   +   Property in   +   No inequitable result –
relationship   traceable form   *Re Diplock* (1948)
                                                                                                    Foskett v *McKeown* (2000)

| Mixed funds | Debts – not traceable | Overdrafts payment into overdrawn a/c = traceable – Re Tilley's WT (1967) | Improvements – Re Diplock (1948) | Profits |

effect of   +   position of
tracing   present
                                          possessor
                                          (has notice?)

Trustee –
O'Sullivan v
*Management
Agency* (1985)

Volunteer –
Re Tilley's WT
(1967) v *Re
Diplock* (1948)

Trust + trustee
money
– *Re Hallett* (1880)
– *Re Oatway* (1903)

Trust A + Trust
B – *Clayton's*
Case (1816)

Trust + volunteer
money
– *Clayton's Case*
(1816)

Personal remedy against the recipient confined to administration
of estates – *Ministry of Health* v *Simpson* (1951)

20.1 Introduction

Whenever a breach of trust occurs, the question of remedies must be addressed and so the topic is relevant to almost every aspect of trusteeship covered in the last half of this book. A personal remedy against the trustee does not raise any difficult concepts. The proprietary remedy of tracing is, however, one which students often have problems with – in many cases, this is due to a fear of the mathematical nature of the rules, concerning tracing into a mixed fund. Such a fear is easily overcome by a step-by-step approach to and practice of problems on the subject.

20.2 Key points

If a beneficiary is seeking a remedy for breach of trust, he must first sue the trustee(s) personally, and only to the extent that this remedy is unavailable or is insufficient will the proprietary remedy of tracing be possible: *Re Diplock* [1948] Ch 465. In cases concerning the administration of estates a personal remedy against the recipient of the trust property may be available as a last resort: *Ministry of Health* v *Simpson* [1951] AC 251. The court made it clear in the case of *Target Holdings Ltd* v *Redferns (A Firm) and Another* [1995] 3 All ER 785 that the trustees would not be liable unless loss was caused by their fault and was not attributable to some other reason. *Armitage* v *Nurse* [1997] 2 All ER 705 is authority for the principal that an exclusion clause in a settlement can protect a trustee from liability for gross negligence. *Wight* v *Olswang* (1999) The Times 18 May considered whether paid trustees of a settlement, in this case solicitors, were able to rely on exemption clauses in a settlement – so as to escape liability in respect of alleged breaches of duty. There were two exclusion clauses, one general and the other restricted to unpaid trustees. It was decided that the solicitors would not be protected by the clauses.

Personal remedy against trustee

Position of beneficiary vis-à-vis the trustees

The trustees are jointly and severally liable and so the beneficiary can sue any or all of them: *Attorney-General* v *Wilson* (1840) Cr & Phil 1.

If a trustee is liable and is also a beneficiary, he will not be able to claim any beneficial interest until he has made good his breach.

There are several important defences available to a trustee against an action for breach of trust.

a) Consent of, or confirmation or release by the beneficiaries.

Whether a beneficiary has consented is a question of fact which will depend on the circumstances. In order to consent a beneficiary must be sui juris and must have known of all the relevant facts although he need not know that he is, in fact, consenting to a breach of trust: *Holder* v *Holder* [1968] Ch 353. After a breach of trust by a trustee the beneficiaries could either confirm his action or release him (as in *New Zealand Guardian Trust Co Ltd* v *Brooks* [1995] 1 WLR 96) the effects of which are to protect the trustee from a legal action.

b) Instigation or request or consent in writing of a beneficiary.

It is established both as an equitable principle and under TA 1925, s62 that if a beneficiary instigates or requests a breach of trust, his beneficial interest may be impounded – he will have to indemnify the trustee out of his beneficial interest. To rely on the equitable principle, the trustee must show that the beneficiary benefited in some way from the breach. This is not necessary under s62, although the section does require consent to be in writing, and knowledge of the relevant facts by the beneficiary: *Re Somerset* [1894] 1 Ch 231.

c) The Limitation Act 1980.

The Act provides that no action can be brought against a trustee more than six years after the right of action accrued. This is subject to two important exceptions in s21(1) – there is no period of limitation if the breach of trust was fraudulent or if the trustee is still in possession of either the trust property itself or its proceeds. In the case of a beneficiary who is an infant, the six year period does not begin to run until he attains majority. Similarly, in the case of a reversionary interest under a settlement, the period does not begin to run against the remainderman until the interest falls into possession.

d) The Trustee Act 1925, s61.

Under s61 it is a defence that the trustee acted 'honestly and reasonably' and 'ought fairly to be excused'. Whether he did so will depend on all the circumstances including adherence to any relevant statutory guidelines such as those concerning advice in the sphere of investments (see Chapter 15). The importance of the 'reasonably' requirement was underlined in *Re Stuart* [1897] 2 Ch 583 in which it was said that it would be relevant to consider whether the trustee would have acted similarly had he been dealing with his own property.

e) Discharge in bankruptcy.

Once an order of discharge has been made in respect of the trustee, he is no longer liable unless the breach was fraudulent.

Position of the trustees inter se

The TA 1925, s30(1) provides that a trustee is not liable for breaches of trust committed by his co-trustees unless the breach somehow occurred through his own 'wilful default' as defined in, amongst others, *Re Vickery* [1931] 1 Ch 572. The practical effect of this is that if an innocent co-trustee is sued for a breach for which his co-trustee was wholly liable, he will not be liable provided that he was in no way guilty of a breach of trust himself – for example, in the supervision of the trust as in *Bahin* v *Hughes* (1886) 31 Ch

D 390. In practice it is likely that if one trustee has been active in committing the breach, his co-trustee will be liable for failure to check his actions.

In addition to the s30 protection, a retired trustee will not be liable for breaches committed by his successors unless he knew that a breach of trust would follow his retirement: *Head* v *Gould* [1898] 2 Ch 250. Similarly, a new trustee will not be liable for breaches committed by his predecessors unless he discovers such a breach and fails to remedy it.

Measure of liability

The amount for which the trustee will be held liable is generally the amount of loss caused to the estate. In the sphere of unauthorised investments:

a) if breach of duty to sell unauthorised investments, is liable for the difference between what he would have received if he had sold at the correct time and the amount received when it was in fact sold;

b) if breach is that a proper investment was improperly sold, the liability is the difference between the amount received and the value at the commencement of proceedings or at the date of judgment (it is unsettled which is the correct date), plus any income which would have been received from the proper investment;

c) if breach is that the trustee made an unauthorised investment.

Any profit made as a result of the breach must be held on trust. In addition to liability for loss, the trustee will be liable to pay interest at a fixed rate if the income received on the property is lower. If it is higher, the trustee is liable to account for the actual income. If the income which should have been received is higher, then the trustee will be liable for this amount.

If the trustee has committed more than one breach, the loss made on one cannot be set off against a profit made on another except in the limited situation when the breaches stem from a single investment policy: *Bartlett* v *Barclays Bank Trust Co Ltd* [1980] Ch 515.

Proprietary remedy – tracing

Tracing trust property is possible both at law and in equity. It is, however, generally done in equity as the legal remedy does not recognise a beneficiary's equitable interest (and so a beneficiary cannot trace against a trustee and would have to join the trustee as a party when tracing against anyone else). Nor does the legal remedy allow tracing into a mixed fund.

In *Foskett* v *McKeown* [2000] 2 WLR 1299, Lord Millet in the House of Lords presented a general review of the law and this included the idea that tracing has to be distinguished from following. Following involves going after the same asset, whilst tracing involves substituted assets. This is a change of terminology rather than substance. In the case, premiums on a life assurance policy had been partly paid for out of a mixed fund which contained money subject to a trust. Such payments were in breach of trust. Following the analogy of mixed bank accounts, the beneficiaries were entitled to a proportionate share of the money payable under the life policy.

To be able to trace trust property in equity, the beneficiary must show three things.

Initial fiduciary relationship

This requirement was restated in *Westdeutsche Landesbank Girozentrale* v *Islington London Borough Council* [1996] 2 All ER 961, and the emphasis is on 'initial', as once an initial fiduciary relationship such as trustee – beneficiary is established it does not matter that the person who is in possession of the trust property is in no such relationship to the beneficiary.

The number and variety of situations in which a fiduciary relationship may exist is limitless: *Re Hallett's Estate* (1880) 13 Ch D 696. This reduces the impact of the requirement.

The trust property must be in a traceable form

It need not be in the same form as it was when it left the trust but it will not be traceable if it has been consumed or dissipated: *Re Diplock* [1948] Ch 465. In the case of *Westdeutsche Landesbank Girozentrale* v *Islington London Borough Council* it was decided that stolen money could be traced.

a) Payment of debts

If trust property or its proceeds are used to discharge a specific debt, the trust property will not be traceable: *Re Diplock*. However, if the property is rather paid into an overdrawn account, this will not be the case and the property will continue to be traceable: *Re Tilley's Will Trusts* [1967] Ch 1179.

b) Improvements to property

The property will only be traceable if the improvements result in an increase in the value of the property: *Re Diplock*. Even then, the court may not allow the beneficiary to trace if it would be inequitable to do so (see (c) below).

c) Profits

If the person in possession of the trust property makes a profit on it, whether he will be liable to account for such profits will depend on his relationship to the beneficiary.

i) If he is the trustee and is, therefore, in a fiduciary position to the beneficiary, he will be liable for any profits made on the trust property (see Chapter 14). If he mixes trust property with his own, the same should be true if he acted in breach of trust. It was suggested in *O'Sullivan* v *Management Agency* [1985] 3 All ER

351, however, that if a trustee acts with complete honesty he may be allowed to retain a share of the profits.

ii) If he is an innocent volunteer and the fund is unmixed, *Re Diplock* [1948] Ch 465 would suggest that he is entitled to keep any profit made on the trust property. Dicta in *Re Tilley's Will Trusts* [1967] Ch 1179 suggest though, that he should in fact account to the trust for such profits, and thus, that he should account for a proportion of the profits if made on a combination of trust property and his own.

d) Mixed funds

i) If a trustee mixes trust property with his own property the trust is entitled to the value of the trust property used and if any doubt exists as to quantity, it is to be resolved in favour of the trust: *Indian Oil Corporation* v *Greenstone Shipping SA* [1988] QB 345.

If the trust property is mixed with the trustee's own money in his bank account and amounts are withdrawn from the account then the first rule to apply is that the trustee is deemed to withdraw his own money first: *Re Hallett's Estate* (1880) 13 Ch D 696 – although if this results in an inequitable result, the rule was modified in *Re Oatway* [1903] 2 Ch 356 and, in fact, the trust will have a charge over both the funds in the bank account and over any traceable property purchased with money withdrawn from the account.

It is important to note that if a trustee pays more of his own money into the account after the original mixing and withdrawals, the trust will not be able to trace against this subsequent payment in unless it was intended to repay money spent: *Roscoe (James) (Bolton) Ltd* v *Winder* [1915] 1 Ch 62, sometimes called the 'lowest intermediate balance' rule. Two cases have supported this view: *Bishopsgate Investment Management Ltd (In Liquidation)* v *Homan and Others* [1994] 3 WLR 1270 and *Re Goldcorp Exchange* [1994] 3 WLR 199.

ii) If money from two or more trusts are mixed, their claims rank pari passu to each other. If there are insufficient funds in the account to satisfy both claims, the rule of convenience in *Devaynes* v *Noble: Clayton's Case* (1816) 1 Mer 572 will apply – the withdrawals are deemed to be made in the order of the payments in, using the first trust money paid in first, if the mixing takes place in an active continuing bank account, eg a current account. The Court of Appeal made it clear, in the case of *Barlow Clowes* v *Vaughan* [1992] 4 All ER 22, that this rule of convenience would not be used in all cases – for example it would not be used where it would be impractiable or if it would cause injustice.

iii) If the trust money is paid into a bank account of an innocent volunteer, the same rules apply as between the volunteer and the trust as between two or more trusts above.

No inequitable results

Even if a tracing remedy is available above, the court will not grant relief if it would be inequitable to do so. As a result, tracing is not available against a legal purchaser without notice, of the trust property. Similarly, if trust property has been used by a volunteer to improve his house, the court will not enforce a sale of the house so that the trust could realise the trust property if this would cause the volunteer undue hardship.

Personal remedy against recipient

This remedy is used as a last resort and its application is limited to the administration of estates and is, thus, of limited value: see *Ministry of Health* v *Simpson* [1951] AC 251.

20.3 Key cases and statute

- *Foskett* v *McKeown* [2000] 2 WLR 1299
  Lord Millet – tracing and following – change of terminology rather than substance

- *Holder* v *Holder* [1968] Ch 353
  Consent of the beneficiaries – full age – informed

- *Re Diplock* [1948] Ch 465
  Tracing in equity – must be in a traceable form – no inequitable result

- Trustee Act 1925, s30 – trustees only liable for each other; where wilful default; contribution and indemnity

20.4 Questions and suggested solutions

QUESTION ONE

Under the terms of the will of a testator who died in 1983, a fund of £3,000,000 was left to trustees upon trust to distribute the capital amongst such charitable or worthy causes and in such shares as the trustees should in their absolute discretion think fit and the residuary estate was left to the XY Charity. On various dates since the testator's death, the trustees dealt with the fund as follows:

a) £1 million was paid to the AB hospital which spent £500,000 on dialysis machines and computer equipment and invested the balance in government stock which is now worth £550,000;

b) £1 million was paid to the CD University which applied the money towards the cost of a new library building: the total cost of the building was £2 million;

c) £1 million was paid to the EF Foundation for the Relief of Poverty. It paid this sum into its bank account which at the time was £200,000 in credit. The following day, the EF Foundation drew out £500,000 and applied it in providing hotel accommodation for the homeless. One week later, it received a donation of £500,000 and paid this sum into its account. Since then, further sums have been drawn out and the present credit balance is £400,000.

Advise the XY Charity.

University of London LLB Examination
(for External Students) Law of Trusts June 1991 Q7

General Comment

For anyone with even a passing knowledge of the law of tracing, this is a good question to answer. It really revolves around *Re Diplock* [1948] Ch 465 and the examiner might well think in retrospect that the question was too easy.

Skeleton Solution

Tracing – conditions – *Re Diplock* – *Re Oatway* – personal remedies – loss of tracing.

Suggested Solution

The issues raised in this question are similar in many respects to those discussed in the landmark decision on the law of equitable tracing: *Re Diplock* [1948] Ch 465. We are asked to advise the XY Charity, obviously with a view to this charity (as residuary legatees) recovering any assets wrongly paid out by the executors. Our first priority is, therefore, to establish that the executors/trustees of the testator have wrongfully distributed the assets subject to the trust. There is no difficulty in this. The trust is expressed to be for 'such charitable or worthy causes' as the trustees think fit. However, in order to be charitable a trust has to be exclusively charitable. As seen in *Chichester Diocesan Fund and Board of Finance Inc* v *Simpson* [1944] AC 341 (concerning the will of Caleb Diplock), a trust for 'charitable or benevolent' purposes was held void on the grounds that the trustees could choose objects which were benevolent but not charitable in law. The same is true in our case and the gift is not charitable, not being exclusively devoted thereto. Thus, the trustees have wrongfully distributed the funds. Can the XY Charity recover the property?

The first point to note is that the XY Charity as residuary legatee must sue the trustees personally. They will be liable personally for all the loss, although with such large sums it is unlikely that they could meet this liability in full. Only, however, when they have exhausted this remedy (eg the trustees are bankrupt) may the XY Charity resort to tracing in equity and the *Re Diplock* special in personam remedy.

Equitable tracing

The conditions for the existence of the right to trace in equity were reasonably clearly laid down in *Re Diplock*; there must have been a fiduciary relationship and the plaintiff must have an equitable proprietary interest in the property he or she is seeking to trace. In this case, there clearly is a fiduciary relationship between the XY Charity and the trustees (note the relationship does not have to be between the immediate parties to the action) and as residuary legatees the charity has an equitable interest in the trust. Both the conditions are satisfied.

a) The hospital has given no consideration for the payment of the £1 million and therefore cannot avoid tracing on the ground of being a bona fide purchaser for value. Of course, if the AB Hospital had notice of the breach of trust, they would be constructive trustee of the property and liable to repay the money in full. Assuming however no notice, they are innocent volunteers. *Re Diplock* [1948] Ch 465 makes it clear that if the innocent volunteer has retained the plaintiff's property (more correctly the property in which the plaintiff has a proprietary interest) in recognisable form – even if different from the original form – then the plaintiff may trace to it and recover. Here specific property has been purchased – dialysis machines/computers and government stock. Subject to the general rule that an equitable remedy will not be permitted to do inequity, the XY Charity can recover this property, or in the case of the equipment ask that its monetary equivalent be returned. Further, in the case of the government stock, it appears from *Re Tilley's Will Trusts* [1967] Ch 1179 that the plaintiff may be able to claim the increase in value of the property, ie the extra £50,000. This is because tracing is a right in rem – a right to the thing which is your property irrespective of the value it holds at the moment. Note, however, that *Re Tilley* was decided in the context of an action against a trustee and the court may adopt a more lenient attitude where the tracing is against an innocent third party, especially if that third party has used skill and judgment to increase the value of the property. There is an argument that the profit should be shared: *Boardman* v *Phipps* [1967] 2 AC 46.

b) Again, prima facie tracing is available. The University again appears to be an innocent volunteer. However, in *Re Diplock*, some of the money had been spent on the alteration of old buildings and the erection of new ones. The Court of Appeal held that in these circumstances no action would lie because it would be inequitable to force an innocent third party to surrender such an asset, especially where the innocent party also contributed substantially to the cost of the property with its own money – as here. Essentially, the plaintiff's property has become untraceable, although this is something of a fiction because if the defendant had been the original trustee it is clear that the plaintiff would have had an enforceable charge over the property as a reflection of its interest: *Re Oatway* [1903] 2 Ch 356.

c) Where an innocent volunteer mixes trust money (ie XY's) in a bank account with his own money – as here – the court in *Re Diplock* decided that a beneficiary did not deserve the special protection afforded by the rule in *Re Hallet's Estate* (1880) 13 Ch D 696 which applied to mixing by trustees. The rule in *Devaynes* v *Noble: Clayton's Case* (1816) 1 Mer 572 applies so that the money spent on untraceable assets (here the hotel accommodation) is spent on the basis of 'first in first out'. Thus, the first £200,000 of the £500,000 spent on hotel accommodation was EF's own money, the next £300,000 belonged to XY. EF then received £500,000 by donation and the balance in the account stands at £400,000. Under the rule in *Clayton*, this £400,000 must be the remains of the last £500,000 to go into the account (ie last in, last out). It therefore belongs entirely to EF and XY has no claim under tracing to the balance in the account.

In personam

If the personal action against the trustees and equitable tracing fails to secure the return of trust property – as is likely in our case – the XY Charity can fall back on the special in personam remedy of *Re Diplock* [1948] Ch 465. This is a remedy of last resort and it appears to be available only when there has been a wrongful distribution of assets under a will (or possibly a liquidated company: *Re Leslie (J) Engineers Co Ltd* [1976] 2 All ER 85). In effect, it means that although XY cannot receive back its specific property by means of tracing, it can sue the recipients of that property personally for its value. What is more, it is clear from *Re Diplock* that there is no defence of 'change of position' (ie that the money has been innocently spent) to this action and therefore the three charities will be liable. Note, however, that if this action is really a species of unjust enrichment, the case of *Lipkin Gorman* v *Karpnale Ltd* [1991] 3 WLR 10 may provide some comfort, for in that case the House of Lords has recently held that the defence of 'change of position' is available to an unjust enrichment claim.

QUESTION TWO

By his will made in 1988, Fred leaves all his personal property to Brian and Bertrand. The will also states that he leaves all his real property to Cyril 'on trust for such person or persons as I shall communicate to him'. Last year, Fred handed Brian an envelope with the instruction that it was not to be opened until after his (Fred's) death. Unknown to Brian, the letter states that Fred's personal property should be held by Brian and Bertrand on trust for Gloria, Fred's mistress. At the same time, Fred telephones Cyril and tells him that the property he will receive under Fred's will should be held by him on trust for Roger, Fred's illegitimate son. Cyril agrees that he will do this.

Fred has now died. Advise Gloria and Roger as to any interests they may have in Fred's estate.

University of London LLB Examination
(for External Students) Law of Trusts June 1995 Q5

General Comment

Problem questions of this nature require the student to address the issues raised and apply the appropriate legal rules to them. The advantage of this type of problem is that it provides its own framework for the answers.

Skeleton Solution

Take each bequest in turn – half-secret trust problem – fully-secret trust.

Suggested Solution

There is a distinction between the real property and the personal property left by Fred after his death. Fred's will states that his real property is to be left on trusts to be communicated by Fred to Cyril. Fred does communicate the terms of this trust to Cyril in a telephone conversation. The property is to be held on trust for Roger. Cyril agrees to be a trustee on this basis. There is an issue here therefore of a secret trust. It is required by s53(1)(b) Law of Property Act 1925 that trusts of land must be evidenced in writing. Similarly, the Wills Act 1837 requires that testamentary dispositions of this sort must be made in writing.

The issue arises whether the precise terms of the trust must be evidenced, or simply that there is such information as to enable the parties to find out the terms of the trust. The issue is, therefore, whether the oral trust should be enforced, or whether the legatee should be required to hold the property on resulting trust for Fred's estate. The general rule is that the trust will be enforced in favour of the beneficiary Roger: *Thynn v Thynn* (1684) 1 Vera 296. On these facts, the secret trust should be enforced because the testator validly declared an inter vivos trust during his lifetime, and the trust thereby became constituted by the vesting of the property on his death in Cyril, the legatee.

However, this theoretical underpinning has not been the approach which the courts have taken in seeking to enforce secret trusts in these circumstances. The approach taken in the courts was that it would be a fraud if the legatee, Cyril, were allowed to retain the property: *McCormick v Grogan* (1869) LR 4 HL 82. This theory eludes the argument that the Wills Act 1837 is not being enforced if the trust is given effect without the observance of the relevant formalities. In these circumstances, the fact that the will states that Cyril holds only as trustee means that the property can be validly held for Roger's benefit as sole beneficiary under the trust, as in *Blackwell v Blackwell* [1929] AC 318.

With reference to Gloria's interest, there is a problem revolving around the conflict between the terms of Fred's will and the purported instruction handed to Brian that Fred's personal property be held for Gloria's benefit by Brian and Bertrand after his death. The will, made in 1988, states quite clearly that all of Fred's personal property is to pass to Brian and Bertrand. The written instruction to Brian, the content of which is undisclosed at the time it is given to Brian, was created in 1994. The issue therefore is whether the subsequent written instruction will override the bequest in the will.

There is no issue here that there would be a fraud if the property were to be passed to Bertrand. However, Brian is informed that the instruction exists but he is ignorant of the terms of the letter. Therefore, it can be said that Brian is bound by the terms of such instruction. For Brian to deny to be bound by those terms after Fred's death would permit him to perpetrate a fraud on the trust, because it might be that, had Brian objected to being bound by any such instruction, Fred would have made alternative arrangements for that property.

The general rule is that the legatee will hold the property on resulting trust for the estate. In *Re Boyes* (1884) 26 Ch D 531, where a solicitor had undertaken to hold a property on trust according to instructions he was to receive by letter, Kay J explained that the legatee accepts property on the basis of a trust which it would be a fraud for him not to carry into effect. Here there is no communication of the terms of the trust, as with Roger's gift, before the time of death, and therefore the property must be held on resulting trust rather than being passed on to Gloria.

QUESTION THREE

By a settlement made by Smith, the trustees, Dum and Dee, were directed to hold a trust fund consisting of shares and debentures in Alpha plc, a public limited company, and certain government stock, on trust to pay the income to Adam for life remainder to his children. The settlement contains no special investment clause except a provision that, before making any change of investment, the trustees should first obtain the consent in writing of Smith.

In 1987, Dum and Dee, with the consent in writing of Smith, sold the shares in Alpha to one of themselves, Dum, for £200,000 (their quoted value) and invested the proceeds in the purchase of shares in Beta plc, another public limited company.

In 1988, Dum and Dee, with the consent in writing of Smith, sold the government stock for £500,000 (its quoted value) and invested the proceeds in the purchase of freehold offices in Docklands.

In 1989, Dum and Dee, without the consent of Smith but with the encouragement of Adam, sold the debentures in Alpha plc for £100,000 (their market value) and invested the proceeds in shares in Delta plc, another public limited company.

The shares in Alpha plc are now worth £300,000; the shares in Beta plc are now worth £100,000; the shares in Delta plc are now worth £200,000 and the freehold offices are worth £250,000.

Advise (a) Adam's children, (b) Dum and Dee jointly as trustees, and (c) Dum individually, as to their respective legal positions.

University of London LLB Examination
(for External Students) Law of Trusts June 1991 Q5

General Comment

This is a typical question on liability for breach of trust, especially since it involves some consideration of powers of investment. Such questions usually look much harder than they actually are and should be attempted by any candidate with a reasonable knowledge of the law of personal liability of trustees.

Skeleton Solution

Personal liability for breach of trusts – standard of care – measure of damages – remedies and defences – some knowledge of Trustee Investments Act 1961.

Suggested Solution

The issues raised in this question concern the individual liabilities of trustees for breach of trust – both collectively and individually – as well as the possible remedies available to a beneficiary whose interest has been adversely affected by such breach. It is, of course, the duty of trustees to invest trust property so that income will be produced for the beneficiaries (eg *Stone* v *Stone* (1869) 5 Ch App 74) and trustees will be liable for failing to do so within a reasonable time of the establishment of the trust. This is not the case here. However, trustees may also be liable for breach of trust for investing contrary to their powers of investment or by failing to meet the standard of care required of trustees when dealing with beneficiaries' property. These are the matters in issue here. There are no express powers of investment in this case and therefore, the power of investment is governed by the Trustee Investments Act 1961. It is unlikely that the requirement of Smith's consent excludes the statutory power (if it did there would be no power to invest!), but rather places an additional limit on the trustees in the exercise of the powers under the Act. This means that the trustees cannot exercise the powers of investment under the Act without Smith's consent, but also that Smith's consent cannot make lawful an investment which the Act does not authorise.

Of course, if investment is undertaken (which in this case, if at all must be under the Act), the trust fund must be divided into two equal parts – the narrower range and the wider range part. This is a precondition of the exercise of investment powers under the Act and it is clear that on sale of any of the existing investments of this particular fund, the fund would have to be divided. (Note: there is no breach of trust merely by retaining unauthorised investments when the trust was created, because this is not investment.)

a) The sale of the shares in Alpha to one of the trustees – Dum – and the investment of the proceeds in Beta plc. Adam's children are beneficiaries under the trust and are therefore concerned by the fact that the value of the investment has halved after the sale of Alpha shares and the purchase of Beta shares. However, in order to establish liability for breach of trust – so as to recover the difference in value – they must establish some breach of trust. It is clear that there has been no breach of any express stipulation, for Smith's consent has been obtained. However, there is no indication that the fund has been divided into two halves as required by the Act and, therefore, the investment in Beta shares may be unauthorised. Likewise, there is no indication whether Beta plc fulfils the conditions stipulated in the Trustee Act 1925 for investment in public companies (viz not less than £1 million share capital, dividend paid on relevant shares for preceding five years, shares quoted on Stock Exchange, shares fully paid and incorporated in the UK).

Again, trustees investing in wider range investments must obtain and consider advice (s6(2) Trustee Investments Act 1961) as to the suitability of the investment and its suitability in the overall investment profile of the trust. Importantly, however, there is also the general duty of care imposed on trustees when investing trust money. The trustee must act as an ordinary prudent man of business would act if he were minded to make investments on behalf of other people: *Re Whitely* (1886) 33 Ch D 347. If any or all of these breaches of trust have occurred, it is clear that both Dum and Dee will be jointly and severally liable to make good the loss to the trust fund, ie the difference between the value of the unauthorised/unwarranted/ imprudent investment and the value of the fund before such investment was purchased: *Fry* v *Fry* (1859) 27 Beav 144. Here, £100,000.

In addition, however, Dum may have incurred further liability as constructive trustee because of his purchase of the trust property. Under the 'self-dealing' rule a trustee must not be both a vendor and purchaser of the trust property and any such sale is voidable at the instance of the beneficiaries within a reasonable time – irrespective of how fair the transaction may have been. Smith's consent is irrelevant as it is the beneficiaries' interests that are prejudiced. If Adam's children act within a reasonable time, Dum will be held constructive trustee of the Alpha shares, including their increase in value. It is thus better for the children to pursue this avenue, as they would effectively have an asset worth £300,000, instead of an asset worth £100,000 (Beta shares) plus the £100,000 damages awarded for breach above. If Dum is bankrupt or otherwise unable to meet this constructive trust liability, it may be that Dee could be held liable for his co-trustee's breach of trust either because he was in 'wilful default' within s30 Trustee Act 1925 or because he failed in his own duty to supervise Dum.

b) This case is much clearer. A trustee may only invest money in the purchase of land if he is expressly authorised by the trust instrument or by some other statutory provision such as the Settled Land Act 1925, see eg *Re Power's Will Trusts* [1947] Ch 572. Neither of these is applicable here and therefore there has been a breach of trust and the trustees are jointly and severally liable for the loss. Smith's consent does not absolve the trustees as, as explained above, the consent is in addition to the requirements of the Trustee Investments Act 1961. It does not replace them.

c) The same general considerations apply to the purchase of Delta shares with the money obtained from the sale of Alpha investments as were relevant in (a) above. It is, however, clear that the provisions of the 1961 Act have been breached because the Alpha debentures were Part II narrower range investments and the proposed Delta investments could only be Part III wider range. The income from the sale of narrower range investments should be invested in investments authorised under that Part.

Similarly, Smith's consent has not been obtained and so there is a breach of the clear terms of the trust. Adam's encouragement does not affect his children's ability to sue for breach of trust for any loss sustained, but it would be open to the trustees to plead his instigation as a bar to a claim made by him: eg *Life Association of Scotland* v *Siddall* (1861) 3 De GF & J 60. Moreover, under s62 Trustee Act 1925, the trustees may seek to impound Adam's beneficial interest to help meet their liability on the ground that Adam instigated or requested a breach of trust with knowledge that he was so doing: *Re Somerset* [1894] 1 Ch 231. This is in effect a form of indemnity for the trustees. They may also try to plead s61 Trustee Act 1925, on the grounds that they should be excused liability being (in relation to this breach) honest, reasonable and ought fairly to be excused. This is unlikely given their deliberate disregard of the consent requirement.

QUESTION FOUR

Charlie is a director of Principal Ltd, and is authorised to make payments out of the company's bank account. Feeling underpaid, he decides to pay for his annual holiday from company funds. He arranges the holiday through a travel agent, Supertravel. To avoid any reference to Supertravel in Principal's records, Charlie transfers the amount due, £2,000, from Principal's bank account by cheque into the account of Bogus Ltd, a company owned and controlled by Bertie, a friend of Charlie. Charlie tells Bertie that the transfer is part of a clandestine scheme to evade corporation tax and must be kept secret. Bertie then arranges for the payment of £2,000 by electronic transfer into Supertravel's account. Bogus Ltd is wound up soon afterwards and ceases to exist.

On his return from holiday, Charlie gives his nephew, David, a graduation present of £500 in cash. In fact, the money had been stolen by Charlie from Principal's safe. David pays the money into his bank account, raising the balance to £750. He later pays in £250 received as a present from his parents. David then draws out £500 and uses it to buy two cases of vintage wine. He holds a party at which one case is consumed. The other case remains.

Charlie has now disappeared. Advise Principal as to any claims they might have against Supertravel, Bertie and David.

University of London LLB Examination
(for External Students) Law of Trusts June 1997 Q8

General Comment

This is a problem-question concerning following and tracing.

Skeleton Solution

Supertravel cannot be made liable either as a constructive trustee or through the following and tracing – Bertie is probably not liable as a constructive trustee – clearly the money cannot be followed or traced into his hands – David is almost certainly not a constructive trustee – £250 seems to be traceable into his hands.

Suggested Solution

Clearly Charlie acted in breach of trust and could therefore be sued to make good the losses which he has caused Principal Ltd. This applies to both the £2,000 misappropriated for his holiday and the £500 stolen from the safe. This remedy is, however, of little use as he has disappeared. The question then becomes whether

Principal can claim against Supertravel, Bertie or David either on the basis that they are constructive trustees or under the rules relating to following and tracing.

There is at present no evidence on which Supertravel could be made into a constructive trustee. There is no evidence that they acted in any way which was dishonest or fraudulent: *Barnes v Addy* (1874) 9 Ch App 244 per Lord Selborne LC, where it was held that liability as a constructive trustee is imposed on those who 'assist with knowledge in a dishonest and fraudulent design on the part of the trustees'. There is no evidence here that Supertravel were aware of any irregularity or that this was anything other than a perfectly ordinary sale of a holiday. The only thing which might have aroused their suspicions is the manner in which the payment was made to them, but it is submitted that the evidence at present available does not go far enough to make them liable even on that basis. On the present evidence all the cases concerning banks being turned into constructive trustees (eg *Karak Rubber Co Ltd v Burden (No 2)* [1972] 1 WLR 602) are all distinguishable and not relevant to the instant case.

Bertie plainly did know that there was 'a dishonest and fraudulent design on the part of the trustees'. The difficulty with making him liable is that he did not know that the victim was Principal. Indeed he probably believed that the victim was the Inland Revenue and that Principal was the beneficiary.

It seems most unlikely that David can be made liable as a constructive trustee, since there is no evidence that he acted in any way dishonestly or improperly.

The question then becomes whether Principal can follow and trace its money. Tracing in equity can only take place when three conditions are satisfied. These are as follows.

a) There must be an initial fiduciary relationship: *Re Hallett's Estate* (1880) 13 Ch D 696.

b) The property must be in a traceable form. As Lord Greene MR said in *Re Diplock* [1948] Ch 465 the money must still exist 'either as as separate fund or as part of a mixed fund or as latent in property acquired by means of such a fund'. For example, money spent on a dinner (Lord Greene's example) or a world cruise is no longer traceable. Where a trustee or innocent volunteer uses the money to pay off debts it cannot be traced. Money paid into a bank account, on the other hand is normally eminently traceable. Where an innocent volunteer uses trust money to improve an asset (eg repairing or extending a building), money spent on labour only is apparently not traceable, nor is money spent without bringing any increase in value to the property, but otherwise improvements are apparently traceable, provided it is not inequitable so to do: *Re Diplock*.

Special rules apply where the money has become mixed. This can apply in three cases: (i) where the trustee mixes trust money with his own money; (ii) where an innocent volunteer mixes trust funds; and (iii) where a trustee mixes funds belonging to two or more trusts.

Where an innocent volunteer receives trust money without notice and mixes it with his own money, the right to trace still exists, but with qualifications.

Where the innocent volunteer mixes the trust money with his own in an active bank account, the pari pasu rule does not apply, but the rule in *Devaynes* v *Noble: Clayton's Case* (1816) 1 Mer 572 applies: see *Re Stenning* [1895] 2 Ch 433. This is the FIFO (first in, first out) rule, whereby the trustee is presumed to draw on money in the order in which it is paid in, and thus on any money in the account before the trust money is paid in before the trust money is withdrawn.

c) No inequity results.

In the instant case there is plainly an initial fiduciary relationship, since Charlie is (or at least was at the relevant time) a director of Principal Ltd.

However, it is submitted that in the case of Supertravel the property is no longer in traceable form, nor would it be equitable to allow tracing as they gave value (in the form of a holiday) for what they received.

David is plainly an innocent volunteer. Presumably the £250 initially in his bank account was his own money. If so, no question of mixed trust funds arises. Therefore it is simply a case of trust money being mixed with David's own money. That being so, the FIFO rule applies. Thus the when he drew out the £500 to pay for the wine he is presumed to have drawn out the £250 which was already there first and then on £250 of the trust money. Thus there is £250 of the trust money left, which is amenable to tracing.

It is perhaps worth mentioning in passing that the money spent on one case of the wine (assuming it was deemed to have been bought with trust money) would not be amenable to following and tracing as it had been drunk.

There seems to be no inequity in allowing the remedy of tracing against David.

Principal should be advised accordingly.

Old Bailey Press

The Old Bailey Press integrated student law library is tailor-made to help you at every stage of your studies from the preliminaries of each subject through to the final examination. The series of Textbooks, Revision WorkBooks, 150 Leading Cases and Cracknell's Statutes are interrelated to provide you with a comprehensive set of study materials.

You can buy Old Bailey Press books from your University Bookshop, your local Bookshop, direct using this form, or you can order a free catalogue of our titles from the address shown overleaf.

The following subjects each have a Textbook, 150 Leading Cases/Casebook, Revision WorkBook and Cracknell's Statutes unless otherwise stated.

Administrative Law
Commercial Law
Company Law
Conflict of Laws
Constitutional Law
Conveyancing (Textbook and 150 Leading Cases)
Criminal Law
Criminology (Textbook and Sourcebook)
Employment Law (Textbook and Cracknell's Statutes)
English and European Legal Systems
Equity and Trusts
Evidence
Family Law
Jurisprudence: The Philosophy of Law (Textbook, Sourcebook and
    Revision WorkBook)
Land: The Law of Real Property
Law of International Trade
Law of the European Union
Legal Skills and System
    (Textbook)
Obligations: Contract Law
Obligations: The Law of Tort
Public International Law
Revenue Law (Textbook,
    Revision WorkBook and
    Cracknell's Statutes)
Succession

Mail order prices:	
Textbook	£14.95
150 Leading Cases	£11.95
Revision WorkBook	£9.95
Cracknell's Statutes	£11.95
Suggested Solutions 1998–1999	£6.95
Suggested Solutions 1999–2000	£6.95
Suggested Solutions 2000–2001	£6.95
Law Update 2002	£9.95
Law Update 2003	£10.95

Please note details and prices are subject to alteration.

To complete your order, please fill in the form below:

Module	Books required	Quantity	Price	Cost
		Postage		
		TOTAL		

For Europe, add 15% postage and packing (£20 maximum).
For the rest of the world, add 40% for airmail.

ORDERING

By telephone to Mail Order at 020 7381 7407, with your credit card to hand.

By fax to 020 7386 0952 (giving your credit card details).

Website: www.oldbaileypress.co.uk

By post to: Mail Order, Old Bailey Press at Holborn College, Woolwich Road, Charlton, London, SE7 8LN.

When ordering by post, please enclose full payment by cheque or banker's draft, or complete the credit card details below. You may also order a free catalogue of our complete range of titles from this address.

We aim to despatch your books within 3 working days of receiving your order.

Name

Address

Postcode   Telephone

Total value of order, including postage: £

I enclose a cheque/banker's draft for the above sum, or

charge my   ☐ Access/Mastercard   ☐ Visa   ☐ American Express
Card number

☐☐☐☐ ☐☐☐☐ ☐☐☐☐ ☐☐☐☐

Expiry date   ☐☐☐☐

Signature: .... Date: ....